T0334006

The Discipline of Data

Pulling aside the curtain of 'Big Data' buzz, this book introduces C-suite and other non-technical senior leaders to the essentials of obtaining and maintaining accurate, reliable data, especially for decision-making purposes. Bad data begets bad decisions, and an understanding of data fundamentals – how data is generated, organized, stored, evaluated, and maintained – has never been more important when solving problems such as the pandemic-related supply chain crisis. This book addresses the data-related challenges that businesses face, answering questions such as:

- What are the characteristics of high-quality data?
- How do you get from bad data to good data?
- What procedures and practices ensure high-quality data?
- How do you know whether your data supports the decisions you need to make?

This clear and valuable resource will appeal to C-suite executives and top-line managers across industries, as well as business analysts at all career stages and data analytics students.

Jerald 'Jerry' Savin FIMC, CPA is President/CEO of Cambridge Technology Consulting Group, Inc., a consulting firm based in Santa Monica, California. A professional information systems consultant with decades of experience, Jerry's practice combines information systems with public accounting and business expertise to support his client companies in such areas as data architecture, business intelligence, enterprise resource planning, project management, and IT auditing and compliance. He has been elected an Academic Fellow of the International Council of Management Consulting Institutes and a Fellow of the Institute of Management Consultants (FIMC). He brings his years of experience in industries from aerospace to healthcare to telecommunications to his work as a lecturer at California State University Northridge, University of California Riverside, and UCLA Extension.

The Discipline of Data

What Non-Technical Executives Don't
Know About Data and Why It's Urgent
They Find Out

Jerald Savin

Routledge
Taylor & Francis Group

NEW YORK AND LONDON

Designed cover image: Getty

First published 2023
by Routledge
605 Third Avenue, New York, NY 10158

and by Routledge
4 Park Square, Milton Park, Abingdon, Oxon OX14 4RN

Routledge is an imprint of the Taylor & Francis Group, an informa business

© 2023 Jerald Savin

Library of Congress Cataloging-in-Publication Data
A catalog record for this title has been requested

ISBN: 978-1-032-28078-3 (hbk)
ISBN: 978-1-032-28076-9 (pbk)
ISBN: 978-1-003-29522-8 (ebk)

DOI: 10.4324/9781003295228

Typeset in Bembo
by Taylor & Francis Books

Contents

Illustrations

Figures

Tables

Chapter 1

Preface

This book is intended for decision-makers, especially Business Executives, Business Owners and Senior Managers who depend on data to make informed strategic and tactical decisions, which in turn impact daily operations and longer-term strategies. These decisions, directly or indirectly, are ultimately aimed at increasing profit, businesses' life blood. This interdependence was a linear relationship in the past. Today, however, it is increasing exponentially. Look at the growth patterns of businesses at the beginning of the COVID-19 pandemic. Some businesses experienced meteoric growth, others shuttered, hopefully only temporarily, and these changes occurred in a matter of months. I recall a senior manager saying, 'the pandemic has done more for sales (in a positive sense) than our salesforce did last year.' Today, business changes happen quickly; hence, having good data is essential for making good business decisions quickly.

The design of this book is to highlight the issues that regularly arise when working with Data. This book is intended to be a reasonably comprehensive enumeration of these issues, their impact on decision-making, and 'good practices' that identify effective approaches and techniques to address these issues. As a side note, I personally believe there are many 'good practices' but I am often skeptical of 'best practices' for three reasons. First, are 'best practices' really the best or just one of several alternatives? Second, the 'best practices' assertion is often used by third parties to coerce adoption of certain practices. If the third-party said, 'this is how the software works and changing it could be costly', that would certainly be more transparent. Third, a 'best practice' may not fit in every situation. The old rule 'it all depends' still applies.

Why should you read this book? A significant aspect of our practice is litigation support. A common theme in many lawsuits is misunderstandings because of different expectations regarding products and services. The goal of this book is to provide a common language with which to discuss the factors and forces that affect Data, Data Quality, and hence the Quality of our Decisions.

Maybe closer to home are executive disputes where several executives are in sharp disagreement regarding 'what the data says.' Potentially, each

DOI: 10.4324/9781003295228-1

executive has his/her own facts and interpretations. No wonder wild disagreements arise. This 'my-own-set-of-facts' is also evident in national discourse. Whether in executive meetings or nationally, being able to agree on a common set of facts, Data, is the first step to making appropriate, reasoned decisions.

When encountering disagreements, when making important decisions, when trying to understand a situation, significant questions include: What happened? How did it happen? Why did it happen? What does it mean for the future? To answer these questions, we need a common vocabulary regarding data and how to use and interpret it. The intention of this book is to provide a common vocabulary and to identify common issues and methods. Inevitably such as discussion involves technical terms and concepts. My objective is to inform and empower executives who ultimately manage and use their organization's data to chart the direction of their respective businesses and their effectiveness and profitability.

Throughout the book there are numerous references to Customers, Suppliers, Items or Products, Employees, the Revenue or Sales Cycle, and the Expenditure or Purchasing Cycle. Why? Because these elements are basic to business and relate to every business. Yes, there are other examples, but these are easily recognized examples.

A special thank you to Dr. Pouyan Eslami, a colleague at California State University Northridge. Dr. Eslami graciously reviewed the book and provided very helpful feedback. Thank you. Also, a special thank you to my clients who over the years have reminded me of their needs and the things that can go wrong, and finally a thank you to my students, who constantly ask provocative questions. Teaching is a great opportunity to structure and re-structure the content of Information Technology, the wellspring of my teaching. A special Thank You to my very special proofreader, my spouse, Anne Sirota, who completes me on several fronts and who graciously agreed to read the manuscript (several times). To all, a big THANKS.

Chapter 2

Data – Introduction

The Nature of Data

Data is fundamental to business and to life. It is as fundamental today as it has been from the beginning of time. The big difference today is digitalization and readily available data, at least until you can't find something you are searching for.

Let's turn the clock back, way back, way before computers, way before the Internet, way before televisions and telephones. Suppose you were planning to go out and were wondering whether it was going to rain or not. The only information you had at that time was your personal observations. Based on the temperature, humidity, the clouds outside and your previous experiences, you decide. You can't call your neighbors, no telephone. You can't read the newspapers, no newspapers. You can't check the Internet, no Internet. The only data available to you then were your personal observations and your perceptions about the weather. That was all. Going way back, writing was confined to images carved in stone or pieces of clay, obviously we have gone way back. The point: Your sense of reality is based on your personal experiences. Your experiences and your remembrances of those experiences, they were your information vault.

Today, reality is highly abstracted. Movies create entertaining realities where even gravity is seemingly defied. We hear music without musicians. We see realities via images without being in those realities. We can see earth from above without being launched into space. All of this would be magic to our ancestors. Today we take it for granted. We live in a world where reality is abstracted. Our knowledge is no longer limited to our personal experiences.

It is time to give Data its due, its respect. The intent of this book is the following:

- To explain the language of data, especially for those not steeped in data technology.

DOI: 10.4324/9781003295228-2

- To introduce tools for managing data and making it useful in our business and personal lives.
- To understand data as both descriptive and as a basis for decisions that empower the future.
- And finally, to remind readers of the power of data to abstract reality.

As this book is written, 'metaverse' is an emerging technology and concept, which will take us further into abstraction, a reality that exists digitally where fact and fantasy become blurred. One must wonder what future vacations will be. Will be sitting at home and be miraculously transported to a place of our dreams?

Abstraction enables us to see things and not be there, to can hear things and not be there, to experience things and not be there. We can make decisions based on events in which we did not participate; we are able to make decisions based on interactions we did not have. Our decisions can be based on the accumulation of many experiences, situations, and entities of which we were not a part. What this means is that we live in an abstracted world and constantly understand the world and make decisions based on abstractions.

Two Simple Use Cases

Assume you are responsible for stocking stores for an upcoming season. Your business objective is to stock the stores with items customers want and will buy. The worst-case scenario is not having the items the customers want. The in-between scenario is having a collection of items some customers want and some don't want. At least we were partially right. This activity plays out routinely among buyers for large retailers and trickles down to owners of small businesses as well that can only afford to stock items their customers will purchase. BUT this decision is an estimate, dare I say a guess. What will customers want during an upcoming season or event or routinely? Their needs and wants change over time as does the merchandise that is available. Against this backdrop decisions are made.

Consider your favorite restaurant. Some customers want the same experience time after time, so the restaurateur develops recipes and decor to ensure the same experience every time. However, some customers, count me in this group, are looking for something new and different, not the same 'mac-n-cheese' every time. How does the restaurateur accommodate this? The same way merchandisers choose the items they stock, the restaurateur picks new menu items. Some restaurants go as far as a new menu daily, a taste treat for their customers. The merchandisers' decisions were based on data. The restaurateurs' decisions were based on data ... and maybe a little 'art' as well.

Going back to our buddy in the stone age, how did he decide what to wear tomorrow? Will the weather be hot or cold, rainy or overcast, freezing or sweltering? What are the chances the weather could change while he was out? The stone age person was probably much more in tune with nature and what is happening outside his/her home than we are today. Today, the conditions inside our homes can be very different than outside. Yes, we can look out the windows or step outside to get an idea, but we can also check the weather forecast, whether in the newspaper, or on television, or on our smartphones, and 'see' beyond our immediate situation. In a more extreme example, we are deciding what to pack for our upcoming vacation. Suppose the vacation is a summer vacation and we are heading to a beach for 'fun in the sun'. How likely are we to be greeted by rain? This happened to us earlier this summer. We were rained out of three events we planned to attend. This summer we were more concerned about the virus than the weather. But the weather forecasts today are amazingly accurate for longer periods of time thanks to enormous number crunching. Consider the hurricane forecasts where forecasters lay out not one track but a series of potential tracks for the hurricane. The multiple tracks form a cone around a track that is most likely, in the language of statistics, most probable.

For the merchandiser, selecting what to stock for an upcoming season or for us deciding what to wear or to pack, data plays a critical role in our decisions. Yes, there can be some 'art' to our decisions, but they tend increasingly to be based on data that is an abstraction of reality. The data becomes the 'springboard' for decisions, which could be a gracious swan dive into the future or a frantic cannonball into the future.

With these examples in mind, let's return to some basic questions about data:

- How does data come into existence? Consider a brief history of data as we look to the future and technologies such as Artificial Intelligence, Machine Learning, Deep Learning and more.
- What are different forms of data? How different can these abstractions be?
- What happens to data after it comes into being? How does it get from place to place? How is it processed? What is its lifecycle?
- What is the language, the words and terms, that are used by those who work with data making it available and useable for us?
- What is data worth; what is it really worth? Can we put a price tag on data? What is the market for data?
- In essence, why read this book?

Changing Data Landscape

Going back to the Stone Age, data was initially stored in memories and passed down through stories and images and text on pottery and stone and eventually as written records, relatively modern in the larger arc of history.

Today we have images and sound recordings, and the ability to store and process images and recordings digitally, largely a Twentieth Century phenomenon. The point is simply that data has existed from the beginning of human history. Data is not new, only how it is recorded, increasingly in digital formats. Recordings have evolved from stories and clay tablets to written documents and now are entries in databases. Consider live music, the records, then CDs, now streaming. Music, as an expression, hasn't changed but the format certainly has.

Hence, a central theme of this book is that data does not exist in a vacuum. It came from somewhere. It may be useable as is; it may require effort to make it useable. This effort is often referred to as 'data wrangling,' which will be discussed in its own section and throughout this book.

While data's form has changed, our reliance on it has continued. It has remained a basis for decisions. Data is a record of past entities and events, a contemporary call for action and an indication of what might be done in the future, i.e., Past, Present and Future. Data has always, without regard to its current emphasis, been used to describe the past, to inform the present, to predict the future and to prescribe, or at least suggest, what should be done in the future.

These aspects of Data have not changed over the millennia. What has changed are the following:

- Our ability to record data in new forms and formats.
- Our ability to use that data in new ways in commerce and in life.
- Our ability to predict the future and define future courses of action in uncertain situations.

I leave to the anthropologists the stories that were passed down from generation to generation to explain past events and situations and the written records that evolved to provide permanence to this data and our understandings of its meaning.

What is Data?

To ask what data is, is both simple and complicated. The simple answer is that data is the stuff stored in databases. The data were previously captured by computer applications, by websites, or by sensors and placed in databases for operational use and for future analytical use. A more nuanced definition of data considers factors such as where the data came from, where it is stored, how it will be used, how it might predict the future. This are a long way from data as a bunch of zeros (0's) and ones (1's).

Data comes in many forms as diverse as lists of transactions, lists of entities, directories, numerical counts, webpages, posts, audio files, video files, and much more.

Certain data has a very special place in business and in our personal lives, specifically data that identifies us and describes who we are, our habits, and our values. This is generally lumped together in the category of Personally Identified Information or PII.

Facts and Data

From the perspective of data, the word **Fact** is an interesting word. **Facts** attaches the concept of reality to data, i.e., that data are true factual abstractions of reality, the opposite of which is 'fake news,' a current in vogue term, or 'old wives' tales.' Per Merriam-Webster, old wives' tales are 'an often-traditional belief that is not based on fact', i.e., a superstition. Maybe the word 'superstition' is really looking down on ancient experiences through a modern lens and maybe, just maybe, missing the underlying realities of our ancestors. It is interesting to wonder about the life experiences on which these tales are based. Clearly, or unfortunately, we are well acquainted with the various disasters nature can unleash on us. We now understand earthquakes and droughts and don't attribute them to upset gods. 'Fact' may in fact be the relatively new way to identify situations which have persisted for millennia, such as natural disasters.

Staying in the present, nearly everything that happens today is recorded in ones and zeroes, the basic language of computers. It is hard to think of anything that isn't being recorded today although a lot isn't, such as our daily lives. A lot goes unrecorded, at least we hope it is unrecorded. A variation on the question, 'if a tree falls in the forest and no one hears it fall, did it make a sound?' Do events require witnesses? We become acutely aware of this problem when we look at data, asking questions of data which is incomplete or sheds little or absolutely no light on a subject at hand.

Keeping with this theme, Data will be discussed along three dimensions:

1 The Past – Data as documentation, as records of past entities, events, and situations.
2 The Present – Data as the mechanism that moves business processes, and our personal lives, forward. Data is an activator or catalyst or impetus to action.
3 The Future – Data as the basis for Predicting the Future and Prescribing Future actions.

Today popular books on data focus on a variety of viewpoints – Data Analytics, Artificial Intelligence, Machine Learning, Data Science and more. These approaches often take for granted the quality or lack of quality of the data upon which these methods rely.

You may be familiar with the expression 'Garbage In Garbage Out.' It was a well-known phrase, maybe overworked, but built on the concept of 'good' data. How can we expect to make effective decisions based on poor data, or dirty data, on erroneous data or misleading data? Maybe the phrase should be updated to 'Bad Data In, Bad Decisions Out.'

Artificial Intelligence (AI) and Machine Learning (ML) are hot topics today as AI and ML move from imagination to reality in business and in our personal lives. A recent webinar title reminded me of the importance of Data to Artificial Intelligence and Machine Learning. The title included the following phrase: 'AI & Data.' Simply put, 'No Data No AI', 'No Data No Machine Learning'. These technologies rely on data. Data is their foundation. No Data, No Technology. It is as simple as that. Hence, data and these technologies are inherently joined like Siamese twins.

We all have an idea of what data is. It is constantly mentioned in the news. The expression 'the data says …' has become commonplace. Parenthetically, as this book is in its final stages or preparation, Open AI's DALL-E and ChatGPT have leaped from development to newscasts, to newspaper headlines, to full blown popular articles on artificial intelligence.

The Value of Data

Data has become the currency of the 21st Century. It has become Digital Gold, not cryptocurrency, but nevertheless an object of great value. To limit 'Digital Gold' to cryptocurrency is much too limiting. The idea behind data as the 21st Century currency is the recognition that data is essential to commerce and to our personal lives. We check our email before we go to bed; we check our email when we get up the next morning … to be sure we don't miss anything. Jokingly, I wonder what would happen if the world ended and we didn't get an email telling us that. If the answer to this conundrum is found anywhere, it would mostly likely be in science fiction.

I was recently appalled by an organization that justified imposing additional late renewal fees based on the need to re-enter expired members' data. What? Does that mean that the organization discards member's data when members don't renew? This makes no sense.

This example raises an interesting question. How valuable is our data? For a glimpse into the value of data, consider the gambling industry and the bankruptcy of Caesars Entertainment. The data in Caesar's Total Rewards loyalty program was estimated to be worth over $1 billion. [– Bernard Marr, 'Big Data At Caesars Entertainment – A One Billion Dollar Asset?', Forbes, May 18, 2015.] For another example, consider the value of the three credit reporting agencies, Experian, Equifax, and TransUnion. As of the beginning of 2022, the three agencies had a total valuation of over $75B. [Calculated in January 2022 based on information supplied by www.stockopedia.com and www.macroaxis.com.] Does data have value? You bet it does!

Today there are businesses whose business in whole or in part is directly related to data, such as the major credit reporting agencies. Other Data Businesses include Data Aggregators and Data Brokers. They buy data, organize and re-organize that data, and then re-sell that data to buyers who most likely use that data to market products and services to us. That data was our data; that data was data about us.

Consider the case of search engines. Their activity is founded on data. Every piece of data on the Internet, directly or indirectly, is cataloged. Every search is recorded and categorized. The data is 'read,' is categorized and organized to be useful. These records allow us to ask for documents, images or sounds based on categories as well as keywords. For example, we can search for movies based on titles, subject matter content, even the actors, a common activity during the pandemic as we found ourselves in front of the TV more than ever. More astonishingly we can create images based on words, phrases, descriptions. DALL-E can transform your words into a painting worthy of the masters or a photo-realistic image. DALL-E is described as 'Text-To-Image AI'. That's incredible.

Data has uses and value. Today the call is for businesses is to 'monetize' their assets. One of the biggest and easiest business assets to monetize is data. Consider the Caesars Entertainment bankruptcy. Data was the biggest single asset in the bankruptcy. Today there is an active market for data, for our data, that is in many respects outside our view even though the data is our data.

Consider a simple case – shopping online. We look at an item and the system suggests other similar or complementary items to buy. These recommendations are based in part on our previous purchases and in part on the previous purchases of others. The system draws conclusions based on sales history and other data to make these suggestions. The tricky part is that while this may seem helpful, is it really unbiased? Whose interests are served by these recommendations, our interests, or the interests of the sellers?

This behoves us to know, to really know, our data. We need to know our data, who has it and how out data is used. Why? Because this data affects how we view the world and the choices we make. TikTok has increasingly become a platform of interest because of the data it collects about its users and how TikTok uses that data to decide which videos it makes available to its users. TikTok may have started out as a platform for silly, benign, entertaining videos, but it has become more sophisticated, dare I say more aggressive, in its data collection and in its use of that data. TikTok, like other social media platforms, are having impacts far beyond their original design. TikTok has become a platform of interest because of how it molds its users' worldviews and more widely because of its effects on society in general. Are TikTok and other social media platforms still benign or are they forces that need to be reckoned with?

Final Thought

Consider the following:

> Trying to make sense of the economy over the past 18 months or so has felt like a fruitless endeavor most of the time. Sometimes all you need is cold, hard numbers. Every week, Bloomberg Opinion's Robert

Burgess '... wades through the deluge of data to find just one number that can help us make sense of it all ... even if it only brings comfort for a few days.'

> – Bloomberg Opinion, 'The Most Important Number of the Week is ...', July 18, 2021.

The intention of this book is to 'make sense of' data and the roles it plays in business and in our personal lives. The intention is to reasonably cover the topic of data from its inception to its final uses. This lifecycle begins with the generation of data, extends through its processing, which includes organizing and re-organizing and enhancement, through multiple uses to its ultimate archiving or deletion.

A Passing Footnote:

At the point in time of this writing, COVID-19 has upended our lives and we are trying to get back to normal, granted a new normal. For an extended period, we sheltered-at-home. Even now some continue to restrict their movements while many attempt to resume the lives they knew before the pandemic. Remote working has become an alternative for those who can work remotely; however, frontline workers from grocery store workers to medical personnel have little choice but to continue working on site in grocery stores and medical institutions in fear of or in resignation of the virus.

By the time you read this book, the pandemic and its aftermath may be history, maybe ancient history, BUT the pandemic was an incredible example of data playing out in our lives, front and center. The pandemic was inescapable. It was on television, in the newspapers, on social media and in our daily interactions. We were living epidemiology, (the study of the distribution and determinants of disease and health-related states and events). For epidemiologists, data and statistical analysis are essential resources and skills. Statistics were no longer a remote branch of mathematics reserved for data nerds. Statistics were determining our lives.

Information about the pandemic was impossible to avoid. Dr. Anthony Fauci, then Director of the NIH's Division of Infectious Disease, was a constant on news outlets. His favorite expression was 'the data says'. International, national, state, and local policies were determined by this data. Our daily lives were determined by this data. From the public's perspective, data science was no longer theoretical; it was omni present and continues to be present. Data Science provided many examples to which we can all relate.

We continue to hope, or wish, to resume normal activities as the virus always seems to have something new for us to deal with. As has been said, 'we are ready to be done with the virus, but the virus isn't ready to be done with us.' Only as time passes will the full impact of COVID-19 on our business and personal lives be known. There will be a normal, but it will be different than the previous normal.

Chapter 3

The Many Facets of Data

Section Outline:

- Introduction
- Basic Concepts
- Basic Terms and Terminology

Introduction:

Thinking about how to 'tee up' the subject of Data, I am reminded of gemstones. A single gemstone may have many different facets, a nod to One-to-Many relationships, which will be discussed later in the book.

So, it is with Data. Data can be viewed through many different lenses from many different perspectives such as:

- How the data was Generated or Captured.
- How the data was Processed.
- How the data was Changed.
- How the data was Stored.
- How the data was Enhanced.
- How the data was Analyzed.
- How the data is used in Decision-making.

Data is the same as a gemstone – One Stone Many Facets; One Topic, Data, with many different perspectives through which the data can be viewed. This multi-facet, multi-dimensional aspect of data is evident in the Data Management Association's (DAMA) summary diagrams. Note Figure 3.1 is the original image; Figure 3.2 is the current evolved image. Figure 3.2 showing a more complex version.

Accordingly, this book begins with common terms and concepts. Most books put this list in the back of the book. Instead, this list is in the front so readers will be familiar with these terms and concepts. Without a basic knowledge of these concepts, readers may miss their significance. Feel free

DOI: 10.4324/9781003295228-3

Figure 3.1   DAMA Original Data Governance Model
Reproduced with permission of DAMA International

to skip through the list looking for unfamiliar terms or concepts. In any case, all these terms and concepts are part of the narrative about data. Understanding this narrative is difficult without an appreciation for these items; hence, the list is at the beginning of the book instead of being relegated to the back of the book.

As with every business and profession, data has its own language, its own terminology, its own lingo, which were specifically developed to give voice to various aspects of data. In this respect, data is no different than any other discipline.

So, the book begins with an enumeration of Basic Concepts followed by an enumeration of words that have a particular meaning, i.e., these words are 'terms of art.' Each concept or word is a facet, a lens, through which to access data, its meaning, and its use.

Each of the terms discussed below has a specific meaning. While it isn't necessary to be fluent in the language of data, being familiar with these terms and the concepts will give readers a deeper understanding of data, its management, and its use. This is in two parts: Beginning with broad terms and concepts and then moving to specific terms and terminology followed by a chapter discussing domains, broader topics that involve multiple specific terms and ideas.

Figure 3.2 DAMA Revised Data Governance Model
Reproduced with permission of DAMA International

A sidenote, NIST, the National Institute of Standards and Technology, a division of the U.S. Department of Commerce, maintains a superb glossary at https://csrc.nist.gov/glossary. If this link becomes invalid, this happens from time or time when documents are moved, merely Google NIST Glossary and you should get an updated link for the Glossary. NIST's Glossary goes far beyond the terms and concepts listed below.

3.1 Basic Concepts

Data

Data are facts, things, events, circumstances, relationships.

For example, data includes Prospects, Customers, Suppliers, Items, Locations, Subsidiaries, Divisions, Purchases, Sales, Shipments, Returns, Transfers, Bills of Materials, Routings, Work Centers, People, and their activities, social, professional, economic, entertaining, sounds, images, the list goes on and on. If you can Google it, it is Data.

Data plays a crucial role in business processes. **Data** both documents business processes, i.e., business events, and moves them forward in their workflow. In workflow, **Data** triggers subsequent steps in the workflow. For example, when an item is purchased online by approving the Shopping Cart, a group of actions are triggered. They happen beyond our view. They include approving our credit, picking the items ordered, packing them, shipping them, and ultimately delivering them to us. The process, at least from our perspective, culminates in the delivery of the items ordered at our front door. The data may also be used outside of our knowledge to determine inventory levels, pricing and whether to continue stocking items. Hence, data identify entities and events that occurred, and it causes additional actions to occur. Ultimately, in the background, data empowers analysis and decision-making.

Information

Information is the meaning we attach to Data, especially to things and events in contrast to their identification. The distinction:

- **Data** are the Raw Facts.
- **Information** is the Meaning and/or Significance we attach to the Raw Facts.

Consider the example of online shopping again. **Data** identifies us, the items we purchased, and the steps that ultimately resulted in the delivery of the items we ordered. **Information**, in contrast, talks about the economic impact of the sale and the potential need to resupply the inventory, especially if we ordered items that are routinely sold by the seller, to say nothing of our satisfaction with the items we ordered.

While in Greece during our summer vacation an interesting example of the difference between Data and Information caught my attention. While driving, I glanced at the car's clock. The time was 16:22. To make sense of 16:22, I had to convert it to 4:22 pm, aha, late afternoon. Reflecting on this situation, the distinction between Data and Meaning was clear. I am accustomed to the 12-hour clock, not the 24-hour clock. To make sense of, to assign meaning to the data, I had to convert the data from one format to another format with which I was more familiar. The **Data** was 16:22 or 4:22 pm; the **Meaning** was late afternoon. Hopefully this example illustrates the difference between **Data** and **Information** and suggests that transformations may be required to make data meaningful, to make data useful.

Data Governance

Data Governance is an enterprise's overall approach to, commitment to and oversight of Data Management. It encompasses the enterprise's Goals, Objectives, Strategies, Policies, Procedures, Practices, Standards, Guidelines, Rules, and Requirements that apply to data and the monitoring and oversight of these elements. Data Governance stresses the organization's commitment to adequately fund data, to comply with the organization's overall goals and objectives related to data and its use, to ensure effective management of its data and, not the least, to conform to applicable compliance requirements associated with the data.

The big challenges for Data Governance are the following:

- Ensuring appropriate Data Policies, Procedures, Practices, Standards, Guidelines, Rules, and Requirements.
- Ensuring that these elements are effective throughout the organization.
- Ensuring Data Integrity, Data Quality, and active remediation of issues related to Data Corruption.
- Ensuring that Decisions are made based on data that are appropriate, relevant, and reliable.
- Ensuring that the Data Infrastructure and Resources, including skilled technicians, are adequately funded and resourced.
- Ensuring data is adequately protected, including data that is the intellectual property of the business, customer, and user, and complies with relevant requirements, such as PCI DSS, HITECH, GDPR, CCPA or similar data protection regulations.

  PCI-DSS = Payment Card Industry Data Security Standard.
  HITECH = Health Information Technology for Economic Clinical Health Act.
  GDPR = General Data Protection Regulations of the EU.
  CCPA = California Consumer Privacy Act.

Summarized in slightly different language, Data Governance is the organization's mandates and monitoring of those mandates to ensure high quality data, properly used in decision-making, and effective protection of data from unauthorized access, use or exposure.

Data Architecture

Data Architecture is the intentional design and standards related to the generation and/or capture of data, its retention, manipulation, and subsequent use.

The Open Group in its Architectural Framework (TOGAF) defines Architecture as follows:

3.7 Architecture

1. The fundamental concepts or properties of a system in its environment embodied in its elements, relationships, and in the principles of its design and evolution. [Source: ISO/IEC/IEEE 42010: 2011]

2. The structure of components, their inter-relationships, and the principles and guidelines governing their design and evolution over time.

– The Open Group, The TOGAF® Standard, Version 9.2,
2018, p. 22.

In the context of data, Data Architecture refers to the fundamental concepts, design, and evolution of the data platform, including its components, their inter-relationships and the principles and guidelines that govern data and its collection and use.

Usually, the term architecture is applied to physical infrastructure, but as used here, we are talking about the broader concepts of goals, objectives, strategies, policies, procedures, practices, standards, frameworks, and the staffing that maintains data and ensures its integrity and appropriate use, i.e., this is much more than just the databases that hold the data.

Data Management

Data Management is perhaps the broadest most encompassing term covering all domains, disciplines, techniques, and tools used to manage data. Data Management is a widely used, overarching, all-encompassing term. In other words, Data Management includes everything involved in managing, manipulating, storing, and using data.

DAMA defines the goals of Data Management as follows:

- Understanding and supporting the information needs of the enterprise and its stakeholders, including customers, employees, and business partners
- Capturing, storing, protecting, and ensuring the integrity of data assets
- Ensuring the quality of data and information
- Ensuring the privacy and confidentiality of stakeholder data
- Preventing unauthorized or inappropriate access, manipulations, or use of data and information
- Ensuring data can be used effectively to add value to the enterprise.

– DAMA-DMBOK: DATA MANAGEMENT BODY OF
KNOWLEDGE, 2nd Edition, p.18.

Notice the recurring themes:

- Supporting Enterprise Needs
- Providing Value to the Enterprise
- Capturing, Storing, and Processing Data
- Ensuring Data Integrity and Data Quality
- Ensuring Data Privacy and Data Confidentiality
- Ensuring Data Compliance, and
- Controlling Data Access, i.e., Limiting access to data

Data Wrangling or Data Munging

Data Wrangling is a similarly broad term. It refers to working with data from inception through use. Data Wranglers are the technicians and engineers that manage an enterprise's data on behalf of the Enterprise, the Data Owners and Stewards, and the Users. Broadly speaking, Data Wrangling includes at least the following activities:

- Generating/Creating/Discovering Data
- Manipulating Data
- Aggregating and Merging Data
- Structuring and Re-structuring, Organizing and Re-organizing Data
- Cleaning/Correcting Data
- Managing Data Gaps and Missing Data Elements
- Enriching Data
- Validating Data
- Publishing Data
- Broadly Managing Data

A Harvard Business Review post refers to Data Wrangling as the 'processes designed to transform raw data into more readily used formats.' [– https://online.hbs.edu/blog/post/data-wrangling.] This is a reasonable but overly limited view of Data Wrangling.

A broader view of Data Wrangling and Data Wranglers includes all aspects of data, except for the management of the applications that generate, manage, and use data for their specific purposes. The application can easily be a cooperative responsibility involving the business owners of the applications and the Data Wrangler. Data Wranglers often export and reprovision application Data for purposes beyond the applications themselves. The engineers and technicians that provide these services generally self-identify as Data Wranglers.

From the perspective of tools, a wide variety of tools are available to assist Data Wranglers, including but not limited to Altair, Alteryx, csvkit, Microsoft EXCEL, Power BI and Power Platform, including Dataverse, Tableau, Talend, Trifacta/Google Dataprep, and statistical platforms such as

R and Python. There are also products for specific sources or targets, such as Datameer (built specifically for Snowflake) and Tabula for data in PDFs. With any list of products such as this, remember products evolve over time. New products emerge; older products disappear. For an aspiring Data Wrangler, do research and see which products are currently widely used. When selecting tools also consider how they will help you get your job done with some thought to what might happen to these tools in the future.

3.2 Basic Terms and Terminology

Abstraction is conceptualizing data where the focus shifts from individual data elements to general concepts, categories, or types, of which the individual items are examples. The Data Management Association (DAMA) describes **Abstraction** as '… the removal of details in such a way as to broaden applicability to a wide class of situations while preserving the important properties and essential nature from concepts or subjects.'

[– DAMA-DMBOK: DATA MANAGEMENT BODY OF KNOWLEDGE, 2nd Edition, p. 151.]

For example, a baseball, a basketball, a football and so on are examples of balls. Consider, for example, Athens, Berlin, Buenos Aires, Cairo, Chicago, London, Los Angeles, New York, Paris, Sydney, and Tokyo. They are all cities, each with its own personalities, nuances, peculiarities, location and so on, but they are all cities. Some are seaports; others are landlocked; hence, 'city' is the highest level of abstraction, and 'seaport' or 'landlocked' are characteristics of 'city'.

ACID – BASE – CAP

ACID is a model to ensure dependable Data in relational databases. The individual elements of ACID are:

- **A**tomicity
- **C**onsistency
- **I**solation
- **D**urability

Atomicity requires transactions either succeed or fail. There is nothing in between, i.e., partial success does not exist in the ACID model.

Consistency requires transactions to meet all appropriate business rules; hence, again avoiding partial data, i.e., it's all or nothing at all.

Isolation means that each transaction is separate and independent of all other transactions, which means they don't interfere with each other.

Durability means transactions cannot be changed once they are completed. However, transactions can and are routinely updated, which can include off-setting transactions that alter or adjust the original transactions.

ACID is an underlying design principle for relational databases.

BASE

BASE is the opposite of ACID. **ACID** is pessimistic in the sense that it enforces consistency at the end of every operation. In contrast, **BASE** is optimistic in the sense that it believes that consistency will eventually emerge. **BASE** reflects the emergence of unstructured data and the need to read-optimize the Data without the constraints imposed by ACID. **BASE** also supports partitioned databases and scalability by not insisting on consistency at the time transactions are entered.

BASE stands for **B**asically **A**vailable, **S**oft State, **E**ventually Consistent. For an in-depth discussion of **BASE** see 'Base: An Acid Alternative' at https://queue.acm.org/detail.cfm?id=1394128.

Table 3.1 ACID and BASE compared

	ACID	*BASE*
Database	Schema Restricted	More Flexible & Dynamic
Structure	Tables & Columns with Data types	Tags, Key-Value Pairs, Graphs stores dissimilar data
Consistency	Consistency Enforced	May be Strong, Eventual or None
Focus	Transaction Processing (TP)	Unstructured or Semi Structured Data
History	Traditional Approach	Modern, Works with Unstructured Data
Scaling	Depends on Product & Design	Automatic Scaling

CAP

CAP is another alternative. **CAP** refers to **C**onsistency, **A**vailability and **P**artition Tolerance.

The **CAP** Theorem arose in response to Distributed Systems where Consistency and Availability are not necessarily required and Partitioning, Partition Tolerances, is allowed. This theorem is typically expressed as the 'Pick Two' choice, where we can't have all three constraints at the same time. This is illustrated in Figure 3.3 below.

As the equilateral triangle shows, the three choices are of equal importance and two of three options can be picked but not all three.

Consistent Data – Constant Data Availability – Partition Tolerance

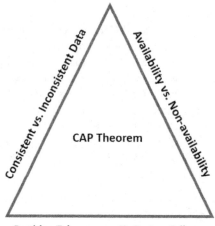

Figure 3.3 CAP Theorem

The Cap Theorem says one must compromise on one of three choices, either Inconsistent Data or a Storage System that is not Always Available or allowing for a Partitioned Environment. This choice is characterized as an Optimistic choice, optimistic in the sense that ultimately, eventually all data is fully stored.

ACID is the traditional approach found in relational databases while **BASE** and **CAP** support newer types of Data and Data storage mechanisms especially the emergence of Big Data, unstructured Data and decentralized storage.

Application Programming Interface (API)

Application Programming Interfaces, APIs, are the gateways that allow data to move into and out of applications. The objective of APIs today is to share data across multiple applications and platforms. APIs have become universal gateways among applications and platforms.

As originally conceived, APIs were intended to provide gateways into applications. They allowed data to be imported directly into applications instead of having to go through conventional manual data entry screens. Suppose one has a thousand names and email addresses that need to go into a CRM system. Being able to upload a file is much easier than having someone enter a thousand names and addresses manually into a CRM system using its data entry screens.

Today APIs are bidirectional gateways, which means they can be used to both import and export data, which allows data to be easily shared among multiple applications and platforms, a quantum leap forward.

APIs are intelligent in the sense that they have access to the validation rules and know how and where to store and retrieve, especially when data is spread across multiple tables.

A critical constraint: Modern business transaction processing systems store their data not in one or two database tables but in many tables. If the data were stored in only one or two tables, importing and exporting data would be relatively simple, but as the number of tables increases so does the complexity of importing and exporting data. The APIs handle this problem; they know the rules and process the data appropriately whether the data is entering the system or leaving the system. This is fantastic and provides opportunities for data automation that move data among applications and platforms.

Data Analytics

Data Analytics is today's bright shiny object. It is the ability to analyze data and, in the process, discover meaning and, hopefully, an understanding that shows a path forward. As businesses amass data regarding their customers and their habits, the insights hidden inside this data are both necessary and irresistible. Businesses search for tools and techniques to understand why customers buy what they buy, when they buy and how this information might be used to better serve the organization's customers. This is Data Analytics in operation.

Data Analytics can be divided into four general technical types:

- Descriptive Analytics – The goal of Descriptive Analytics is to describe, to understand, previous circumstances and situations based on Data.
- Diagnostic Analytics – The goal of Diagnostic Analytics is like Descriptive Analytics with an emphasis on 'causes and effects,' i.e., moving from 'symptoms' to 'causes.'
- Predictive Analytics – The intention of Predictive Analytics is to predict future situations based on similar prior situations. For example, what will our customers want to purchase in the future, what portion of our sales will occur in specific time periods, such as seasons, how much inventory should be stocked for specific seasons, and so on. In general, we are trying to predict future numerical quantities, for example the business will sell 510,000 pieces during the next busy season.
- Prescriptive Analytics – The intention of Prescriptive Analytics is to suggest a course of action, a response, based on based on prior history.

Predictive Analytics makes predictions whereas Prescriptive Analytics suggest courses of action based on these predictions. Prescriptive Analytics is the next step beyond Predictive Analytics.

Sticking with the previous example, if the system projects sales of 100,000 pieces, then we may want to start the season with at least 100,000 pieces. If this quantity is unusually higher than normal sales, extra marketing efforts may be in order. We may also want to make alternative plans if demand is less than or greater than the predicted 100,000 pieces.

Consider a public company's stock price. It can be evaluated over an extended period. That data could be analyzed for movements in the stock price to identify trends and unusual stock movements, outliers. This is Descriptive Analytics. The analysis could focus on the ups, downs, and sideway movements of the stock to determine what caused them, maybe new products and services, maybe stale products or services that reduced sales, maybe external events such as a pandemic that affected the business' stock price positively or negatively. This is Diagnostic Analytics. Based on what is known, predictions could be made about the future price of the stock. This is predictive analytics, and finally recommendations could be made regarding potential positions in the stock. This is Prescriptive Analytics.

Data is the subject matter of Data Analytics (DA). From this analysis flows understanding based on the data to which the Analysis is applied. There are any number of books about data analysis and various data analytic tools and techniques. The focus here is on the data that is the basis, the foundation, for understanding and for decision-making, especially the preparation of the data for analysis and evaluation.

Data Attributes

Data Attributes are the **Data Elements**, the **Characteristics,** associated with **Entities** and **Events**. For example, the entity Customer has a name, an ID number, at least one if not many addresses, telephone numbers, email addresses, and so on. These are Attributes or Characteristics of the primary object.

Some of the attributes may be classifiers like make and model. Some of the attributes may be reporting dimensions that allow the data to be 'sliced and diced,' where slicing and dicing refers to breaking a dataset into subsets. For example, take customers and slice them by sales volume, by items purchased, by location, by frequency of purchases, or other attributes. Whenever you hear 'slicing and dicing,' think attributes and dimensions as large datasets are broken down into subsets, into subgroupings, based on shared characteristics.

Big Data

Big Data is a big deal. Maybe Yes and Maybe No, depending upon the circumstances. This is said in the context of '**Big Data**' is a big deal, which may not necessarily be true. Big Data is not necessarily an issue for all businesses; it could represent big opportunities. And newer technologies are making Big Data more accessible to businesses regardless of size or resources.

What distinguishes Big Data? This question was usually answered in terms of V's. Originally there were three V's but over time the number of V's has grown to 8 or 9.

The original 3 Vs were:

- **Variety**
- **Velocity**
- **Volume**

Variety refers to significant diversity and variability within datasets. This easily occurs in business, health, and financial data to say nothing of social media, which is inherently diverse. For example, think of the data collected by the credit reporting agencies or the vastness of social media posts.

Velocity refers to torrents of data. Consider the daily volume of social media interactions. Everyday new data, new statistics are generated, collected, and analyzed. It truly is an onrushing flood of data.

Volume refers to the enormity of the data. Consider the daily sales of larger retailers; consider all healthcare agencies worldwide and the volume of data they collect daily; or consider Data Brokers that maintain contact data for individuals and businesses worldwide.

As originally coined, the term 'Big Data' referred to

- An abundance of data
- With a great deal of variety
- Coming at us at the speed of on-rushing asteroids.

The emphasis is on how businesses handle this kind of data in contrast to the more orderly data accumulated by businesses through in-house applications.

But Big Data is more than Variety, Velocity and Volume. Over time other V's that were added, such as:

- **Veracity**
- **Value**
- **Validity**
- **Vulnerability**
- **Volatility**
- **Visualization**

Validity and Veracity ask if the data is valid and creditable? Can this data be relied on for decision-making? Volatility focuses on fluctuation versus consistency. Is the data in a state of constant flux? How quickly can systems react to changes in the data? Does the volatility make the Data more useful or less useful? Vulnerability refers to the Data's attractiveness to bad actors.

Large Data farms could be irresistible to malicious actors who recognize the potential Value of the Data. Visualization has been added to the list by some commentators to include how Data is displayed and consumed.

Collectively, these are slightly different, but potentially overlapping dimensions.

For business, the big questions are:

- Can this data help us be competitive, potentially more competitive?
- Can this data help us increase revenue?
- Can this data help us control costs?
- Can this data help us increase profit?
- Can this data make us more effective?
- What is the cost of this data?
- How much work must be done to make this data useful?
- What resources are required to manage and manipulate this data? Do we have the tools and skills to easily manage this data, and if we don't, how can we get them?

Data Brokers

Big Data is big business. **Data Brokers** are the companies that acquire, process, and resell Big Data. They are in the business of Big Data. The most recognizable Data Brokers are probably the credit reporting agencies. They collect, aggregate, organize, cleanse, and distribute financial information about consumer and business financial activities, but they are not alone. There are many other companies in the Big Data Pipeline.

The originators of Big Data are very familiar. They collect and/or generate and resell business and personal data. We certainly recognize, Google, Facebook, Instagram, TikTok, Amazon as well as other big players in search, social media, and retail spaces. We also recognize the banks, the supermarkets, the big box stores, and other retail establishments with which we interact daily. Their business activities are sources of Big Data.

How can we get a glimpse 'behind the curtain'? Getting a glimpse is relatively easy. Search for an unusual product or service, unusual for you, or go to a website and look at products that are unusual for you. Then continue working on the Internet and see how long before ads appear for the items you looked at only minutes or hours before. Obtain a loan or a new credit card and see how quickly this affects our credit score. This is the Big Data industry constantly at work.

The 'Data Superhighway' is open for business at warp speed. We don't have to do anything to see our data flying around the Internet. This is one reason for Europe's General Data Protection Regulations (GDPR) and the California Consumer Protection Act (CCPA). For more information on either of these regulations, go to https://gdpr-info.eu/ or https://www.oag. ca.gov/privacy/ccpa.

For current purposes, the objective is merely to recognize the existence of this industry. Our businesses may already be using this industry for information about our customers and potential customers, for lead generation and for competitive analysis, at the least.

Part of what fuels this industry is the push to 'monetize' assets. 'Monetizing' assets is another revenue stream for businesses. It allows, it encourages businesses to convert their business information into cash. So, there is a complete supply chain for data: Businesses eager to sell their data for cash, Data Brokers that are eager to get business data which they can in turn sell to their customers, and finally businesses eager to buy this data for a variety of purposes. This is a perfect storm in which we are the commodity, our data is the commodity, that is routinely bought and sold.

Capability Maturity Model Integration (CMMI):

Capability Maturity Model Integration may seem a little off topic but reserve judgement. **Capability Maturity Model Integration** asks how mature, how developed, how sophisticated an organization's policies, procedures, practices, and standards are. This easily applies to data. Aside from the specifics of CMMI, which are available at https://cmmiinstitute.com, the maturity integration model stresses the effectiveness of an organization's policies, procedures, practices, and processes and its ability to refine and improve these capabilities. CMMI embodies the notion of continuous improvement, increasingly a requirement of a hypercompetitive marketplace.

The ideal is explicit policies, procedures, practices, and processes, which, in turn, provides a basis for evaluating the effectiveness of these items and initiating improvements to them. The exact opposite of a mature organization is an organization lacking formal policies, procedures, practices, and processes. For them, every issue, every problem is something new that needs an ad hoc resolution. In other words, the organization is constantly 'fighting fires.'

The takeaway is that sophisticated formal policies and procedures allow organizations to constantly re-evaluate their performance and refine their practices to improve performance. Lacking this, an organization is likely to rush from one problem to another. As a practical matter, most organizations are somewhere between the extremes hopefully working to improve.

Data Capture – Data Collection

Data Capture or **Collection** deals with the beginning of the data pipeline, the data's point of origin. The data may be generated by systems or somehow captured. The source could be an internal or external system. For example, when we ship an order, we 'generate' shipping information. At the same time, we receive information from the carrier, which was generated by the carrier's system. In the end, we end up with a mix of data generated by our system and by the carrier's systems.

Data Capture or Data Collection refers to the systems in businesses that initially recognize data was generated by our systems and/or obtained from external sources. In either case, the data is stored in our systems. Data Capture or Generation is an inherent aspect of business systems.

Data Catalog – Data Dictionary – Data Glossary

Data Catalog, Data Dictionary, Data Glossary are similar overlapping terms.

The common aspects are information about data including at least the following items:

- Name
- Description
- Associated Metadata used to Identify and Classify Data
- Related Attributes
- Where the data is Produced/Generated
- Where the data is Stored
- Where the data is Consumed

Data Dictionaries generally contain the names and meanings of tables and data elements in the tables in the databases. A **Data Glossary** is similar including names and descriptions of the data elements. A **Data Catalog**, though similar, also may also tell us where the data and its elements are stored. In common practice, these distinctions blur.

Nevertheless, the items listed above are important because they identify and explain the data, its elements, and tell us where they reside. Without this information, we are left to guess, which is not necessarily quick or accurate, especially in large databases and data repositories. Knowing where Data resides is crucial to storing, accessing, and effectively using data.

Data Chain of Custody

Chain of Custody is a legal term, which is useful beyond its legal definition.

Data routinely moves from one place to another place, around and among various systems and storage facilities. The idea behind **Data Chain of Custody** is the assurance that the data moves intact, that data integrity continues. **Chain of Custody** emphasizes Data Integrity as data moves from place to place. This becomes particularly important when the data moves through multiple systems and hands and in the process can become compromised or corrupted or at least be of uncertain integrity.

The big questions then are:

- Was the Data corrupted?
- Where did the corruption occur?
- When did the corruption occur?
- What is the nature of the corruption? Is this merely a matter of spelling or misspelling or something more complex?
- Were values changed?
- Were values added or deleted? If so, by whom for what purposes?

In a legal environment, **Chain of Custody** is important for evidentiary purposes. In a business environment, the **Data Chain of Custody** and **Data Integrity** are important if we plan to use the data downstream for decision-making purposes where good answers are essential. We could make wrong decisions because the data was corrupted. The sooner the nature and extent of the corruption is identified, the sooner decisions can be adjusted.

Misinterpreting data is our mistake. Incorrect data is not necessarily our mistake but, in the end, we 'own' our decisions whether they are based on good data or bad data; hence, the concept **Data Chain of Custody** is critical. It emphasizes Data Integrity as data passes from system to system, from entity to entity so we can 'own' good decisions.

Data Cleansing/Data Cleaning, a.k.a., Data Correction

Data Cleansing is fixing data, where the data is inaccurate, incomplete, incorrect, invalid. It is the process of detecting and correcting errors. At its simplest, **Data Cleansing** or **Data Cleaning** is:

- Identifying Errors in data
- Fixing these Errors

Cleansing begins with identifying erroneous data.

The erroneous data can be fixed in place, in situ, or it can be moved to another area and fixed there, say a quarantine area, either approach is fine. If the questionable data is separated from the principal dataset, this is typically referred to as quarantining the erroneous data. Identifying errors is especially the case when data moves through a 'pipeline.' One objective is to ensure that erroneous data does not become mixed in with error-free data. Another approach is to clearly identify errors, i.e., tag the errors, so that they can be easily cleaned up later.

Correction can involve several different actions:

- Modifying, Correcting, Changing, Editing existing erroneous Data Elements
- Adding missing Data Elements, i.e., completing the Data
- Deleting erroneous Data if they cannot be corrected
- Good practices suggest keeping a record of the changes. Sometimes changes must be rolled back, and the data has to be re-cleansed.

When it comes to erroneous data, there several special cases worth noting:

- Classification related Issues
- Missing Data
- Duplicates

Classification Related Issues:

Classification Data is important for reporting and for analytic purposes. It can be inaccurate or missing. Either way, reporting or analysis may be compromised and potentially misleading.

When talking about Classification Data, think about how often Classification plays an important role in summarizing or analyzing data. Take a simple example of customer sales. If you wish to summarize or analyze customer sales by customer type or item type, the summarization or analysis is much easier if all the customers and all items have types, and the types are correct. Lacking the types or dealing with incorrect types makes accurate summarization or analysis difficult and potentially misleading. For another example, what about summaries and/or analyzes of employees. Summaries or analyses in this area may require multiple different employee categories. So, having that data, or access to that data, is crucial for a complete, accurate analysis.

In any discussion about Data, missing Data values are a problem, doubly so if the missing data elements are classifiers. Partially missing Classification Data limits analysis; completely missing Data means no analysis or at least no analysis that depends on that Classification Data. If the Classification Data is only partially missing, then the analysis is only partially compromised, which can render the analysis inadequate or worse misleading.

The next aspect reminds me of an adaptation of CS Lewis' Alice's Adventures in Wonderland, 'If you do not know where you want to go, it doesn't matter which path you take.' The adaptation is 'If you don't know where you are going, you won't get there.' All of this suggests that Classification is extremely important and generally needs to be known in advance. Trying to add Classification Data on the fly may be difficult, time consuming, arduous, and potentially misleading. So, better to figure that out in advance and bake the Classification data into the applications that generate the data in question.

A minor twist to Classification Data, is the problem of exclusive categories versus overlapping categories. Consider Returned merchandise. For sake of this discussion, let's say the merchant's first question is whether the merchandise can be sold or not, and the second question is why the consumer returned the merchandise. Was it a matter of taste, or fit, or age, or proper functioning or something else? Knowing whether the merchandise can be resold or not, whether the merchandise is defective or not, whether it can be fixed or not, whether it can be checked and put back on the floor or not, are all important questions. In this case, is the 'or not' true? If the customer didn't like the merchandise and the merchandise is still intact, can the merchandise be resold? Processing refunds on a massive basis requires a group of Classifiers that sort through the various choices. Some classifications are independent of each other; some are interdependent or overlapping. Setting this up requires understanding the merchandise and the alternatives available to the retailer. A sad case that is mostly behind us is the case of returned software. If the media was writeable, occasionally the software came back to the store with malware attached waiting to infect the next customer that installed the software. Gladly this option is now behind us.

No discussion of classification is complete without a brief discussion of more complex cases such as apparel. Garment classification could include any combination of the following classifiers: type, gender, size, color, style, pattern, season, material, line or label, use, and specific characteristics such as long sleeve versus short sleeve, neckline, hemline, crease or no-crease, cuff or no cuff, and the list goes on. See, for example, Amazon's Apparel Product Listing currently at https://sellercentral.amazon.com/gp/help/external/M6YJ5XPA58U99XM.

'Missing' is a special case when we get to numerical data.

Is zero, 0, the same as no value? Remember 0 is a value as much as any other number. Can we assume that a 0 is the value of a field or does it really mean there was no number. Can a zero replace a null value? In some cases, the answer may be yes, in other cases the answer may be no. To understand the situation, let's consider several use cases.

Is a summation affected by a zero or a blank? Not necessarily. Is an average affected by a zero or a blank? Yes, if the average interprets the zero as a number, the denominator, the count, is larger than it would be if the zero was ignored making the average larger. The system that originally captured the data may automatically insert a zero in a numeric field if the field is left blank, i.e., nulls are not allowed. The numerator is the unchanged, but the denominator is larger. The denominator is larger if zeros are included in the count, smaller if they are excluded from the count.

In various situations, null, NA, or a distinctive character, such as #null, may be used to clearly indicate that a particular field is blank, i.e., that there is no value in this field.

Another interesting question: What is the impact of a blank in a particular field relative to the rest of the data? Should that record be excluded from analysis because a particular field is blank or not?

Duplicates can also be problematic. Are they really duplicates? Maybe yes, maybe no, maybe we can't tell.

Problems include:

- Identifying duplicates
- Identifying duplicates when the data is the same versus when the data is different
- Determining how and why duplicates occurred
- Deciding how to appropriately treat them depending on the situation and subsequent uses

Are they truly duplicates or different instances of the same facts? Did the customer buy the same item or items more than once or was the original purchase accidentally duplicated?

Fuzzy Logic can be used to find duplicates where the elements in question are similar but not completely identical, such as proper names with multiple different spellings. Soundex is an example of a system that indexes names based on sound rather than spelling to identify potential misspellings or alternative spellings of a name.

By way of a final off-hand remark, even a broken clock is correct twice a day (assuming a 12-hour clock) … but that doesn't mean the clock isn't broken.

Data Cleansing operates on at least two levels:

- Purity
- Fitness for subsequent downstream

Purity seeks the most complete, consistent, correct, accurate data, while downstream use may require data modified and/or enhanced for a specific purpose. No fixed answer here, simply different situations with different questions.

And this is only a sample of the issues that can arise during Data Cleansing. Remember, in the end the data is being changed hopefully for the better but possibly, just possibly, for the worst.

Data Compliance

Strictly speaking, **Data Compliance** is compliance with applicable laws, regulations, and protocols. In a larger context, **Data Compliance** extends to sensitive data that while outside of regulatory compliance, is still important to businesses.

Data Compliance encompasses two use cases:

- The first use case is Compliance with the applicable laws, regulations, and protocols regarding data, such as PCI-DSS or GDPR.
- The second use case is Conformance with business objectives and standards regarding this data, which is frequently referred as 'sensitive data,' 'trade secrets,' or 'intellectual property', everything from customer lists to customer data, to price lists, to product formulas, and more.

In the first use case, the business is legally liable for failing to comply. In the second use case, there may be no legal liability per se, but the nature of the problem can be just as impactful. Consider something like the formula for Coca-Cola. I suspect Coca-Cola wouldn't want that formula floating around the Internet. Intellectual Property or Trade Secrets involve recognition that the data is super sensitive and warrants great protection. Typically access to such data is very restricted. In an automated environment, multiple hurdles, such as network segmentation, and special authentication procedures can be implemented with the ultimate objective of limiting access to the data to a very small number of individuals.

Data Corruption

Data Corruption is the state of data being erroneous, incomplete, inconsistent, or invalid. As noted above, **Data Cleansing** is the process of dealing with **Corrupted Data**.

Data may have been corrupted at its source or become subsequently corrupted as the data was processed and/or moved among various locations, applications, and databases. The question of Data Corruption boils down to two questions:

- Did the business receive corrupted Data?
- Did the business corrupt previously uncorrupted Data?

If the business received corrupted data, the business needs to deal with the parties from which the data came. If the business corrupted the data, the processes to which the data were subjected need to be reviewed and resolved.

Ultimately, **Data Corruption** is the exact opposite of **Data Quality**.

Data Custodians

Data Custodians are the personnel that manage and operate the databases and repositories in which data is stored. Also see Data Stewardship and Data Stewards, which are below.

Data Stewardship distinguishes among **Data Custodians, Data Owners,** and **Data Stewards**. In larger enterprises these roles and responsibility may be delegated to different personnel; in smaller enterprises single individuals may have 2 or 3 of these roles.

Data Custodians are the keepers of the data, but they are not necessarily 'subject matter experts' regarding the data. Their primary responsibility is the safe keeping of data; hence, the unsung heroes that work in the shadows outside the view of users keeping their data safe.

Data Degradation/Rot

Data Degradation or **Rot** refers to the diminishing relevance, usefulness, and value of data over time. This is especially important when data is being used analytically. Does the data still have the value it previously had or has the value deteriorated over time because relationships and patterns changed. The data may be relevant and important but over time this relevance and importance can decline. Regardless of this decline, the business may wish to keep the data in its current state with an expired flag or separately in an archive environment. Given the cost of data storage today, there is less reason to throw away data to save money. Segregating the Data may be the best option. Instead of tossing the data out, put the data in a separate environment, potentially at a lower cost, but outside the data that is normally used for operations and analysis and retrieve the data in question whenever it is needed ... if it is ever needed.

Consider data on the Spanish Flu. Who would have imagined the lessons that the Spanish Flu might teach us today dealing with COVID-19?

Data De-identification

Data De-identification is 'anonymizing' data, i.e., hiding the identity of sensitive information, such as Personally Identifiable Information (PII). This process is also called Obfuscation or Redaction. The purpose is to hide the identity of a person or entity. An alternate approach is to mark data as 'secret' or 'confidential' to limit its distribution and consumption.

To keep data useful, Raw Data may be profiled or classified along certain dimensions such as type of entity, or geographic region, or other entity characteristic. The data can then be analyzed along these axes without disclosing the identities of the entities involved.

Data Masking is another technique. This technique is frequently used to obscure social security numbers and credit card numbers where only the last 4 digits are visible. The fragment is enough to alert us to the complete number but does not disclose the entire number.

Data Tokenization is another technique. It is discussed below. Tokens take the place of the actual values.

Ultimately, **Data De-identification** is about making the data available but hiding the identities of the entities involved.

Digital Transformation, Document Management, Content Management

Thanks to **Digital Transformation, Document Management** and **Content Management** are moving in new directions as documents are increasingly replaced by 'digital data', i.e., digitized data. Yes, 'digital data' may sound redundant, but the intent is to emphasize the contrast between data on physical documents and data available via electronic means. In the early days of **Digital Transformation**, Digital Transformation meant moving away from paper documents to Data stored in databases, i.e., going 'paperless.' This ultimately has a major impact on **Document Management** and **Content Management**. Documents disappear and content is managed entirely digitally.

A basic tenet of **Digital Transformation** is moving from paper documents to digital data, which can be available to anyone at any time, in multiple formats subject to authorization. **Digital Transformation** aims to transform business processes such that the process is increasingly digital with little need or reliance on traditional documents. A good example is buying stuff online. Normal business documents have been replaced by messages, alerts, and emails. Business documents, such as Purchase Orders, Sales Orders, Work Orders, Invoices, and Shipping Manifests still exist but only digitally; not that they cannot be printed and distributed if needed, but today these items remain primarily digital. One example is Return Material Authorizations (RMAs). Until recently, RMAs were included with shipments to facilitate returns; however, increasing returns are handled by the supplier's website providing a QR code or a scannable number. In these environments, traditional RMAs are no longer used. The object can be taken to a shipping point that tracks the return based on the number embedded in the QR code or available in scannable form.

Another example is vaccination cards. People can carry their cards with them, or they can carry an image on their cellphones. If the cellphone is lost, no big deal, just get a new phone and transfer the image onto the new phone rather than trying to replace a lost physical card.

At some point in the future, **Document Management** and **Data Management** will effectively become one and the same, i.e., the management of the data, which was the subject matter content of the documents. If documents are required, they can be easily created, or re-created. If there is a future for Document Management systems, it is the management of physical documents that need to be created and saved or cannot easily be re-created if the original copy becomes unavailable.

A heads up, NoSQL databases are categorized in 4 types of databases of which one is 'Document Database.' The word 'Document' as used in this context does not refer to what we normally regard as documents, such as forms or reports. This will be discussed in greater detail in the section on Databases and NoSQL.

Even **Data Visualizations** can remain digital. Visualizations don't have to be printed on paper. They can remain digital to be displayed when needed. In this form, 'Drill Down,' the ability to jump from summary to detail and back, is easily implemented.

Having said this, paper isn't going away, at least not immediately, but more and more content will be digital. Remember the simple example of online returns where codes replace physical documents to track returns. Either way the data is available online and paper is present only when and where necessary.

Content Management

Content Management has its origins in paper documents. **Content Management** systems were devised to store documents and index them in such a manner that the paper documents could be easily and quickly retrieved.

Today, as documents disappear, databases and search engines are relied upon to find and retrieve data. What does that mean for Content Management systems in the future? We will have to wait and see. Remember the Dewey Decimal System and Libraries; keyword searching replaced Dewey and his Decimals. Search technologies will either replace or radically overhaul content management.

Database

Databases are the workhorses of data. They are the repositories where captured data is stored. The capture and processing happen in applications, storage happens in databases. This topic has many aspects. Accordingly, it is discussed separately in the Domains section of the book in the Database Domain.

Database Administrator

Database Administrators (**DBA**s) are the technical engineers that design and maintain databases. In the realm of Application Software, such as ERP Systems, this function is pretty much handled by the designer and developer of the ERP system leaving little for DBAs to do; however, when ERP data is exported out of the ERP Database into other data repositories, DBAs may be intimately involved and responsible for the data storage facilities.

Traditional DBA responsibilities include database design, data integrity, data reliability, backup and recovery, system performance, and database maintenance. DBAs play an important role in situations involving continual data availability especially for applications that are continuously available, i.e., 24 hours a day, 7 days a week, 365 days a year.

Data Dictionary

Data Dictionary defines a '... collection of names, definitions and attributes about elements that are being used or captured in a database.' [– https://www.dataversity.net/data-dictionary-demystified/#.]

Three major uses for Data Dictionaries are:

- Clarifying the contents of data elements. Consider different types of dates, such as, distinguishing creation date and last-update date, or explaining abbreviations such as LName for last name, FName for first name and MName for middle name.
- Being able to locate different data elements in a database.
- Being able to assemble queries and reports based on relationships and the location of the data. Depending upon the structure and complexity of the database, this can be challenging.

Data Egress and Ingress

Data Egress and **Data Ingress** refers respectively to exporting or importing data. Other words that are frequently used in this context are inbound versus outbound data and uploading versus downloading data. These terms are typically used in connection with moving data into, out of or among various systems and databases, especially into or out of various applications.

Operationally, these terms refer to moving data among various systems; however, in a security context, there is a major focus on whether outbound data is being compromised. In this latter context, the term **Exfiltrate** is also used to refer to the extraction data from business systems potentially for nefarious purposes.

When Data leaves an enterprise, the enterprise should be aware of the outbound movement and should have given permission.

Simple recurring examples of Data Egress and Ingress include backing up data on-premises, backing up data to a cloud storage facility, downloading from cloud storage to an on-premises facility, importing third-party data, such as data from Data Brokers, and moving data among applications and repositories. These actions occur in the context of normal operations including retaining copies of data for backup purposes.

Data Elements vs Data Values

This contrast focuses on the difference between **Data Elements** and their **Values**.

Generally, a **Data Element** is an attribute or characteristic while the **Value** is the actual contents of the **Data Element**. For example, Customer Name, Customer Telephone Number, Customer Email Address are **Data Elements** while the name, telephone number and email address are the actual **Values**. The essential difference is the difference between the name of something and the actual **Value** of the item named.

Taking this distinction one step further, an **Entity**, such as a Customer, or an Item, or an **Event**, such as a sale or a purchase, may have several associated **Data Elements**, such as Customer Name, Customer Telephone Number, Customer Email Address, Item Name and Number, or Sales Order Number and the associated Customer Number and Items purchased. The Data Values are the actual contents of the Data Elements.

The Data Elements related to Entities and Events are typically referred to as **Attributes** or Characteristics of the primary item.

An interesting example of **Data Elements** and their **Values** are an ordinary ballpoint pen. The pen is the Entity, which comes in different Sizes, Colors, and Configurations. The different pen-point sizes, the different ink colors and the different packaging configurations are the **Values** associated with a particular pen.

Data Enrichment or Enhancement

Data Enrichment is a fascinating data process. Implicit in this concept is the notion of adding additional data to pre-existing data to provide a fuller, more complete picture of pre-existing data. Data Enrichment typically occurs to increase the completeness of the data and/or to provide additional information that will be important for downstream data consumption.

An interesting example of enrichment is movie box-office data. Starting with theatre box-office data, we know which movies a theatre showed, the ticket sales by auditorium, by ticket category, by date and by show times. If the theatre is a multiplex, the movie may be shown on multiple screens and each screen will have its own box-office data.

If we plan to subsequently analyze this data, we can easily geolocate the theatre down to latitude and longitude and easily see what movies were shown in adjacent auditoriums and theatres. But there are other dimensions that would make our analysis more informed, more explanatory, and potentially more useful ... if we only had that data. The good news is that this data is readily available and could include any or all of the following data elements: Movie Theme, Movie Genera, Movie Franchise (if part of a Franchise like Star Wars), MPAA rating, Viewer ratings, the Distributor, the Director, the Stars, the Producers, the Release Schedule and more. Collectively, this additional information greatly expands our analysis and give us much greater insight into the movie and potential future demand for this movie and similar films in the future. The good news is that this data is widely available from platforms like IMDb.

While this might seem straightforward, it isn't completely because of theatres with the same names in different locations, because of movie titles that overlap, because of reissued movies, and so on. But this additional data makes basic box-office information much more relevant.

Data Ethics

Data Ethics defined:

> Data ethics are the norms of behavior that promote appropriate judgments and accountability when collecting, managing, or using data, with the goals of protecting civil liberties, minimizing risks to individuals and society, and maximizing the public good.
> – https://resources.data.gov/assets/documents/fds-data-ethics-framework.pdf, p. 9.

This is the US Government's definition. This definition works as well for business enterprises.

To summarize this definition, Data ethics relates to the ethical collection, maintenance and use of data, especially personal data and data upon which businesses rely and upon which they place special emphasis, such as trade secrets. Ethics include responsibility and accountability for unethical actions and practices.

This data may contain information about customers, suppliers, employees, internal processes, formulas but is not limited to these types of data.

Data Ethics encompasses policies and procedures related to Appropriate Use, Privacy and Confidentiality of data that could be either personal data or business-related data.

Given the emphasis on monetizing Data, especially customer and personal data, Data Ethics can easily become a hot topic of conversation especially if the movement and sale was neither appropriate nor approved.

Data Fabric

Data Fabric is a newer term that emphasizes data accessibility across diverse environments. Ideally, data should be equally accessible across a business despite multiple different environments and architectures within the business.

Talend, a Data tools vendor, defines Data Fabric as:

'...a single environment consisting of a unified architecture, and services or technologies running on that architecture, that helps organizations manage their data. The ultimate goal of data fabric is to maximize the value of your data and accelerate digital transformation.' [– https://www.talend.com/resources/what-is-data-fabric/]

IBM offers an alternate definition:

'Data fabric is an architecture that facilitates the end-to-end integration of various data pipelines and cloud environments through the use of intelligent and automated systems.' [– https://www.ibm.com/topics/data-fabric].

The metaphor is that of 'fabric' stretched over a decentralized data environment that allows for 'frictionless', 'seamless' movement, access, and processing across a distributed environment. The theme is the ability of users to access data anywhere based on a common architecture. If this sounds too esoteric, think about being able to easily access data across a complex, fragmented environment without having to call in the technicians to assemble the data being sought.

Talend identifies its ultimate strategic objective as follows:

'... to change the way the world makes decisions. We take the work out of working with data and make data useful for all organizations.' [– https://www.talend.com/about-us/]

Gartner first identified Data Fabric in February of 2019 as one of its top data trends for 2019. At that point in time, Data Fabric was number 6 on Gartner's Data 'hit parade.' Gartner used the phrases 'frictionless access' and 'consistent distributed data environment' to describe Data Fabric. [– https://www.gartner.com/en/newsroom/press-releases/2019-02-18-gartner-identifies-top-10-data-and-analytics-technolo].

From an engineering standpoint, this can be accomplished by having a single, overarching 'data-centric architecture that responds to the constant rate of change.' [– https://www.gartner.com/en/newsroom/press-releases/2019-02-18-gartner-identifies-top-10-data-and-analytics-technolo].

Data Fidelity

Data Fidelity refers to having faithful copies of the original Data. **Data Fidelity** is like **Data Integrity**.

A more technical definition would address the movement of data among various nodes and the retention of the data's original meaning and granularity.

When you hear the term Data Fidelity, you may want to ask the speaker exactly what is intended. Is the speaker talking about exact copies of the original data? If so, what about appropriate additions and alterations? How do these changes affect Fidelity? Are they allowed if they do not change or diminish the original meaning of the data?

Data – Geotagging

Geotagging refers to assigning Latitude and Longitude coordinates to Entities and Transactions. Geotagging answers the 'where' question, which is often important in determining who gets credit for sales, for sales commissions calculations, for sales patterns and trends, and for determining densities, such as where sales are strongest, where customers are located, and the question of whether customers are clustered in certain areas or regions, and so on.

Geotagging has become increasing important for operations and Data Analysis.

Data Glossary

Data Glossary defines key Data characteristics. It provides a common, shared vocabulary; hence, a Data Glossary may also be referred to as a 'Business Glossary' because it connects data and the business. A **Data Glossary** provides a shared vocabulary between the Business and IT. An example of a Data Glossary is the W3C Linked Data Glossary, at https://www.w3.org/TR/2013/NOTE-ld-glossary-20130627/. Data or Business Glossaries can be tailored to specific businesses and the everyday language of the business.

Golden Image

A **Golden Image** is an accurate copy of Data at a previous point in time. Golden Images typically come into consideration when determining the completeness or correctness of a copy of the data. A Golden Image is created when data is determined or agreed to be complete and correct. That copy of version is subsequently used as a benchmark against which to validate future copies of the data. The saved validated copy of the data is the 'Golden Image'.

Data as History/Historical

Data is **History**. Business Data is the history of a business, including, but not limited to, all of the entities, internal and external, with whom and about which the firm interacts and all of its business events.

The History should be complete and up-to-date stored in such a manner that the business can easily see the business' trends in a chronological format.

For example, how do current sales, revenue and profit this year compare with last year, compare with the last 5 years, compare with the last 10 years? What are these trends over extended periods of time?

Data Integrity – Data Quality

Data Integrity is a subset of **Data Quality** encompassing accuracy, correctness, reliability, and trustworthiness. The opposite of **Data Integrity** is data that is not dependable, is not reliable, is not trustworthy. See the **Data Quality** domain for further discussion of **Data Quality**.

Data Liberation

Data Liberation may sound like an obscure concept; however, it is becoming increasingly important. In short, **Data Liberation** teaches us to maintain our data in 'native format' outside of the applications that generate and maintain that data, especially where SaaS services are involved. The concept is that of liberating data from the applications that generate it and maintain it; thus, allowing users to access and use the data outside the applications.

In the case of Software as a Service (SaaS) application, i.e., cloud applications, our data is under the control of the SaaS cloud vendor. Liberating the data means making a copy of the data outside of the SaaS applications and their databases and maintaining that data in a repository over which we have control. This repository could be on-premises or in another cloud storage facility. Either way, a copy of the data that is maintained outside the SaaS application under our control rather than the control of the SaaS vendor. Should anything happen on the SaaS side, we at least have a copy of our data.

Liberating our data from the control of others requires a regular, routine process, ideally automated, that copies the data, especially the latest Data, out of the SaaS applications into the alternate repository.

For example, take a business that maintains its customer data in a SaaS CRM system, of which there are many choices. Data Liberation teaches that businesses should have copies of its data outside of the SaaS CRM system for at least 4 reasons.

- First, to protect that data
- Second, to ensure access to that CRM data regardless of circumstances
- Third, analysis may be done more easily outside of the constraints of the SaaS system
- Fourth, we will never know completely how the SaaS vendor is maintaining and protecting the data (despite whatever the vendor's marketing literature says.)

Not picking on anyone but consider this example. A client used a cloud ERP provider that had a SAS70 certification, the predecessor to today's SOC (System and Organization Control). The SAS70 certification was highly touted by the service provider. Upon examination, we discovered that the auditor, a major accounting firm, expressed no opinion regarding the vendor's assertions because the auditor was unable to confirm the controls were implemented and were effective. The SAS70 detailed the company's policies and procedures, but the auditor was unable to confirm the operation of these controls. As a practical matter, the SAS70 was useless. Remember the maxim, 'The road to hell is paved with good intentions.'

Data Lineage

Data Lineage asks the question: From where did the data come? What were its origins? The importance of Data Lineage lies in several aspects depending upon whether it is internal data or externally generated data.

- If the data is internal data, then the organization ought to be able to determine the origin of the data and by extension ought to know or be able to know the Quality of that Data.
- If, on the other hand, the data comes from outside the organization, its origin may be impossible to determine, which in turn raises potential questions about the Quality of the Data.
- A corollary to the second use case is being able to know what happened to the data as it moved from its origin through multiple hands into the organization's control.
- In the second case, the big questions are:
  - From where did it come?
  - How was it originally collected?
  - Who and how many parties handled the data between its origin and our final receipt of it?
  - And ultimately has the data changed as it moved through the pipeline?

While **Data Lineage** answers the question, 'From where does the data come?' **Data Lineage** is often a proxy for **Data Quality**. In other words, knowing the history of the data gives the user some sense of its potential quality or lack thereof. If the lineage is uncertain, greater skepticism may be warranted. If the lineage is certain based on knowledge of the entities that captured and processed the data, users of that data may have more comfort with respect to Data Quality and appropriate potential uses for that data.

In a '**zero trust**' world, all external data is best treated skeptically because ultimately users cannot be sure of what happened to the data and its Quality between its origin and current uses.

Tools to document Data Lineage include Data Flow charts and Source and Target analyses.

Data Location

Data Location deals with the question of where Data is located. Where is it stored? And how is it stored?

Data Location becomes important when enterprises catalog their data, which is often the first step in consolidating data across multiple platforms and environments and may be the first step in a cybersecurity initiative. Nothing is worse than unprotected data, especially if the data is not protected merely because the organization forgot to or failed to determine where the data resides.

Why is Data Location important? If we don't know where the data is, we can't use it, we can't protect it. To make matters worse, data may be stored in multiple locations, such as various transactional databases, data warehouses, data marts and archives. Duplicate copies of data not only raise cybersecurity issues but data synchronization issues as well. Multiple locations may be confusing or wasteful, but they also protect data from accidental loss.

By way of clarification, **Data Location** does not generally refer to **Geotagging**, i.e., identifying the location of entities and events by latitude and longitude, i.e., 'lat long'.

Data Mapping

Data Mapping is a technique for controlling the movement of Data, i.e., copying of data from one place to another place. Typical Data Mapping terms include **Source** and **Target**, where the **Source** is the data repository out of which the data is being moved and the **Target** is the location into which the data is being copied. For example, consider data that is being copied out of an application, such as an ERP system, into a Data Warehouse.

The requirement for the Source and the Target can easily be different. For example, a Data Warehouse may be formatted differently than the source application; hence, the data may need to be reorganized, may even need to be enhanced. The Source and Target may have different data requirements at the field level. For example, the Source may store customer names in a single field, i.e., Prefix + First Name + Middle Name + Last Name + Suffix, while the Target may store each piece of data in a separate field, i.e., FirstName, MiddleName, LastName and so on. Furthermore, the Source may contain data elements that are not included in the Target and the Target may require data elements that are not in the Source.

The purpose of **Data Mapping** is to surface these differences and force a determination of how these differences will be handled. Depending upon the nature of the differences, different data manipulation techniques may be required, such as re-formatting, enrichment, quarantining and other techniques.

The Chapter on Data in Motion includes a detailed example of the types of differences that can occur. Experience teaches these differences are the rule, not the exception.

Data – Masking

Data may be **Masked** to obscure its original value. For example, replacing passwords with asterisks. In some cases, the mask can be removed, and the actual value can be observed. An alternative approach is **Data Tokenization**, which is discussed below.

Data Maturity

Data Maturity builds on the concept of continuous improvement where, in this case, the improvement is in the capabilities to handle data and manage its quality.

Various authors and frameworks describe this process differently, but the underlying message is the same, i.e., implementing formal processes to establish and improve Data Quality. See Figures 3.4 and 3.5:

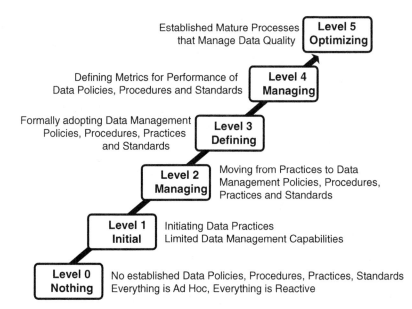

Figure 3.4 Data Maturity Model

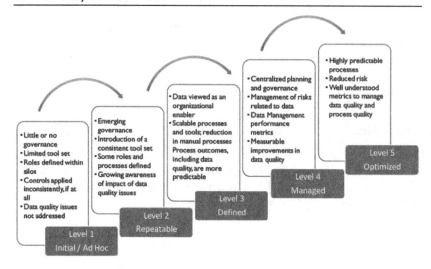

Figure 3.5 DAMA Data Management Maturity Model
Reproduced with permission of DAMA International

At lower end of the spectrum is ad hoc fixing or, in colloquial language, 'firefighting'. At the upper end, the mature end, of the spectrum, procedures, and processes for capturing, maintaining, and ensuring Data Quality and usefulness function effectively including formal reviews of how the data was handled and how the procedures and processes can be improved.

Another way of saying this is at the bottom-end of the spectrum, established policies, procedures and standards do not exist so every issue that occurs is dealt with as a single episode, sort of like the game of whack-a-mole.

At the top end of the spectrum, the organization's data policies, procedures, practices, and standards are fully implemented, and the organization reviews its actions to improve them, i.e., the organization learns from its experiences. The objectives are to ensure the high-quality data and to ensure its data policies and procedures are established and functioning effectively. In between the bottom-end and the top-end of the spectrum, businesses have partially implemented policies, procedures, practices, and standards with room for improvement.

For additional information on Capability Maturity Model Integration (CMMI), see ISACA's CMMI Institute at https://cmmiinstitute.com/.

Data Mining

Data Mining is the process of examining data looking for unusual patterns or correlations. This technique is typically associated with large datasets. Data Mining is commonly used in Data Wrangling, Data Analysis and Data Science technique.

Data Mining focuses on unusual situations or relationships that are not otherwise obvious. A common business problem is customer 'churn' where existing customers go to other suppliers. I recall one data mining example involving a credit card enterprise asking the question: which customers are likely to switch to another credit card. As I recall the example, data mining discovered that credit card holders that regularly split bills were more likely to switch to other credit cards. Data Mining is looking for proverbial 'needles in haystacks.'

Data Modeling

Data Modeling is an essential diagnostic and design technique for discovering, understanding, analyzing, designing, and visualizing datasets. The results are Data Models.

In practice, **Data Models** are either structure oriented or process oriented. A structural model shows relationships among entities and events. A process model focuses on transactions and events and shows workflow processes from beginning to end with an emphasis on producing, manipulating, and consuming data.

Entity Relationship Diagrams (**ERD**s) are an example of structure diagrams. **Data Flow Diagrams** (**DFD**s) are an example of process diagrams.

Entity Relationship Diagrams (**ERD**s) play an important role in designing and documenting Entities and Events and relationships among them. ERDs show how various elements are structured and how they relate to each other. For example, an ERD can show the relationships among customers, their orders, their returns, their payments, and their refunds. In contrast, Process Diagrams show the steps and decision points in business processes. Relational Databases rely on, embody, Entity Relationship Models.

Data Flow Diagrams (**DFD**s) focus on the process that produces, manipulates, and consumes data. For example, if a process step requires approval, the process stops at that decision point until approval is given. Depending upon approval, the process may continue, or it may send the item back to a prior step in the process, or the item may sit where it is with alerts to the various parties affected by the disapproval.

Data Flow Diagrams can show a single process, or set of processes, or it can show an entire lifecycle from beginning to end. For example, the DFD can show the customer placing an order or the DFD can show the entire customer order process from beginning to end, including placing the order, approving the credit, picking the items ordered, packing the items ordered, shipping the items ordered, culminating in the customer receiving its order.

DAMA's DMBOK lists

'the six most used schemes [models] are: Relational, Dimensional, Object-Oriented, Fact-Based, Time-Based, and NoSQL. Models of

these schemes exist at three levels of detail: conceptual, logical, and physical. Each model contains a set of components. Examples of components are entities, relationships, facts, keys and attributes. Once a model is built, it needs to be reviewed and once approved, maintained'.
– DAMA-DMBOK: DATA MANAGEMENT BODY OF KNOWLEDGE, 2nd Edition, page 124.

Hence, models can be different with respect to type and detail. Data Models include 'Metadata', which is described separately in this section, and is critical for Data users.

Data Models visualize data and datasets. They are extremely useful ways to see data, its constituent parts, and the relationships among these parts.

Data Models include:

- Entities and their Attributes, including Categories, and
- Events and their Transactions.

Entities are the objects being modeled. They can easily be identified by some combination of the reporters' six questions:

- Who
- What
- When
- Where
- Why
- How

Or they can be thought of in terms of an expanded version of person, place and thing:

- Person
- Place
- Thing
- Object
- Event
- Action, in the sense of a sale or a purchase including the people and things involved in the actions

In general, Entities tend to be nouns, i.e., the subjects of sentences, the objects associated with various actions, which are the verbs. Obvious business Entities include customers, suppliers, products, items, locations, people, and so on. **Attributes** are the adjectives that characterize Entities such as names, locations, credit limits, contact information, sizes, types, and so on.

A brief note – To be useful, Entities need to be clear, unambiguous, and easily recognized. This can be a problem for Entities with similar names such as customers, suppliers, or employees that have identical or nearly identical names. How can one be sure which employees are which when their names are similar, maybe even identical? The quick answer is their IDs in database parlance their Primary Keys (PK's).

Events are typical business occurrences such as sales, purchases, making items, moving items, borrowing money, loaning money, promoting business, and so on. **Transactions** are events with a series of steps or activities that together comprise a Transaction. Issuing a Purchase Order is an Event, but it is only part of the Purchasing Cycle; issuing a Sales Order is an Event but it is only a part of the Sales Cycle. In both cases the Purchase Order and the Sales Order start a chain of events that culminates in purchasing something or selling something.

Attributes are not limited to Entity characteristics. There are also characterize Events such as the items bought or sold, their quantities and prices, shipping instructions (how and where), payment instructions, and so on. These are **Transaction Details**.

And there are certain Attributes that have a downstream importance. These are Categorical Attributes, i.e., **Categories. Categories** are particularly significant because they group entities, events and transactions based on similarity or equality and at the same time discriminate between entities, events and transactions that are neither similar nor identical. These differences can be reduced to two words: Inclusion and Exclusion. Categories group items together, inclusion, and separate items that are not members of a group, exclusion. These elements are major considerations in downstream Data Analysis. How can businesses stratify their customers without distinguishing their sales volumes? Examples of broad Categories are Customers, Suppliers, Products or Parts, Manufacturing Formulae, and Employees. Products, for example, can be further distinguished by Productline, Product Type, Product Source, Product Category, Product Use, and so on.

One might argue Categories are a minor issue; however, an ERP system could theoretically have a single 'entity table.' that included customers, suppliers, items, employees, account numbers, and more, all in the same master table. This is unusual, but it does occur. SAP, for example, includes the concept of Business Partners which in turn includes customers, suppliers, and other types of business partners. All are entered using the same set of Data Entry screens.

As noted above, **Categories** have an important downstream role in querying, reporting and business analytics where items are separated into groups based on various categories, often for the purpose of arriving at counts such as how many customers are in different geographic areas, which customers buy which items in which quantities, the quantity of items stored in different locations and the volume of items shipped via different carriers and methods. These examples rely on multiple Categories or perspectives through which customers and their actions can be evaluated.

The Data Management Association (DAMA) offers a slightly different model, which identifies three types of business information:

- Resource Information – This category encompasses profile data for Customers, Suppliers, Products/Items, Accounts, and so on.
- Business Event Information – This category includes event-specific information related to sales orders, purchase orders, work orders, cash deposits and withdrawals, and so on. This information could be described as event artifacts.
- Detail Transaction Information – This category includes point-of-sale details, Internet of Things sensor data, social media data.
  – DAMA-DMBOK: DATA MANAGEMENT BODY OF KNOWLEDGE, 2nd Edition, pages 126 and 127.

Before leaving the topic of Data Modeling, an important element to discuss is **Relationship**. This typically involves the use of IDs, in the case of relational databases, Primary Keys, which 'connect' related elements in different tables, data subsets. The illustration below, Figure 3.6, combines 2 simple use cases, buying and selling, in a single diagram.

The right-hand side of the diagram shows the relationship between Customers and the items sold to them. The left-hand side shows the relationship between Suppliers and the Items purchased from them.

These use cases answer the questions of who buys specific items and from whom were those items originally purchased? **Relationships** link Entities related by virtue of Events. **Relationships** also link Entities with their associated characteristics.

Parenthetically, Graph Databases use different language referring to relationships as 'edges' that connect 'nodes,' entities, to each other.

In **Relational Data Modeling, Relationships** are indicated by repeating an item's Unique Identifier, which resides in Parent or Master Table, in a Subsidiary or Child Table. The Unique Identifiers are referred to as **Keys** or **Ids**. In the Relational Model, these elements are referred to as **Primary Keys** (**PKs**) and **Foreign Keys** (**FKs**) where the Primary Key is the Entity or Event identifier, and the Foreign Key is the repetition of the Primary Key in a subsidiary table, hence establishing a

Figure 3.6 Relationships Diagramming

Relationship. Typical Primary Keys are CustomerID, SupplierID, ProductID, LocationID, and so on.

Two final comments regarding Data Modeling, **Data Models** may contain one or more diagrams, where each diagram captures or focuses on specific aspects of a Model. Accompanying documentation typically explains the terms used in the diagrams and may identify issues or questions related to the Model that remain to be resolved.

Data Modeling for Non-Relational Databases differs by database type. In some cases, the model is simply two columns where the first column contains a Key that uniquely identifies a Value in the second column. The Key may be random, or it may bear some relationship to the Value.

Tagging is another method where tags are used to identify items. In this method, tags name data elements. So, for example the tag 'employee' could be followed by the name 'Fred Smith' where Fred Smith is an employee of the business. This approach can quickly become very detailed and complex, but every value is clearly identified by its tag. An example of this in business is XBRL, eXtensible Business Reporting Language, which is a freely available international standard for exchanging business information. XBRL is based on XML (eXtensible Markup Language) standards.

Another approach involves Graphs in which 'lines' connect 'dots.' The dots are objects, i.e., entities, which are referred to as nodes and the lines connect the dots, the nodes, to each other showing the interconnections. The lines are referred to as 'edges.' So, in Graph parlance, the 'edges' connect the 'nodes'.

These models are quite different than relational models, but ultimately, they all involve entities or objects, their attributes, their relationships, and the business processes of which they are parts.

Native Format

Discussions about Raw Data, Data Quality and Data Fidelity inevitably end up with questions regarding the Data's original format, i.e., its **Native Format. Native Format** emphasizes the importance of being able to access data in its original, unprocessed form. This allows analysts to see the impact of the processing on data and the changes that occurred as the data moved from its original state into subsequent states, stores and uses.

Consider time-series sensor data. The Native Format is the stream of sensor data as it comes from the sensor. The data could be visual data from a camera which subsequently undergoes image processing or temperate readings from a thermometer or thermostat. In the first case, the Native Data is the video stream from the camera before image processing occurs. In the second case, the temperature readings are the data stream, which may be evaluated by an application to determine if the readings are normal or abnormal. If subsequent questions about the data arose, one might need to go back to the original data and re-process it to confirm accuracy.

Having Data in its original format allows the data to be re-examined and re-processed later if needed.

Normalization, Denormalization

Normalization is a basic technique associated with relational databases. The goals of **Normalization** are to eliminate duplication and ensure consistency, i.e., to avoid inconsistent Data. This is typically done via the organization of tables within relational databases.

A good way to explain **Normalization** is through a simple example.

Take a customer and its Data. Customer Data typically includes at least a customer 'number', a customer name, addresses, contact information, payment options, shipping instructions, and so on. In simpler times, all of this data might be contained in one, or two, tables. Today, each type of data may be in its own table. As a result, we end up with different tables for addresses, contact information, payment information, shipping information, and so on.

Parenthetically, in older business systems, a single table might limit customers to two addresses: a billing address and a shipping address, which would fit in a single customer table, but what happens when customers have multiple addresses, not just two? The obvious solution is to create a second table that can handle multiple addresses without being constrained to just 2 addresses.

Back to **Normalization**, consider customer names. Do systems include customer name in every subsidiary table? No, normalization says the customer's name exists in just one place. If the Customer Name was present in multiple tables, there is a possibility that the values could be different in different tables causing errors downstream.

Normalization eliminates this possibility by providing only 1 field for Customer Name. Without going into all the details, this approach avoids the problem of multiple different values for the same field in different tables.

Parenthetically, customers names can change. To handle name changes, the Customer Name may be time-stamped with Beginning and Ending dates and/or using Aliases. For fun, get a copy of your Credit Report and see how many variations are listed on the report for your name.

Normalization comes in degrees: First Normal Form (1NF), Second Normal Form (2NF) and Third Normal Form (3NF). Third Normal Form is the 'gold standard.'

Where things get interesting is when this process is reversed. **Denormalization** transforms normalized data into tables with redundant data. Sticking with our example, Customer Names might appear in every order in a denormalized database. Hence, the Normalized SalesOrder and SalesOrderLines tables are combined in a Data Warehouse or Data Mart, so that the Customer ID, the Customer Name, and the Sales Order number are repeated on every Sales Order Line. Why do this? Why make seemingly unnecessary copies of the same data? The reason is typically performance. If most, or all, of the data related to a single sales transaction is stored in a single record, there are fewer reads. Fewer JOINs are required to query the data. [Note: JOIN is the SQL command to 'join' the contents of two tables based on a Foreign Key.] This reduces system workload when queries or reports are generated.

Normalization and **Denormalization** are techniques that serve important functions. Users don't need to understand how to normalize and denormalize datasets to be beneficiaries of these techniques.

Data Optimization

Data Optimization is a collection of techniques applied to data with the goals of increasing the data availability and maximizing data effectiveness. **Data Optimization** can refer to techniques applied to data to make querying and reporting more efficient, i.e., quicker, and **Data Optimization** can refer to more general techniques that prepare the **Data** for its subsequent use. One of these techniques is 'Views' or 'virtual tables,' which pre-format data for a particular query without replicating the data; hence a 'virtual' duplicate without the overhead of actually duplicating the data. As the expression goes, it is something like 'having your cake and eating it too.'

Essentially Data Optimization focuses on techniques to increase the effective use of data, including speeding up the process of assembling data for operations, analysis, and/or decision-making.

Data Orchestration

Data Orchestration is the management and execution of **Data Processing** tasks, especially the automation of these tasks. **Data Orchestration** refers to at least the collection, assembly, and organization of data, if not all actions applied to data by multiple processes. The orchestration plans and controls the processes and their execution. The processes may run serially or in parallel. Data Orchestration is particularly relevant when data must be collected from multiple applications, and their associated databases, and assembled in a new instance often for reporting or analysis purposes. **Data Pipeline** is a related concept.

Data Organization

Data Organization refers to how data is organized and any subsequent re-organization of that data. All Data is organized somehow. The problem is the organization may not suit our purposes and so we re-organize the data.

Depending upon the type of data and how it is used, data typically has a basic or native organization, which reflects how the data was initially generated or collected. If the data in question is Sales Data, its natural organization reflects the customer order process. If the data is sensor output, the data stream is its basic organization potentially timestamped.

As data moves from its transactional area to permanent storage, especially for subsequent analysis, the data could easily be re-organized several times for different purposes. For example, Sales Transactions could be organized differently depending upon whether the use is Sales related versus Customer related versus Item related versus Marketing related.

The typical reason for re-organizing data is to make the data more useful. Data organization and reorganization extends throughout data's lifecycle serving various purposes at different stages.

Data Ownership/Owner/Stewardship

Data Ownership and **Data Stewardship** are two closely related concepts. Who ultimately **owns** the data and who is **accountable** for the data? The relevant question is typically: Who is responsible for data and its quality … or lack thereof?

Data Ownership can be viewed through two lenses: legal ownership and business 'ownership.' In latter case, business ownership refers to the party or parties that are responsible for the data. For example, Sales Data is typically 'owned' by the sales department. In a practical sense, those who know the data best are often its owners. The legal definition is just that, who is legally responsible for the data.

Data Stewardship refers to the people or departments that are responsible for maintaining the data, especially maintaining its quality and availability. The stewards may be the owners, but the stewards may be different. Stewardship typically involves technical knowledge and skills to ensure accuracy, accessibility, safety, and trustworthiness.

These two concepts may intersect, sometimes they diverge. The owners may know the data better than the stewards, but the stewards may have technical skills that the owners don't. So, the distinction comes down to 'Subject Matter Experts' (SMEs) that own the business data versus the engineers that maintain the databases and use various technical tools and techniques to ensure the data is of the highest quality and availability.

Where this distinction gets confusing is when IT is a principal player or custodian. While IT may have custody of the data and may process it, the owners and stewards of the data are usually its business users because it is their data even though IT may be immersed in its lifecycle. The owners may be more likely to identify errors and mistakes than IT. The more involved IT is, the longer IT is involved, the more experienced IT becomes, but the owners may still be the best judges of Data Quality and Usefulness.

When third parties, i.e., parties other than owners and stewards, work with the data, they should be in touch with the owners and stewards especially when questions arise regarding accuracy, validity, and usefulness.

Data Pipeline

Data Pipeline refers to the processes and steps that move data from one place to another, such as from its original sources to its final destinations, and the automation of those processes. **Data Pipeline** considers the entire process and the individual steps involved in the process. Other related terms include **Data Ingestion** and **Data Orchestration**.

Informatica succinctly describes Data Pipeline as 'an end-to-end process to ingest, process, prepare, transform and enrich structured, unstructured, and semi-structured data in a governed manner.' [– https://www.informatica.com/resources/articles/data-pipeline.html.] In popular use, the term ingestion may include major parts of a data pipeline, more than just the initial upload. Other aspects of a Data Pipeline include data aggregation, the combining of Data from different sources, and the organization and re-organization of data.

The Data Sources may be internal or external, from the perspective of the entity operating the pipeline, and can involve multiple APIs. The Destinations can be Data Warehouses, Data Analytic platforms, and other data storage facilities.

Increasingly these processes are moving from manual to automated processes and can include both on-premises resources and cloud-based, SaaS-based (Software-as-a-Service), resources.

Data Pipeline, as a term, increasingly refers to an automated process. The process could be batch, or, as these processes become increasingly automated, the pipeline could include replication processes whereby the data is simultaneously copied into a data pipeline.

As noted above, the pipeline can include Data Transformations, such as cleaning, standardization, organization, re-organization, sorting, de-duplicating, validation, and verification as the data passes through the pipeline.

Data Privacy

Data Privacy refers to data to which special protections apply because of personal, business, societal or legal regulations or standards. Data Privacy often include 'sensitive' data, which may or may not involve Personally Identifiable Information (PII). Recently I asked a class if they care about sharing non-PII data. While some students said they didn't care, most cared about non-PII as well as PII data, and wished that Data Privacy was the reality more so than it is.

Data may be private because it is personal information and as such is subject to contractual or legal regulations or 'acceptable use' policies. A business' ability to use that data may be subject to a contract between the person and the business or it may be subject to governmental regulations, such as the General Data Protection Regulation (GDPR) of the EU, or the California State Consumer Privacy Act (CCPA), or other jurisdictional laws or regulations.

Sensitive Data may include certain financial and intellectual property, such as financial information or product or engineering formulas. Businesses have obvious reasons to restrict access to these types of Data on a need-to-know basis.

Data Privacy is part of the cybersecurity domain. As such, Data Privacy deals with the types of data covered by privacy, by the various restrictions and controls that apply to that data, and by the remedial actions that are required should those restrictions fail.

Data Provenance

Data Provenance, as defined by NIST, is equivalent to the 'chain of custody' as used in legal settings. 'It involves the method of generation, transmission and storage of information that may be used to trace the origin of a piece of information processed by community resources.' [– NIST, Glossary, Data Provenance.]

From a business perspective, Data Provenance, Chain of Custody, Data Lineage, and the history of data are synonymous. These various terms at a minimum refer to the origin of the data, how it was processed post-origination, and the ability of the organization to know and confirm what has transpired since the inception of the data.

Data Quality – Data Corruption

Data Quality is the 'goodness' of the data, i.e., the absence of flaws and defects. This is typically expressed in terms of multiple characteristics such as

- Accuracy
- Appropriateness
- Completeness
- Consistency
- Relevance
- Reliability
- Usefulness
- Trustworthiness

Gartner defines Data Quality from a tools perspective: 'the processes and technologies for identifying, understanding and correcting flaws in data that support effective information governance across operational business processes and decision making.' [– https://www.gartner.com/en/information-technology/glossary/data-quality-tools]. While the definition is tools centric, it focuses on 'understanding and corrects flaws' in data, i.e., errors and inaccuracies in the Data.

Thomas C. Redman suggests another dimension, 'fit for intended purposes.' In this sense, 'good data' is data that is fit for, appropriate or relevant to the questions being asked of it. Below is an extended quote from T. C. Redman:

> 'These points lead to the following definition of data quality (based on Joseph Juran):
>
> Data are of high quality if they are fit for their intended uses in operations, decision making, and planning. Data are fit for use if they are free of defects and possess desired features (See Figure 14.2).
>
> Note first, that data quality is intimately tied to customers and their uses of data. In a very real sense 'data are of high quality if those who use them say so.' …
>
> Second, data may be put to any number of uses. And it almost always happens that data that are ideally fit for one use are marginally [fit] for a second and poorly fit for a third. … It is about meeting the specific needs of specific customers.'
>
> – Thomas C Redman, Data Driven: The Field Guide,
> Boston: Digital Press, 2001, page 73.

Notice that Redman mentions defects as well as 'fitness.'

In his writings, Redman compares two automobiles, a VW and a Cadillac. The answer to the question of which is better depends on the owner's needs and uses. As data practitioners, we hope the answer is more than perception, but Redman does remind us that appropriateness, applicability, and relevance are important dimensions as well as flaws and defects. These dimensions become particularly important for Consumers of Data and Decision-makers as complex analytical techniques sit between the data and the decisions we make based on the data. I am not willing to say Data has High Quality because a user 'says so,' as Redman allows, but clearly applicability, appropriateness and relevance play critical roles in **Data Quality** as well as accuracy, completeness, validity, and other measures.

What is the opposite of **Data Quality**? The typical answer is Erroneous or **Corrupt Data**, i.e., Data may contain errors or may be otherwise corrupted. The errors can be errors of commission where the Data is clearly incorrect, or the Data may contain errors of omission, i.e., missing elements, as well as being otherwise corrupted. To say Data lacks Quality merely because it is inappropriate sounds a little 'goofy', but nevertheless inapplicable, inappropriate, or irrelevant Data can easily lead to inappropriate Decisions.

Technologists used to talk about GIGO, 'Garbage In Garbage Out.' Today GIGO is an oversimplification of the situation. Data Quality is more than a question of 'garbage'; it is also a question about applicability, appropriateness, and relevance.

Keep in mind that measures of Data Quality extend across the Data's lifecycle. Changes to Data during its lifecycle may make the Data more or less useful.

Related topics include **Data Integrity** which says the Data has not been altered or changed in an unauthorized manner during its lifecycle, from its inception to its final use. **Data Validity,** a similar concept, focuses on the correctness of the Data based on accurately or correctly reflecting requirements and reality.

A comment in passing, **Data** may be of high quality but inappropriate for certain uses; hence, Quality Data but not be fit for all uses as Redman teaches in this final comment, 'Data Quality is not a concept that makes sense 'in the average' [– Ibid.] i.e., Data Quality may be determined on a case-by-case basis.

Data – Raw Data

Raw Data is data at its inception before it is processed, especially if changes subsequently occur.

Sensor Data and Log files are reasonable illustrations of Raw Data. Data directly out of a sensor is Raw Data. It may be subsequently saved and evaluated. If the data is determined to be 'normal,' the actual data may be discarded. If the data is determined to be 'abnormal,' the data may be saved and subsequently evaluated. In this use case, the data that is generated by the sensor is Raw Data. If the stream of data is processed in anyway, it is no longer Raw Data, but Processed Data. It has lost its Rawness. Another example is Log data. Log data are generated by systems as events occur in the system and are typically stored as 'Log files.' Log files can document every event, or they can be limited to abnormal events or situations. Log files often grow to astronomic size relative to other files in a system and are frequently 'pruned.' Log files may contain the actual data at its inception, or they may be a time-stamped historical record of events or situations that occurred with minimal actual data, such as the value before and the value after an event occurred.

The importance of **Raw Data** is the capability it provides to return to the original, unprocessed data and re-examine it bypassing the changes that occurred after the data was originally generated. This sort of analysis can detect unintentional or intentional errors that were introduced in the data after its generation.

Over time new tools and techniques may evolve that enable the data to be evaluated at its inception and analysts may prefer to apply these new tools and techniques to the original data before it is subsequently processed. For additional discussion on Raw Data, see Native Format.

Data Redundancy

Data Redundancy is repetitious data, i.e., copies of the original Data. On first hearing, this may sound like a bad thing, something to be avoided, but **Data Redundancy** is a technique to ensure nothing is lost and is a by-product of organizing and re-organizing data for different use cases.

From a broader perspective, data is routinely backed up to avoid Data Loss, probably not once but multiple times depending on the data's importance.

In terms of transformed data, why is data copied, organized, and reorganized? Sticking with the example of Customer Data, the original data resides in the organization's ERP system. That data is then subsequently copied into a Data Warehouse for subsequent querying, reporting, and analysis. That data may be then copied into separate Data Marts for Sales, Marketing, Purchasing and so on. This means the business has the original data and at least four additional copies. Having multiple copies of data for specialized purposes is a common solution to get the most benefit out of the data. Very quickly the number of copies can multiply especially when storage is basically cheap and unlimited, which is increasingly the case.

From a different perspective, the elimination of Data Redundancy is a central tenet of Relational Databases. The objective of the Relational Database is to distribute data across multiple tables to promote effectiveness, efficiency, and performance. The elimination of Data Redundancy is part of Data Normalization, but when data steps outside of its applications, it may be replicated multiple times.

With multiple copies, synchronization can become a problem. If the data changes, the changes generally need to be replicated to all copies, so the enterprise has a 'single version of truth.' Lacking synchronization, different Departments may have very different versions of the truth which can result in some challenging executive meetings when different parts of the enterprise have very different versions of the same circumstances.

Data Relationships

Data Relationships are the interconnections among Entities and Events. Relationships are absolutely essential to data and its interpretation. If relationships did not exist, the analysis would be an analysis of random items. Everything would be coincidental; nothing would be related to anything else.

Consider our recurring example involving Customers and their purchases.

First, Customers may be interrelated. For example, Customers may be different parts of a larger enterprise. Hence, Customers could be evaluated individually or in terms of the organizations of which they are a part and/or in comparison to each other.

These relationships may be characterized as parent child relationships where the 'children' entities are related to or part of a parent entity, such as an enterprise and its subsidiaries, or they may be siblings, i.e., equal members of a group.

Second, what are Customers without their Orders? Customers are businesses' lifelines. What do Customers buy? When do they buy? Have their buying habits changed? Which Customers are more profitable; which Customers are less profitable? What does yesterday's Customer history say about tomorrow's Customer purchases? All of these questions are based on the relationships between Customers and their Orders.

Data Relationships are essential aspects of Relational Database models and Graph Database models. Relational Databases use the repetition of Primary Keys as Foreign Keys in other tables to identify relationships. Graph Databases use nodes and edges to model the data. The edges connect the nodes to each other.

Data Remediation

Remediation normally refers to repair and in a broader conversation to the actions and techniques employed to repair data. In the first case, **Data Remediation** refers to the correction or repair of incorrect or corrupt Data. The objective of the cleansing, correction or repair is to provide accurate, high-quality Data for subsequent use. In the second case, the term **Remediation** applies to Risk Management where remediation focuses on reducing erroneous, defective data as part of an overall program to reduce risk.

Data Risk

Data Risk extends well beyond the data itself. **Data Risk** considers the impact of **data** on the business. How might erroneous, inaccurate, inconsistent, or incomplete **data** affect operations, financial decisions, executive decisions. **Data Risk** can far exceed the value of the **Data Elements** themselves. Data Breaches, for example, can have significant long-term consequences.

In Risk Management, Impact and Likelihood are the two critical dimensions. In the case of Data Risk, what is the impact of erroneous or misleading data on decisions? By extension, how impactful are these decisions? Impact includes both the effect of erroneous data on decisions and the impact of the decisions on the business. The second dimension asks how likely the data is erroneous or misleading. In other words, how likely are decisions to be adversely affected by erroneous or misleading data and how likely are the decisions to be operationalized.

In terms of Risk Mitigation, Data Owners, Data Stewards, and Data Users are responsible for assessing the accuracy, reliability, and integrity of the data that is used in daily decision-making and longer-term planning and for alerting management if the data does not meet the organization's standards. Silence is not an option.

Roadmap

A **Roadmap** is what you would think it is. It is a plan typically for the implementation of improvements. Roadmaps typically define future directions and situations. Roadmaps describe how to get from the Current State to a desired Future State.

Applying this concept to data teaches businesses to have a formal plan and process for the creation, collection, correction, enhancement of data to optimize decision-making. As noted above, Data Quality does not necessarily shield businesses from applying their Data inappropriately. A reasonable Data Roadmap may include the following:

- First, the business' longer terms vision and direction with respect to data, which includes What the business needs and wants are, What the business is trying to accomplish? And Why?
- Second, a reasonably comprehensive foundation (current state), which identifies the following:
  o List of data assets, and how these assets are currently used by the business
  o The Applications, Storage Repositories, and tools that generate/collect, process, store and otherwise use the data
  o An assessment of the quality of the data
- Third, based on the current state foundation, the improvements the business wants to make, needs to make, in the management of its data assets including
  o Consideration of current technologies and tools, including decisions regarding updating and/or replacing older technologies (transition from current to future state)
  o Consideration of new technologies and their potential roles (future state)
  o Changes to data collection, processing, storage, and use, including impact on tools, technologies, and resources, including required skills and expertise (transition from current to future state)

- Fourth, confirm the business' New Objectives and Outcomes with respect to data and its Uses in the business (future state)
- Fifth, develop the initiatives that need to be implemented to convert the Vision into reality

Obviously, a roadmap is just a piece of paper without a formal process to develop and maintain the Roadmap, especially without involving the Stakeholders, those who are affected by the changes.

Data Science

Data Science is the multidisciplinary approach to data, its assessment and interpretation, including

- The study of data and methods for capturing, storing, processing, and analyzing data
- Advanced analytical and statistical techniques
- The application of a combination of Mathematics, Computations, Statistics, Programming, Data Analysis, Machine Learning and Artificial Intelligence techniques and tools

All for the purpose of gaining insights and making informed decisions.

Arguably the major distinction between Data Science and Data Analysis is the increased use of advanced techniques beyond just analyzing data. This is a compact definition for the hottest topic in data today, a topic worthy of many books.

Data Security and Protection

Data Security refers to the protective measures implemented to address the following security issues:

- Availability versus Unavailability of Data

  Is Data available when and where needed?

- Authorized versus Unauthorized Access

  Is Data Access Controlled and Unauthorized Accesses Prevented?

- Data Corruption

  Is Data protected from unintentionally and as well as intentionally corruption?
  Is Data of the highest Quality suitable for the business' purposes?

- Confidentiality, Privacy, and Intellectual Property

Which Data is Confidential and requires appropriate restrictions regarding Access and Use?

Are Privacy Issues associated with certain Data?

Is the Data Intellectual Property that needs to be tightly controlled like other critical business assets?

- Compliance Requirements

Is the Data subject to specific compliance requirements?

Are the compliance requirements appropriately satisfied?

Data Security considers both Data 'at rest,' i.e., in storage, and 'in motion,' i.e., Data that is moving among various locations both inside and outside an organization. These, for example, are central themes of HIPAA's HITECH requirements.

As with other topics, entire books are devoted to Data Security providing a rich tapestry of resources for organizations be they businesses or other types of organizations.

Service-Oriented Architecture

Service-Oriented Architecture (SOA) is a technical topic that covers a set of principles, methodologies, protocols, and software to share data and/or coordinate Interoperability among multiple applications or services.

Another way of explaining **Service-Oriented Architecture (SOA)** is an approach whereby well-defined service calls isolate the innerworkings of different applications from each other and data is shared through the service calls. This approach allows the applications to be independent of each other and still share data among themselves. A big benefit of SOA is the ease with which interfaces can be updated when changes occur because the changes are handled through the service calls. SOA is a commonly deployed technique.

Single Version of Truth

The idea behind a '**Single Version of Truth**' is that in complex organizations every Division, every Department, every Sector has 'its' Data for analysis and decision-making. These multiple versions of the Truth can lead to some fairly ruckus executive meetings as different executives describe their view of the organization, and the decisions they believe are essential for the organization.

The goal of a '**Single Version of Truth**' is for all parts of the organization to at least agree on the basic facts of a situation. For example, the Accounting Department has one set of figures while the Sales Department has another set of figures both may be correct but from different perspectives. The adoption of one viewpoint versus adoption of another viewpoint can have a significant impact on the decisions that are made. The **Single Version of Truth** should transcend competing versions and, hence, be a superset of data that reconciles the various numbers and factors needed for and used in decision-making. If this is easier said than done, the organization needs to develop methods and initiatives to reconcile the competing datasets.

Data Slicing and Dicing, and Drill Down

Data Slicing and Dicing, and **Drill Down** are commonly used inter-related terms.

Strictly speaking, **'Slicing and Dicing'** is based on the notion of Data Cubes and Dimensions where data can be cut or subset along the dimensions. **Slicing** cuts large datasets into smaller coherent sub-datasets using a specific dimension. Whereas **Dicing** generates sub-cubes, i.e., sub-datasets, based on two or more dimensions.

These are querying, reporting, and analytical techniques that are applied to large datasets to view their contents from different perspectives. Remember the analogy in the preface of the book of a gemstone and its multiple 'faces' through which the gemstone can be viewed. Each face is effectively a different **Slice** and multiple faces taken together is **Dicing**.

Consider Sales Data. Sales Data can be sliced by customer, by group of customers, by customer class or any other customer dimension. The same Sales Data could be diced for a particular set of customers and particular set of products to address the question of which customers bought which products, certainly a familiar business query or report. Who is buying what?

Drill Down is a similar concept not based on data cubes but on Details and their Summaries. **Drilling Down** is going from Summary to Detail; **Drilling Up** is going from Details to the Summary. There are two corollaries to **Drill Down, Drill Around** and **Roll-Up. Drill Around** refers to moving laterally within a dataset, for example moving among the orders of a single Customer. **Roll-Up**, or **Rolling Up** refers to summarization. **Drill Down** and **Roll-up** are exactly the opposite of each other. These became popular terms with advent of ERP systems where users could easily move around inside ERP datasets.

Drill Down, Drill Around, and **Roll-Up** are easily illustrated. Customers purchase items. **Drill Down** moves the inquiry from Customers to their Orders. The Orders for particular Customers can be easily examined by moving among the various Customer Orders, i.e., **Drill Around**. Moving from the Customer Orders back to specific Customers is **Rolling Up**. Simply, **Drill Down, Drill Around** and **Roll-Up** are Down, Around and Back Up, a frequent Sales Department activity.

The Key to **Slicing, Dicing,** and **Drilling Around** is the interrelated-ness of the data. In the example above, the datasets involve Customers and their Orders. This could extend to Customers and their payments, to Customers and their returns, to Customers and the credits issued to them, to Customers and their complements and complaints. Throughout this string of questions, the key is the relationship of the Customer, which is established by the repetition of the CustomerID in the various related datasets.

Data Sovereignty

Data Sovereignty refers to data that is regulated by the laws of the country in which the data resides. Given the ease with which data can move across juridical boundaries, various countries have instituted different laws and regulations governing data and its movement and customers have adopted policies regarding where their data can reside.

From a business standpoint, a business may elect to keep or require the keeping of its data in the business's legal jurisdiction. For example, a business in the United States that has data in the cloud might require the cloud vendor to keep all copies of the data within the United States to limit exposure and to be able to prosecute malicious actors for illegal or inappropriate use of the data.

Given the global nature of things, this is increasingly becoming a business issue. It is often difficult to confirm precisely where data resides because global vendors backup their data across different domains for Data Protection and Data Recovery. These are admirable goals but come with potential unintended consequences. Given this reality, a prudent business practice is:

- Imposing Data Sovereignty requirements
- Monitoring compliance with those requirements and
- Including these requirements and the monitoring of them in the service provider's Service Level Agreements (SLAs)

Data Stewardship

Data Stewardship refers to the management of data, in contrast to Data Ownership that refers to the owners of the data. Stewardship and Ownership may be the same, but they can be different. Staying with Sales Data, the Sales Department may own the data, but technologists manage the data on behalf of the Sales Department so that the data is available to and suitable for analysis by the Sales Department.

Data Stewards are responsible for implementing the policies, procedures, processes, practices, and standards that apply to data. The actual **Data Custodians** are the personnel that manage and operate the databases and repositories in which the data is stored.

Data – Structured, Semi-Structured, Unstructured:

Data is often categorized as:

- Structured Data
- Unstructured Data
- Semi-Structured Data

The obvious distinctions are:

- Data may be structured or organized in a way that is readily discernable.
- Data may not be structured in a readily discernable fashion.
- Data may be somewhere in between structured and not structured, i.e., semi-structured or partially structured.

The term Unstructured may be applied to data where the structure of the data is unknown, incomplete, unsatisfactory, or unusable as is.

The Data Structure may or may not be useful. Structured data may be more useful than unstructured Data because the structure lends itself to the intended use. Unstructured Data may be less useful because it requires different tools and techniques to manage.

This set of distinctions may be slightly different than the distinctions to which you are accustomed. The question of structure is inconsequential if you don't use the data; if however you intend to use the data among the first questions regarding the data are the following: 'What is the structure of the Data?' And what do I need to do to get it into a form in which I can use it?

Shifting to the more traditional view of Data Structure, data is typically described as structured if it has an explicit, consistent pattern or organization. Data in a database or in an EXCEL® spreadsheet is generally Structured, i.e., the Data is organized in a consistent manner, and the organization is obvious. In the case of spreadsheets, the organization appears in the first row of data as 'column headings'. If we are lucky, the contents of the column will be consistent with the column headers ... although sometimes they aren't.

A key distinction that cannot be ignored is that databases impose certain restrictions on tables and attributes in a way that spreadsheets do not. As a result, databases enforce consistency whereas spreadsheets do not. So, as the saying goes, 'buyer beware.' Data in a spreadsheet may be consistent but the spreadsheet may lack enforcement mechanisms to ensure Consistency.

That was easy but what about Unstructured Data? Typically, Unstructured data lacks an obvious consistent organization scheme or at least it lacks an obvious useful organization scheme. Consider product reviews. The 'number of stars' a product or service receives is easier to interpret than an ambiguously written review. Is the review Structured, Unstructured or Semi-Structured? Remember the expression 'Beauty is in the eye of the beholder.' Some reviews are clearly positive, others are clearly negative, and some may be unintelligible, both positive and negative, and some may defy classification. This uncertainty could give rise to the designation of Semi-structured or Unstructured.

To some degree the word 'structure' refers to both the internal organization of the data, and refers to our ability to work with the data regardless of its organization.

Lest we get to tangled up in our definitions, the relevant question might be who cares and why? The real business issue is can we work with the data in whatever form and format it is. If we have the tools and techniques to work with the data for our intended purposes, then whether it is more or less Structured becomes a secondary issue because we can work with the data and in doing that, we can apply an appropriate organization to the data to the extent we require.

Ultimately, the basic underlying questions remain:

- Can the business work with the data?
- Does the business have the necessary tools, techniques, and expertise to work with the data?

If yes, then the distinctions are less important.

One final note, over the last several decades, NoSQL tools and databases have emerged that handle Unstructured Data that would otherwise be a nightmare to handle in Relational Data Models, such as SQL. So, there are better new possibilities for handling Unstructured and Semi-Structured Data as well as traditional techniques for Structured Data.

Data Storage:

When working with Data, we generally must store it. This storage capability can take a variety of forms; hence, the generic reference to **Data Repositories**. The term **Data Repository** can refer to any facility capable of storing Data, i.e., any place data can reside. The storage may be temporary, such as buffers, or permanent such as databases.

Data storage modalities include:

- Data Lakes where a Data Lake is a vast storage facility typically for 'raw Data.'
- Data Warehouses, which tend to be copies of business Data
- Data Marts, which tend to be specialized storage facilities with a singular focus, such as Sales Data, or Research and Development Data, or Manufacturing Data, or Accounting Data.

The actual mechanisms include

- Databases – Databases may be relational database, non-relational databases, and new technologies.
- Spreadsheets – Spreadsheets are limited by size constraints and may be more 'digital workspaces' than a storage mechanism but they persist and are commonplace in businesses.
- Flat files – Flat files, although a legacy technology, are still used to move data among applications and storage facilities. The actual flat files may be retained. The original flat files were either comma separated values (CSV files) or tab separated values (TSV files) or another acceptable delimiter. Today, JSON, BSON and XML are newer technologies, but CSV and TSV files live on.

The storage facility could be online, i.e., an online data repository, or off-line, typically a long-term storage arrangement, such as old dependable magnetic tape or magnetic drives.

The storage facility could be actively used to interactively store data, or the storage facility could serve as a backup resource to protect data and provide a way back to original, pre-processed data.

The question of storage arises the instance data comes into existence. Consider a simple example, a digital thermometer. Let's say the thermometer takes a reading every second. What happens to that reading? Is it lost forever or is it stored? If it is stored, where is the reading stored? Hopefully the reading is stored along with the readings that preceded it and follow it, i.e., in time-series and hopefully the readings are timestamped. Let's say this digital thermometer is in a jet engine. A client made these sorts of sensors for airplanes and their engines. This temperature data could be stored locally on the aircraft and downloaded at its destination like the airplane's 'black boxes', or the data could be streamed to an assessment station, or the data may be processed by the sensor at the time the reading occurs and is published and/or stored only if the reading is abnormal. The later technique is an example of 'Edge Computing.' In Edge Computing, the data is processed as it is generated or collected by remote sensors. Based on an evaluation, the data is stored, and/or streamed, and/or discarded.

Returning to Data Lakes, Data Warehouses and Data Marts, and who knows what new names may be added to this list over time. Data Lakes generally contain enormous amounts of data often before the data is used. As the power of analytic tools increases, analysis of data in Data Lakes is becoming a reality. A Data Warehouse, in contrast, tends to be a company's primary data repository. It tends to be outside the Transaction processing software that generated the data so that its uses do not interfere with normal business processes. This data tends to be predominately, but not exclusively, related to the business generated by the business' internal applications. Data

Marts are like Data Warehouses, but they focus on specific functions or departments, such as Sales Data for the Sales Department, Marketing Data for the Marketing Department, Research and Development Data for the Research and Development Department, Accounting Data for Accounting, and so on.

Inevitably discussions of **Data Storage** get into On-premises Storage versus Cloud Storage. The final decision is up to the buyer. There are arguments pro and con. Without regard to the pros and cons, two things to keep in mind are the following:

- First, when a cloud provider is used, the business is using someone else's computing resources and the business may have little information about how the vendor conducts business. Yes, one could get a Service Organization Controls (SOC), which are Internal Control Audit reports prepared by accounting firms. But at the end of the day, the environment is the service provider's environment and only the service provider knows for sure … and still there are accidents.
- Second, many of the cloud storage services are designed to be 'sticky,' which means they want to get our business and keep our business and our **data**.

  One example of stickiness is their costing model. Uploading **data** may be free of charge while downloading **data** is charged. So, while putting the data into storage is free, we must pay to retrieve our **data** in addition to the service provider's regular storage charges.

Aside from the Pros and Cons of On-Premises and Cloud storage, these are two things to keep in mind in terms of using and monitoring cloud vendors. As the pendulum swings, we are seeing large businesses move some of their workloads off the cloud back on premises. Why? Because of costs.

System of Record

System of Record refers to the official records of a business. This term comes into play in a discussion regarding the question of whether certain data is the official Data of the business or not, or which version of the data is the official version. When ERP systems are used, they are for all practical purposes the business' **Systems of Record**.

Data Tagging

Data Tagging is a process of tagging Data according to certain predetermined categories. The objective is to facilitate subsequent use and data analysis.

Consider the following examples: Most Transactions and Master Data are timestamped, tagged with creation date and last-update date. With versioning or logging functions, changes to Transactions or Master Data can be easily reconstructed based on the timestamps.

Where location is available, such as physical address, data can be Geotagged for subsequent analysis and visualization. Geotagging involves identifying the latitude and longitude of a physical location. Geotagging is frequently colloquially referred as 'lat-long'.

Yet another example might be assigning importance or criticality to data. In other words, is the data Very Important/Very Critical, or Moderately Important/Moderately Critical, or Not Important/Not Critical. Obviously, the organization can determine the number and degrees of importance or criticality. Generally, the more critical something is, the sooner it is examined, resolved, and/or implemented.

All three examples involve tagging to facilitate the subsequent use of data, which can vary depending on an organization's goals and objectives.

Tagging also has a completely different meaning when we get to languages that tag data elements including, XML, HTML, JSON and so on. The tags identify data elements. Different languages implement different rules and formats, but the basic idea is that data can be identified by an associated tag.

Data – Time Series

Time Series Data refers to data that can be sequenced and used or analyzed serially. This could be as simple as a series of transactions that can be sequenced by their order numbers, or their positions in a list or by timestamps. This could also be a stream of data from IoT (Internet of Things) devices whereby the sequence is inherent in the stream and/or the data is time-stamped. Either way the data can be ordered based on physical position in the data stream or a sequential numeric or alphanumeric numbering scheme.

Narrowly, Time Series Data can be defined as time-stamped observations whereby the observations can be evaluated as successive observations or events such as temperature or pressure over time. More broadly, the concept of Time Series Data can apply to any business data that can be arranged in a sequence based on attributes that establish a sequence such as serial transaction numbers or timestamps that allow the transactions to be arranged in sequence and analyzed over the passage of time. This can be especially important in terms of staffing with maximum staff at times of high activity and minimum staff at times of low or no activity. And temperature readings could be an indication of whether a device is operating correctly or not. In this context, over-heating or under-cooling, as in refrigeration, can be problem. Over-heating may indicate the device is malfunctioning or the environment is hostile to the device and its proper functioning.

Ultimately nearly all business Transactions are time series data, i.e., the business transactions can be arranged in sequence over time; hence, the data can be easily analyzed for trends and unusual events.

Data – Tokenization

Data is **Tokenized** to obscure its original value.

The obvious application is tokenizing sensitive data. In this use case, the sensitive data is replaced by its Token. The token may be of the same length and format as the original data or not. For example, replacing passwords with a token. The original password is stored in a secure vault and is only subsequently accessible via the token. If the token is compromised, the password is not necessarily compromised. Another example of **tokenization** involves credit card transactions. When a business wants to issue a credit to a customer, the business can either use the original credit card number or the original bank transaction number. Using the original bank transaction number avoids having to refer back to the actual credit card number. The bank transaction number behaves as a token, i.e., a substitute for the original credit card number and its use is limited to the transaction in question. Humm, so a hacker could initiate additional refunds to a customer … a difficult way to make a living.

A question one may ask is: How does this approach differ from Encryption? Encrypting Data means applying a formula, albeit a very complex formula to the data. Encrypted Data is unlikely to be cracked but it is not impossible, especially with quantum computing on the horizon. Tokens, on the other hand, identify the sensitive data but the token's value bears no relationship to the data's original value. So, decryption techniques do not allow the original value to be discovered. The original value can only be recovered from the secure token vault.

A similar but less secure approach is **Data Masking**, which was previously discussed.

Data Transformation

Data Transformation is the process of transforming, i.e., changing, the format of data typically to make the data more useful. The strict use of the term typically applies to changes to the data, such as organizing and re-organizing Data, for different uses. Used informally, the word transformation may also apply to cleansing and fixing Data. Data Transformation often happens in the context of integrating data from different sources or adapting data for different uses. Some business examples include harmonizing the formats of names, addresses, telephone numbers, dates and so on so that they share a common format, or the format is altered for different uses, such as time in the 12-hour and 24-hour formats or dates in different formats or proper names in different formats.

Trusted Source

Trusted Source refers to a Data Source that is considered authoritative, of high quality, such that the recipients of the data can rely on the data for operational and decision-making purposes. This concept is particularly important when a business receives data from outside parties. Can the third-party be trusted?

There is another related concept in Cybersecurity called 'Zero Trust,' in other words, 'never trust, always verify.' Welcome to the wild world of malicious activity and malicious actors.

Data Types

A discussion of **Data Types** used to be simple. Data mostly mirrored what is on our keyboards. Data was either alphabetic or numeric with the special characters lumped in with the alphabetic characters. Hence, Data was either narrative, i.e., alphabetic, or numeric, the stuff of spreadsheets and financial reports. But today consider the various symbol sets and symbols available in a word processing application, the list is mindboggling.

However, even this oversimplifies the situation. There are simple answers; there are complex answers. What constitutes data is much more complex than the previous simple example suggests. What is common is 'Digital'. Data is stored digitally. The differences lie in the various types of data, including, but not limited to, narrative data, which can be broadly described as alphanumeric Data. What about audio Data, video Data, sensor Data, and so on. Representations are as diverse as text, sound files, image files and sensor streaming data. They have at least one thing in common. They are represented by the proverbial zeros and ones. They are digital artifacts of physical things and events.

Here are some basic distinctions:

- Simplest: Text Strings
- Types of Numbers: Integers, Decimals, Short and Long, Floating Point, Dates and Times
- Numbers versus Alphanumeric Characters versus Images versus Sounds
- Entities and Events versus Characteristics
- Data Analytic related types: Qualitative Data versus Quantitative Data.
- Qualitative: Nominal Data, names characteristics versus Ordinal Data, numeric values
- Quantitative: Discrete Data versus Continuous Data, i.e., a continuous range of values

The distinction between Qualitative and Quantitative is illustrated below:

Table 3.2 Qualitative Data versus Quantitative Data

Qualitative Data		T	Quantitative Data	
Nominal Data		Y P	Discrete Data (Numeric)	
	Expressed in Categories or Types	E S		The number of something, such as number of orders, number of employees, number of customers
	Controversial categories could include ethnicity & gender	of		
Ordinal Data		D A	Continuous Data	
	First, Second, Third in a category	T A		Continuous, such as time, temperature, speed, spatial, vectors, and so on
	A, B, C, ... in a category			
	1, 2, 3, ... in a category			

Data has come a long way from being limited to the keyboard and its character sets. Hence, managing data can become fairly complicated depending on the type of data involved.

Data Validation

Data Validation is the process of determining the validity of the data, especially verifying accuracy, compliance with certain standards and its integrity.

The objective of Data Validation is accurate, clean, verified data. Validation may be determined by requirements, rules, and/or quality benchmarks. Sometimes, Data Validation is referred to as Input Validation, i.e., confirming that the data meets the criteria established by an application or a user for entry into a system. Validation may include data type conformance, range and constraint testing, and questions regarding its structure and format.

Validation may also confirm its origins and how accurately it represents its origins. Validation may be determined by internal consistency or by confirmation with a cross-reference schedule. In other words, data may be determined to be valid based on confirmation by cross-reference or a valid value list or table, such as customer number or item number, which confirm their existence and in that sense their validity, such as telephone area codes and postal codes that confirm the validity of these codes.

Validation could also be determined by recalculating totals and subtotals, i.e., to confirm, for example, that the sales orders lines add up to the sales order totals. In EXCEL® spreadsheets, numbers can foot and be cross footed to verify accuracy.

These are different approaches to validating data, one based on occurrence in a list of acceptable values, based on re-calculating amounts, based on agreeing the totals. Occasionally spreadsheets are discovered to be invalid in the sense the numbers do not foot or do not cross-foot, which means the formulas are incorrect or were over-written.

Data Value:

Data Value is both intrinsic and extrinsic.

Looking at **Data** in terms of its intrinsic value focuses on **Data** as an essential part of the business. Consider Google for example. Google is a Search engine. As such, Google is all about **Data** and making it readily available to consumers as they need it when they need it for their purposes.

Looking at **Data** from an extrinsic perspective, the question becomes how can the data be used? The obvious use is selling the data, monetizing it. The essential question then becomes how much money can Google earn by selling its **Data** … which is really our data?

In the first use case, **Data** is an integral part of the business of Google. In the second use case, **Data** is an avenue to revenue. In both use cases, **Data** is valuable but in different ways.

My favorite example of Data Value involves the bankruptcy of Caesars Entertainment Corp. See the following from the Wall Street Journal.

> 'Real Prize in Caesars Fight: Data on Players – Customer loyalty program is valued at $1 billion by creditors'
>
> 'The most valuable asset in the bitter bankruptcy feud at Caesars Entertainment Corp. CZR 3.62%▲ isn't the casino operator's opulent Roman-themed resort at the heart of the Las Vegas Strip. It's the company's big-data customer loyalty program, valued at $1 billion by creditors.'
>
> Caesars chief executive Gary Loveman, a former Harvard Business School professor, said he devised the Total Rewards program in 1998 as a way to attract customers to the company's casinos without breaking the bank to upgrade them
>
> Mr. Loveman said he purposely made it quick and easy for customers to earn and redeem points, unlike airline loyalty programs requiring several flights to get a free trip. 'In our world, you gamble tonight, you eat dinner tonight,' said the executive …
>
> Caesars, in turn, uses the data it collects from the program to target its marketing campaigns and keep customers playing within its sprawling network of around 50 casinos, driving up overall revenue at the company.'
>
> 'Creditors view Caesars' Total Rewards customer loyalty program as the **single most valuable asset** [emphasis added] under dispute in a bankruptcy fight with the casino operator.'
>
> – Kate O'Keeffe, The Wall Street Journal, March 19, 2015.

This is an interesting case study in the value and use of data. In Caesars' case, data was more valuable to potential buyers than the casinos themselves, which is hard to image, but was the case.

The discussion of Value of Data would not be complete without considering the costs associated with collecting, organizing, and utilizing the data, and the economic impact on the business of not having the data.

Value is ultimately the net of the positive and negative aspects of having, managing and using data.

Data – Views:

Data Views are virtual database tables.

Views assemble data from multiple database tables allowing users to access the data as if it was in a single table rather than a bunch of separate tables in a database. The view can be populated when it is run, or the view can be pre-populated such that the results are readily available whenever they are needed. The later are referred to as 'instantiated' or 'materialized' views. Views allow businesses to customize titles and descriptions and, in that sense, personalize the Views to specific users.

Data Visualization

As popularly used, **Data Visualization** typically involves graphics; however, Data Visualization can include Reports and Queries. Data Visualization is not limited to a particular way of seeing data; it is not limited to graphs.

Traditional graphs include line graphs and pie charts. Sophisticated graphics include Heat Maps for density and the use of GeoTags to locate entities and transactions on maps. EXCEL® contains many of these mechanisms although when we get to Data Analytics, applications such as R and Python offer sophisticated scatter plots. In tools such as R, planes and splines can show data in multiple dimensions without being constrained by traditional two-dimensional x-y plots.

Don't overlook Reports. Reports and Queries are the most common form of Data Visualization. They show the data in an organized arrangement typically some sort of list. They are not as attractive and engaging as graphs, but many line personnel depend on them to manage their daily activities. So, though thought of as old fashioned, reports and queries, their digital cousins, still play an important role in describing situations, identifying issues, and informing metrics.

Applications increasing offer Dashboards as another vehicle to visualize data. Dashboards display a variety of items, graphic and textual. They can be personalized to individual users. Dashboards for corporate executives are typically very different from dashboards for marketing, sales, or production personnel.

Chapter 4

Domain Specific Topics

4.1 Data Governance

Section Outline:

- Governance as a Commitment
- Data Governance Defined
- Practical Data Governance Commitments

Organization culture, direction and commitments come from an organization's leaders, be they a Board of Directors, C Suite Executives or Owners and Founders. Regardless of the organization's structure, its culture comes from the Top. The Committee of Sponsoring Organizations of the Treadway Commission (COSO), 1985, a byproduct of the Foreign Corrupt Practices Act, expressed this principle in the phrase 'Tone at the Top'. Tone at the Top was expressed variously in COSO's Internal Control – Integrated Framework. Here are some examples:

> 'The board and senior management establish the **tone** [emphasis added] for the organization concerning the importance of internal control and the expected standards of conduct across the entity.' [–COSO, <u>Internal Control – Integrated Framework</u>, May 2013, page 3.]
>
> 'The board of directors and senior management establish the **tone at the top** [emphasis added] regarding the importance of internal control and expected standards of conduct.' [– Ibid, page 12.]
>
> "**Sets the Tone at the Top** – The board of directors and management at all levels of the entity demonstrate through their directives, actions, and behavior the importance of integrity and ethical values to support the function of the system of internal control." [– Ibid., page 33.]

'Tone' appears 23 times in COSO's <u>Internal Control – Integrated Framework</u>.

DOI: 10.4324/9781003295228-4

'Tone at the Top' is a primary theme, a central tenet, of Corporate Governance, which includes Data Governance. Data Governance is the application of Governance principles to data, especially commitment to High-Quality Data, which means insistence on appropriate policies, procedures and standards regarding data and adequate funding for High-Quality Data. High-Quality Data doesn't just happen. It is intentional.

Having a policy and not adequate funding, it is tantamount to having no policy.

Data Governance is one aspect of Corporate Governance. Data Governance embodies:

- A business' commitment to data
- Its overall approach to data
- Its Data Management strategies, including commitments to data-related policies, procedures, practices, standards, and resources.

As important as Good Governance is for integrity and good conduct, Good Data Governance reflects the business' approach and commitment to data. Good data doesn't happen automatically. Good data is the result of explicit commitments to have and maintain appropriate data.

Data Governance is a business' formal, explicit commitments to Data inclusive of all aspects of Data's lifecycle and the resources that capture, maintain and store that Data, including regulatory compliance and the appropriate use of Data in the operation and management of the business.

Data Governance typically includes at least the following areas:

- Commitment to appropriate Data Management
- Oversight of Data Management
- Oversight of the organization's strategy regarding data
- Oversight of the organization's policies, procedures, practices, and standards regarding data
- Oversight of standards regarding data and data quality
- Ensuring Compliance with industry and government-imposed regulations
- Oversight of Incident and Problem Management policies and procedures covering the capture, retention, use, and analysis of data

Data Governance is focused on ensuring appropriate management over data and its use. The actual management of data is vested in the organization's executive management, particularly IT management.

Two keys to effective Governance are Intentionality and Commitment. This means the organization is explicitly, intentionally committed to having, processing, and using data appropriately including data acquired from outside sources as well as data generated by the business' systems.

COBIT (formerly Control Objectives for Information and Related Technology) is a specific approach to IT Governance, and by extension, Data Governance. COBIT emphasizes the concept of value creation through alignment. Applying alignment to data, data achieves its maximum value for an organization when the data is appropriate, when the data fits the organization's mission, vision, strategy, goals, and objectives.

The Data Governance Institute summarizes Data Governance in the following diagram:

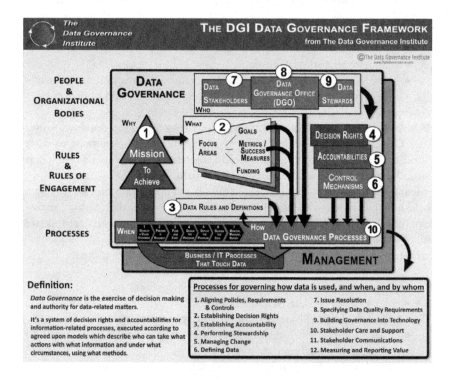

Figure 4.1 Data Governance Institute Governance Framework
Reproduced with permission of The Data Governance Institute

The Data Governance Institute describes Data Governance as follows:

- '… data governance is a system of decisions rights and accountabilities for information-related processes, executed according to agreed-upon models which described who can take what actions with what information, and when, under what circumstances, using what methods.'
  – https://datagovernance.com/the-data-governance-basics/
  definitions-of-data-governance/, July 2022.

- The Data Governance Institute stresses reliability, availability, timeliness, and security.

Moving from advocacy to action, what does Data Governance mean in practical terms?

1   Knowing the business' major datasets, including the sources, storage, and subsequent uses of data. This is usually accomplished by cataloging the business' data.

   o   If the business does not know what data it has and where that data is stored, adequate protection is unlikely.
   o   Or, as Lewis Carrol put it in Through the Looking Glass, 'If you don't know where you are going, any road will get you there.' Paraphrasing Carrol, 'if you don't know where you are going, you won't get where you need to be'.
   o   Knowing the data an organization has is the first step in effectively managing that data.

2   Identifying, implementing, and monitoring the business' data policies, procedures, practices, and standards.

   o   This ensures that the business has appropriate mechanisms in place to ensure high-quality data and these mechanisms are routinely monitored for effectiveness and refined as needed to continue to have high-quality data. The discussion about CMMI, Capability Maturity Model Integration, is relevant here.

3   Recognize that users within the business are the experts with respect to 'their' data; hence, their involvement in data capture, processing, storage, and use is essential for effective high-quality Data. These users may be referred to as SME's, Subject Matter Experts.

4   Managing Master Data is crucial especially when data are aggregated. Does the business adequately manage its Master Data to accurately aggregate data from different entities within the business, be it customer data, supplier data, product data, location Identification, or other data.

5   On the practical side, does the organization have competent technical personnel to implement the business' policies, procedures, practices, and standards for the management of data.

   o   Without adequately trained technical resources, having high-quality data is difficult to maintain especially if the data needs to be 'wrangled', i.e., processed.

6   Ensuring that data is appropriately used.

    o   This idea draws on the notion of 'fitness of use.' Different data is fit for different uses. By extension, different purposes require different data. If data works well for one use, this is no guarantee that it will necessarily address other issues as well, hence the question of appropriateness given different circumstances.

Ultimately, Good Data Governance comes down to

- Having High-Quality Data
- Understanding the Data
- Protecting the Data
- Ensuring the Right Resources are available and adequate to manage the data

Good data, i.e., High-Quality Data, are not accidental. Good data are intentional.

4.2 Data Architecture

Would you build a building without a plan? I suspect my grandfather did but unlikely today. Plans are an essential part of building structures ranging from physical buildings to less tangible items such as Databases, Data Warehouses and Data Marts, hence, a brief discussion devoted to Data Architecture.

First, having a Data Architecture includes planning, design, implementation, and maintenance. Data Architecture does not occur accidentally. Well, not completely, not exactly. Businesses often inherit their Data Architecture by virtue of their primary or biggest applications. Commercial business systems have an inherent Data Architecture reflecting the systems' purposes, processes, and structure. These frequently become an organization's default Data Architecture by virtue of using the system.

The notable exceptions to intentionally designed Data Architectures are three:

First, the Data Architecture that is built into business systems, be they ERP systems or something else.

Second, custom developed applications will, as a normal part of the development process, address data; however, the design is often limited to that specific application, not necessarily with the entire business in mind.

Third, as a byproduct of a specific data initiative. The initiative may involve ingesting data from outside the business, or be a Data Analysis project, or other specific initiatives involving data. As with the second exception, the scope of the architecture is related to the project as opposed to considering the entire business and all of its business systems.

Regardless of the situation, a Data Architecture is a specific, intentional design that encompasses the entirety of the business' systems, databases, and data. DAMA views Data Architecture from three perspectives:

- Outcomes
- Activities
- Behavior
  - DAMA-DMBOK: DATA MANAGEMENT BODY OF KNOWLEDGE, 2nd Edition, p. 98.

This breakdown deals with artifacts, activities, intentions, and roles.

Another approach focuses on the data itself; how it is acquired, how it is processed, how it is stored, and how it is used. In this context, Data Architecture includes:

- The Datasets that exist, or will exist, within the business.
- The Structure of the data, its subsets, and the attributes of data elements within the datasets.
- The Process flows that generate and consume the data.
- The Design and Implementation of the Repositories that hold, organize, manage, and make the data available.
- The Uses to which the data is put.
- And ultimately the Outcomes that occur from the various uses to which the data is put.

The beginning of a Data Architecture is determining the data and datasets that exist, or will exist, in the business. If there is no explicit Data Architecture, this journey begins with discovery identifying the following aspects:

- Data in the Business
- Where Data Resides
- How Data is Organized
- Where Data is Stored
- What Generates Data, typically the applications
- If the Data comes from outside the Business, from where does it come, how is it organized, and how and where it is stored
- Who Owns, Who Manages, Who Uses the Data
- To which Business Processes is the Data related and how is it related to these Business Processes

The next step in developing a Data Architecture is understanding the domains to which the data relates. Is the data related to major business processes, such as buying, selling, or making goods or services? Is the data related to internal activities and/or do these activities involve entities or events outside of the business? Does the data provide insights about entities and activities inside or outside the business, or both?

A major consideration is aligning the data with the business' strategies and objectives. Remember alignment is an essential and core element in multiple IT frameworks.

Based on these understandings and context, a model is designed to express these elements in context. Structure models focus on identifying Entities and their Attributes and on identifying Events and their Attributes. In the relational database world, these are typically Entity Relationship Diagrams (ERDs). Accompanying the diagrams are dictionaries or glossaries that name and describe the various entities and events and their attributes.

In addition to structure diagrams, process or flow diagrams document the lifecycles of data and describe the usage of the data over time. Process Flowcharts, Workflow and Data Flow diagrams illustrate different aspects of the Data Architecture as well as the accompanying documentation that identifies the entities, attributes, and processes and describes how data is generated and used at each step of each process.

Once the Data Architecture is designed, accepted and approved by the business, the Data Architecture is implemented. Part of the Data Architecture design must address implementation. This is often expressed as a 'Roadmap,' a roadmap from the present to the future. Frequently, the words 'current state' and 'future state' are used to identify the present situation and potential future situations, their pros and cons, and their advantages and disadvantages. These become part of the data architecture discussion.

To the extent that a Data Architecture is already in place, this exercise is an opportunity for an expansive consideration of additional uses to which data can be put. How can the business' data be used more effectively to achieve maximum usefulness for the business? What new services or insights can be gleaned from data? What additional data from outside the business can supplement and enrich the business' data to achieve maximum value from that data?

Throughout these steps, the analyst architect is organizing the data and processing the data in a rational system that optimizes data, its storage and use. Inevitably compromises are made as data is used for different purposes to achieve different outcomes. Throughout the process, the Data Architect should be designing flexible structures and processes to accommodate the inevitable changes and drifts that typically occur. As this book is being written, I am conscious of the multiple changes that occurred in response to the COVID-19 pandemic as more data became available, as the nature of the pandemic changed and as people's responses to the pandemic changed. Hopefully future changes will not be as disruptive and profound as those caused by COVID-19.

If your career path takes you into Business Analysis and Data Wrangling, you will get the most points for a flexible, robust design that accommodates the future using previously established alternatives, such as being able to easily accommodate shelter-in-place, remote working, and new retail distribution models, such as delivery services and curbside pickup. Many of these situations and services existed prior to the pandemic on an ad-hoc basis. The pandemic institutionalized them.

A superior Data Architecture should support these new functions at scale without significant changes to the Data Fabric.

This is the beginning of the process. At least here, the intention is to focus on the mechanical aspects of Data Architecture. Other Data Architecture characteristics include the following:

- Data Architectures are conceptual.
- Data Architectures must be consistent with and supportive of the business' goals and objectives.
- Data Architectures need to reflect reality and be realistic.
- Data Architectures need to be able to change over time as requirements and needs change.

There is an inevitable drift of needs and requirements over time, sometimes subtle, sometimes sudden. Either way, inevitably things change. The Data Architecture needs to be flexible enough to adjust to new realities, to adapt to changing requirements and circumstances.

Data Architecture is only one element in the larger world of Enterprise Architecture. The Open Group publishes the TOGAF (The Open Group Architecture Framework). TOGAF identifies four architecture domains, of which data is one domain. Its ADM (Architecture Development Method), '... provides a tested and repeatable process for developing architectures.' [– The Open Group, The Open Group, The Open Group Standard – TOGAF® Standard – Introduction and Core Concepts, Version 10.0, 2022, p. 16.]

TOGAF identifies four architecture domains which are subsets of Enterprise Architecture:

- Business Architecture
- Data Architecture
- Application Architecture
- Technology Architecture

Where Data Architecture '... describes the structure of an organization's logical and physical data assets and data management resources.' [– The Open Group, The Open Group Standard – TOGAF® Standard – Introduction and Core Concepts, Version 10.0, 2022, p. 15.]

TOGAF's Architecture Development Cycle is expressed diagrammatically as follows:

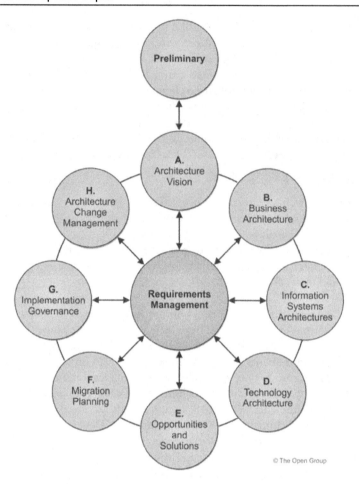

Figure 4.2 TOGAF Architecture Development Cycle
Reproduced with permission granted from The Open Group, L.L.C. - Copyright The
Open Group

Similar to The Open Group, the Data Management Association (DAMA),
describes an Enterprise Data Model as follows:

'Enterprise Data Model (EDM): The EDM is a holistic, enterprise-level,
implementation-independent conceptual or logical data model providing a
common consistent view of data across the enterprise.' [– DAMA-DMBOK:
DATA MANAGEMENT BODY OF KNOWLEDGE, 2nd Edition, p. 104.]

For more information regarding DAMA's Data Architecture Model review
pp. 104ff of DAMA's Data Management Body of Knowledge (DMBOK).

What TOGAF and DAMA have in common is an emphasis upon a unified
model that encompasses both logical and physical models. While at this point

in its publication, DAMA-DMBOK: DATA MANAGEMENT BODY OF KNOWLEDGE, 2nd Edition, pp. 107–110, DAMA emphasizes Data Flow, keep in mind that both Structure Diagrams and Process Diagrams are essential to fully model Data and its lifecycles.

DAMA acknowledges the distinction with which this chapter began, i.e., the accidental Data Architecture brought by applications versus the freedom to work with a 'clean slate.' DAMA acknowledges that very few organizations start with a clean slate. Most organizations are encumbered by past decisions. [– DAMA-DMBOK: DATA MANAGEMENT BODY OF KNOWLEDGE, 2nd Edition, p. 111.] Notice particularly the last sentence.

Other ancillary Data Architecture topics DAMA addresses are:

- Scope
- Dependencies
- Consistent Overall Architecture
- Data Lineage – Traceability
- Replication
- Standards,
- Technology
- Implementation Roadmap

A brief mention of tools is appropriate. Typically, a Data Architect would need at least a graphics tool and a word processor. Words are a poor substitute for graphs, but graphs require narratives to describe context and details. So, not one or the other but both.

Regarding diagrams and graphs, DAMA presents some suggestions for clarity:

- Clear and Consistent Legend
- Matching Diagrams Objects and Legend
- Clear and Consistent Line Direction
- Consistent Line Cross Display Method
- Consistent Object Attributes
- Linear Symmetry

– DAMA-DMBOK: DATA MANAGEMENT BODY OF KNOWLEDGE, 2nd Edition, pp. 116, 117.

To these suggestions, I would add attention to pagination. It is one thing to have a large-format printer. It is quite another matter to use an 8.5 by 11- or 14-inch paper. Without attention to pagination, objects end up being printed on 2 separate sheets of paper, sometimes far removed from each other. This requires pasting together multiple pages often with blank pages in between. Once pasted together, the diagram may be displayed on a large surface, often a wall. Instead of taking the diagrams to the audience, one ends up bringing the audience to the wall.

Two suggestions are using off page connectors and formatting the drawing space in such a manner that one can easily see objects that would otherwise be spread over two pages. Consider the following approach to avoid objects spread over two adjacent sheets.

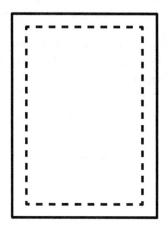

Figure 4.3 Blank Sheet of Paper

The heavy blank line is the page boundary. The dashed inter line is the border for diagramming purposes. Consider the following case:

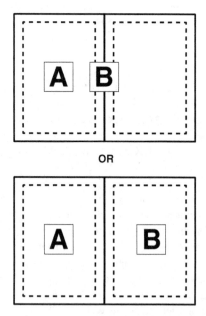

Figure 4.4 Avoid placing components across sheets

In the upper diagram, item B appears on both pages. In the lower diagram, item A is on the left page and item B is on the right page, nothing is on the borders. Something to keep in mind as you do your diagramming.

4.3 Databases

Hold the Data

Section Outline:

- SQL
- NoSQL

Databases are the technical applications designed specifically to hold data.

In the early days of computing, IBM ruled the mainframe marketplace with its IBM System/360 and its IMS^{TM} database, where IMS was the abbreviation for Information Management System. How important was IBM then? The following saying probably best sums up IBM's role in the marketplace then: 'nobody ever got fired for buying IBM.'

In 1969 IBM renamed its Information Control System and Data Language/Interface (ICS/DL/I) IMS. ICS/IMS was born out of the need to track the millions of parts involved in the effort to put a man on the moon. IBM characterizes IMS as 'the world's first commercial database management system.'

'More than 40 years later, the old IBM® IMS^{TM} slogan, 'The world depends on it,' still holds true.'

Arguable.

> And while IBM's pioneering relational database management system — IBM DB2®— became an alternative approach for viewing and extracting value from data in different formats, IMS never lost its popularity as the transactional workhorse for very large workloads. IBM's other transaction processor, IBM CICS ® (Customer Information Control System), was used for web services and online transactions. ... And in many cases these products work together, with IMS used as the back-end database, and CICS providing the front-end online interaction.
> – https://www.ibm.com/ibm/history/ibm100/us/en/icons/ibmims/

Separately IBM engineers developed SEQUEL in the 1970s, which was renamed SQL, to avoid trademark infringement. In the same time frame, Relational Software, Inc, now Oracle, developed its own SQL-based RDBMS (Relational Management Database System). In 1986 and 1987, ANSI and ISO officially adopted standards for SQL, X3.135 now ISO/IEC

9075. [– https://blog.ansi.org/2018/10/sql-standard-iso-iec-9075-2016-ansi-x3-135/]

Ever since, SQL has been the standard for transaction processing applications and their data; hence, much of the material in this book refers to SQL.

But SQL is not alone. NoSQL was developed to compensate for some of SQL's limitations. NoSQL can also be referred to as 'not only SQL,' which in effective confirms the dominance of SQL in the database marketplace.

But today SQL must share the spotlight with 4 other basic NoSQL models. They are:

- Key-Value Data Stores
- Document-based Data Stores
- Columnar-based Data Stores
- Graph-based Data Stores

Each of these models has its own strengths. In general, they have been described as schema-less. Schema-agnostic is probably a better description. Either way, they have flexibility not found in SQL. SQL works great for structured transaction data but what happens when databases are confronted with unstructured data, such as social media posts, other text or narrative content, and the datasets get really large? Enter NoSQL alternatives.

- Key-Value pairs are just that, a Key and a Value, for example, Key = 'ID1001', Value = James. Examples of a key-value databases are MongoDB, Redis, Riak and AWS' DynamoDB.
  Passwords are an excellent use case for Key-Value pairs, where the key is the UserID, and the value is the Password. In a Key-Value database, the system would look up a password based on UserIDs, done, and done fast. If a telephone number is subsequently needed for second confirmation, another Key-Value pair would be UserID and the telephone number.
- Columnar-based Stores store data in columns rather than in rows. The columns are grouped in families, which can be nested; hence, allowing a nearly limitless columnar nested model. Examples include Cassandra, HBase and MongoDB.
- Document-based Stores extend Key-Value by organizing entire documents in groups called collections. They support nested key-value pairs and allow queries on any attribute within a document. Document-based Stores keep all their data in a single table or 'document' generally encoded using XML, JSON or BSON. Here the word 'document' does not refer to objects like Microsoft Word

documents rather the documents are containers, and their contents are encoded. Examples include MongoDB, Couchbase and CouchDB.

- Graph-based Stores use a network model. Graph-based stores employ nodes and relationships. Connecting two nodes establishes a relationship between them. The relationship is represented by an 'edge.' Neo4j is one of the better-known Graph databases. ArangoDB and Tiger Graph are other examples.

  An interesting use case for Graph-based data relates to funneling money to terrorist groups. The graph shows how money moves from entity to entity, from a 'good guy' through a series of intermediaries to a 'bad guy'.

  Coincidentally, products don't neatly classify in a single category. The same product may appear in more than one category. In other words, the categories are not mutually exclusive but partially overlapping.

To the above list, the following could also be added:

- Time-Series Data Stores, such as InfluxDB, TimescaleDB, OpenTSDB, collect series of data elements over time, like a temperature recorder or a traffic monitor.
- Search-based Data Stores enable searches, often key word searches, and their results.
- In-memory Databases store their Data in memory and consequently are extremely fast, such as SAP's HANA.

Typically, businesses use application software to maintain their entities and process their transactions. These applications are essentially business process engines, and their data is typically stored in SQL Databases because SQL uniquely supports transaction processing quickly, effectively. Hence, SQL becomes a common data repository for data analytics and data science. Arguably more challenging or more interesting projects might involve a combination of SQL data and NoSQL data. For example, comparing internal customer activity data with external social media and outside econometric data, to include the impact of external economic events and trends on customer behavior.

Briefly SQL has been incorporated into some of the NoSQL products and SQL has been extended to NewSQL and Distributed SQL. So, SQL isn't standing still either.

Major players in the SQL database market space include Oracle, Microsoft, and IBM with its DB2 product. With Oracle's acquisition of MySQL, Oracle may arguably control the largest segment of the SQL database market, but Microsoft is very common among businesses. It is as if there were really three SQL markets: Microsoft, Oracle, and MySQL, not one market.

Occasionally one may stumble across a MultiValue database where multiple values are stored in a single field. This was popular with the Pick Operating System. Pick passed out of popular use with the premature death of its founder, Richard Pick; however, the product still lives on in UniVerse, a Rocket Software product.

4.4 Master Data and Master Data Management

Threads that Connect

Section Outline:

- Master Data
- Master Data Management (MDM)
- Other Related Aspects of Master Data: Reference Data, Taxonomies, Ontologies and Inference

Master Data and **Master Data Management** emphasizes two major topics:

- **Master Data** identify items uniquely and unambiguously.
- **Master Data Management** manages item identification across diverse systems especially in the absence of unique, unambiguous item identification in different systems.

Master Data are the identifiers within systems that specifically, uniquely, definitively identify items. These entity attributes can be referred to as Identifiers, as ID's, or in the case of the relational model, **Primary Keys** (**PKs**). Their essential function is to identify entities accurately, uniquely, definitively, such as Customers, Vendors, Products, Services, Locations, Organization Components, and so on. These Identifiers include CustomerID, VendorID, ProductID, ServiceID, LocationID, DivisionID or RegionID or DepartmentID, and so on. These ID's uniquely identify specific customers, vendors, products, services, locations, and organization entities.

These Identifiers, or Primary Keys, allow specific Customers and their transactions to be identified for operational, reporting, and analytic purposes. Consequently, they are referred to as **Master Data**. They are the 'keys' that unlock data in databases.

These Identifiers can be generated in 2 ways:

- Either automatically by the system based on an algorithm, or
- Exist outside of a system in conformance to certain rules and restrictions

The simplest algorithm for generating identifiers is serial identification, in the form of $x + 1$. The initial identifier usually begins with 0 or 1, the second identifier is either 0 + 1 or 1, the next identifier is 1 + 1 or 2, and so on. For example, consider check numbers; they are typically sequential. Going a step further, check printers may ask where to begin the sequence number. So instead of 0 or 1, a customer might pick 100 or 1000 or some other number. This numbering scheme is referred as a serial or sequential numbering system.

If the Identifier is not system generated, then constraints usually limit the Identifier's format, such as character type, numeric, alphabetic, or alphanumeric, and length. Consider complex passwords as an example. While they are not Identifiers, they are examples of a complex strings often with some combination of Upper- and Lower-Case Alphabetic characters, Numbers and Special Characters and usually at least 8 characters in length but increasingly websites request passwords that are at least 12 characters in length, hence good candidates for passphrases as opposed to passwords.

Regardless of how the Identifier is generated, the Identifier must be Unique at least within its primary system. The second half of this discussion gets into the question of Unique across multiple systems.

These Identifiers can be random or meaningful. Meaningful Identifiers are often referred to as Intelligent Numbering. In the case of random Identifiers, the Identifier does not have an inherent relationship with the entity. In the case of Intelligent Identifiers, they have some inherent relationships with the entity. Consider a Vehicle Identification Number (VIN):

7FA RW1H9 3 K E 016006

The Vin number is made of six parts, some sources break the number into more than 6 parts,

Where: 7FA identifies the Manufacturer

RW1H9 identifies the Vehicle's brand, body style, engine size and type, model, series

3 is Security Check Digit

K is Model Year

E is Manufacturing Plant

016006 is the Vehicle's Serial Number

The format and content of VIN numbers is maintained by the International Organization for Standardization (ISO). ISO Standard ISO 3779:2009(en) Road vehicles – Vehicle identification number (VIN) – Content and structure. ISO describes the scope of this standard as follows:

This International Standard specifies the content and structure of a vehicle identification number (VIN) to establish, on a world-wide basis, a uniform identification numbering system for road vehicles.

This International Standard applies to motor vehicles, towed vehicles, motorcycles, and mopeds as defined in ISO 3833.
– https://www.iso.org/obp/ui/#iso:std:iso:3779:ed-4:v1:en, July 2022.

This is an example of an external identification authority.

Another example of Master Data is UPC product codes. Many products we buy today have UPC bar codes on them. At checkout, the point-of-sale system reads the UPC to determine the product whose unit price is retrieved from the store's inventory system. This system works reliably to identify products and their correct prices at time of sale, time after time, a nod to one of automation's advantages. Taking this a step further, in our daily shopping we may find the same product at different stores. Upon inspection, we may discover that each store has its own ProductID as well as the Product's UPC code. The UPC code is common across different retailers, but each retailer may have its own SKU, 'Stock Keeping Unit.' In this case, the retailer has both a universal identifier and a separate internal unique identifier. These IDs may have some intelligence built into them like VIN numbers.

Universal Product Codes (UPC) and Global Trade Item Numbers (GTIN) are specifically designed to provide globally unique identifiers that span organizations and international boundaries. For more information on GTINs, go to www.gtin.info. Vehicle Identification Numbers (VIN) are unique identification numbers for vehicles regardless of who or where the vehicle was made and in what jurisdiction the vehicle is registered. Social Security Numbers (SSN) are often cited as examples of GUIDs, but identity theft has crippled their use. My latest Medicare card does not have a Social Security Number on it but a separate number specifically for Medicare purposes.

Not all intelligent numbering schemes are set by standards organizations, such as the VIN number. A former client, an HVAC company, used a 20-character, or thereabouts, number to identify its inventory parts. By looking at the Identifier, an inventory picker could quickly determine exactly which part to pick from inventory, whether the part was ducting, a motor, a fan or something else. As with the VIN number, the characteristics of the part were encoded in its Identifier. There are arguments for and against intelligent numbering, which you can separately research if intelligent numbering appeals to you.

Not to get lost in this discussion is the primary focus of Identifiers, i.e., to Uniquely, Definitively Identify Entities in a collection. In other words, a CustomerID should point to 'one and only one' Customer without ambiguity, without uncertainty, without confusion. You may see the term GUID or its counterpart UUID. GUID refers to Globally Unique Identifier; UUID refers to Universally Unique Identifier. Both terms hint at two properties:

- Uniqueness
- Global Uniqueness

Master Data connects entities and their transactions, such as Customers and their Purchasers, Suppliers, and the items they supply, Employees and their time, Locations and their activities, Warehouses and their contents, and so on. Below are some connection examples:

- Business Partners including

  o Organizations and Individuals
  o Customers and Suppliers
  o Internal or External Business Partners

- Products/Goods and Services including

  o Items, Parts, Productlines
  o Services and Servicelines

- Organization Structures including

  o Subsidiaries
  o Divisions
  o Regions
  o Offices
  o Branches

- Locations including

  o Physical Locations including warehouses and offices
  o Physical Addresses
  o Logical Addresses
  o Latitude – Longitude (Lat-Long) coordinates for GPS use

- Financial Structures including

  o Accounts
  o Assets
  o Reporting Structures
  o Responsibility Structures

The challenges related to Entity Identification are simple. Different people often pick different identifiers for the same items. Identifiers can change over time. Different parts of an organization may identify the same entities differently. The differences could be the result of organizational or geographic considerations. Different parts of an organization may interact with entities differently, like customer in one case and supplier in another case. An example of this in the ERP sphere is Vendor versus Supplier. Some

ERP systems refer to Vendor while others use the term Supplier instead. As the saying goes, 'a distinction without a difference'. In the past, parts of a business may have operated autonomously. There was no need to aggregate data at that point in time and consequently little concern about universality.

Shifting from a focus on Uniqueness to the Management of Master Data, the next topic is Managing Master Data.

Master Data Management (**MDM**) focuses on the scope and extent of the Uniqueness and managing the differences. Relevant questions include the following:

- Is the Uniqueness confirmed to a single system?
- Does the Uniqueness extend beyond a single system?
- Are the Identifiers GUIDs or UUIDs?
- If the Identifier is not a GUID or UUID, how does the business manage the differences?

First, Uniqueness generally is at least within the Entity's primary system, which is to say that a CustomerID is at least unique within the system in which the Customer resides. For example, you have a specific Customer Number at a specific bank. That number is used to identify all of your transactions at that bank spanning your various accounts and transactions. Suppose your bank acquires another bank where you also have accounts. Is your Customer Number at your bank the same as your Customer Number at the other bank? No, not generally.

I say generally because they are often exceptions. An exception I encountered early in my consulting career involved a magazine publisher with well over ten thousand different Identifiers for the United States Post Office. Recollection is far from perfect; the actual number may have been much higher than 10,000 duplicates. Examples of the duplication included US Post Office, USPO, USPS, Post Office, Rockaway Post Office, Post Office Rockaway, Post Office Manhattan, Manhattan Post Office, Manhattan PO ... use your imagination, the list goes on almost without end. Our task was to narrow the number of vendors down to a much smaller number without this sort of redundancy.

Going back to the bank example, your customer number is probably different at each bank with which you do business. I would be really surprised if any two of the customer numbers were the same. So, the customer number is unique within a particular bank but not unique across multiple banks. You can see the confusion when one bank acquires another bank. If you had accounts at both banks, you Customer Number was different and the acquiring bank had to make an adjustment, which could include re-numbering the Customers of the acquired bank, likely preserving the original number somewhere in the Customer Master record, or set up a cross-reference table to connect your various instances. This gets us to the second question.

Second, across an organization with multiple components, be they subsidiaries or just other entities, is the Identifier Unique? Often it isn't, which gets us to the question of scope. The Identifier is Unique within a particular part of the organization but not across the entire organization. What's a good example? Consider a large company such as Disney as a hypothetical example. The Walt Disney Company is well-known across the globe. According to Disney's latest annual report, Disney has major two segments: Disney Media and Entertainment Distribution (DMED), and Disney Parks, Experiences and Products (DPEP). Its annual report lists at least 11 significant lines of business, which are enumerated across approximately 13 pages in the annual report, i.e., the list isn't short. Hypothetically, if you did business with Disney, would your entity number be the same at the Disney Studio as at the Theme Parks as at the Disney Store as at ABC as at other Disney properties? Maybe yes, maybe no. Remember this is a hypothetical example. If the enterprise has a central Entity Identification authority, then maybe yes; if the enterprise doesn't have a central authority, then probably no. This hypothetic example could be further complicated. Supposing you were a customer at some entities and a supplier to other entities. Would you have the same Identifier? Probably not. And a business doesn't have to be a big enterprise to encounter this problem.

Moving back and forth between examples, keep in mind the superiority of Globally Unique Identifiers that extend beyond specific businesses and organizations.

The worst-case scenario, you do business with an organization that includes multiple sub-organizations and in each sub-organization the identifications are different. How is this difference managed? Enter **Master Data Management**. There are a variety of answers:

- Within each sub-organization, your Identifier is different and there is no management of the differences, which is often the case.
- Within each sub-organization, your identifier is different, and these differences are managed through some sort of cross-reference facility.
- Within each sub-organization, your identifier is the same because of a central entity identification authority that issues and manages Entity Identification.

In the second use case, how are the differences managed? If there is no central entity identification authority, the differences are probably managed through a cross-reference mechanism that allows the organization to identify the same entity within different business units despite the presence of different Unique Identifiers within the different units' systems.

If the IDs are different across an organization, how does the organization determine that the Entities with different IDs are really the same? Is there a confirmation process or is sameness determined by inference? If by inference, how accurate is the association? Occasionally, I get duplicate offers in the mail or via email. The duplication tells me the sender has me in its database multiple times with different IDs but the same address. Is the duplication intentional? Is the duplication a matter of inadequate Data Cleansing? Is the duplication a matter of cost efficiency, i.e., the cost of cleaning up the data exceeds the cost of sending duplicates? Is the duplication an inference error? Or is the duplication the result of something else?

Lastly, why is **Master Data Management (MDM)** important? **Master Data Management** becomes extremely important when organizations seek to combine Data from different parts of the organization to see the full extent and scope of interactions with different parties. Maybe several of these outside entities are major customers or suppliers for the enterprise and the enterprise wants to acknowledge that.

Master Data Management argues for a plan to manage master data, i.e., master entities, such as customers, suppliers, employees, products, services, locations, and so on. Ideally, Entity IDs are identical across platforms and organizations. If not, cross-reference mechanisms and inference mechanisms are used to determine equivalence. These mechanisms are not necessarily easy to develop nor are they completely accurate. The last thing that one wants is to introduce errors into the data because of false equivalence.

In a nutshell, **Master Data** refers to Entity Identification and **Master Data Management** addresses Entity Identification Diversity.

Ultimately, **Master Data Management** is an ongoing process to ensure consistency. It is not a 'once-and-done' proposition. MDM is an ongoing commitment to uniformity and consistency to obtain the maximum value from business Data.

Other related aspects of Master Data

- Reference Data
- Taxonomies
- Ontologies
- Inference

In the next page are two examples of simple reference tables. The first relates to a HelpDesk Trouble Ticketing system. The second example relates to the USPS' State Abbreviations.

For the complete list of USPS Postal Codes see: https://www.bls.gov/respondents/mwr/electronic-data-interchange/appendix-d-usps-state-abbreviations-and-fips-codes.htm

Taxonomies

Taxonomies are classification schemes. They are used to organize and standardize Master Data across entities. A business can have its own set of

Code	State	Explanation
01	New	New HelpTicket
02	Assigned	HelpTicket assigned to technician
03	Pending	Additional information is required
04	Work in Process	Technician is working on the problem
05	Escalated	HelpTicket is escalated
06	Resolved	Problem resolved
07	Completed	Requester verifies completion
08	Cancelled	HelpTicket was cancelled

Figure 4.5 HelpDesk Trouble Ticketing Example

State Name	Postal Abbr.	FIPS Code
Alabama	AL	01
Alaska	AK	02
Arizona	Az	04
Arkansas	AR	05
California	CA	06
Colorado	CO	08
Connecticut	CT	09

Figure 4.6 USPS Postal Code Example

taxonomies or, in some cases, use generic taxonomies such as the North American Industry Classification System (NAICS):

2022 NAICS Code	2022 NAICS Title
520000	Finance and Insurance
521110	Monetry Authorities-Central Bank
522110	Commercial Banking
522130	Credit Unions
522180	Savings Institutions ...
522210	Credit Card Issuing
522220	Sales Financing
522291	Consumer Lending
522292	Real Estate Credit
522299	International, Secondary Market ...
522310	Mortgage and Nonmortgage Loan Brokers
522320	Financial Transaction Processing ... Clearinghouse ...
522390	Other Activities Related to Credit Intermediation

Figure 4.7 NAICS Code Example

Over 774,000 entries are part of section 52 for Finance and Insurance. For more information about NAICS, see the following: https://www.naics.com/2022-naics-changes/

A business productline taxonomy might be something along this line:

Productline Taxonomy

Code Value	Description	Parent Code
1000	Sensor	1000
1100	Temperature Sensor	1000
1200	Pressure Sensor	1000
1201	High Pressure Sensor	1200
1202	Low Pressure Sensor	1200
1300	Temp/Pressure Sensor	1000

Figure 4.8 A Productline Example

Taxonomies are established to organize items in consistent groupings. In the above example, the sensor productline is organized into a product hierarchy. Each taxonomy is a different dimension.

Ontologies

Ontologies provide a more sophisticated framework. Whereas Taxonomies classify related items, Ontologies establish classes, relationships, and constraints. Ontologies are overarching constructs that establish relationships among entities such as the relationships between customers and products. The Dewey Decimal System that many of us grew up with is an Ontology. A relational database is an ontology; it is a set of tables with columns and identifiers that comprise the relational schema which can be visualized through an Entity Relationship Diagram (ERD).

Two essential aspects of Ontologies are Metadata and Inference. Metadata, as previous discussed, is 'data about data.' Consider a simple example, Mr. William W. Pendergrass, Senior, is the name of a fictitious person. His name is made up of five parts:

- Prefix
- First Name
- Middle Initial
- Last Name
- Suffix

A more complex analysis might yield something along this line:

Code Value	Metadata	Parent Code
100	FullName	100
110	Prefix	100
120	FirstName	100
130	MiddleName	100
131	MiddleInitial	130
140	LastName	100
150	Suffix	100
160	NickName	100
170	Title	100
171	ProfessionalTitle	170
172	ServiceTitle	170
173	HereditaryTitle	170
180	Number	100
181	JuniorSenior	180

Figure 4.9 Full Name Metadata Example

In this example, the Description becomes the formal metadata for a person's name. The objectives are to decompose Name into its various components and their interrelationships and assign identifiers to each component.

Inference

Consider the following example.

Code Value	Metadata	Parent Code
100	Color	100
110	Red	100
111	Light Red	110
112	Medium Red	110
113	Dark Red	110
120	Green	100
121	Light Green	120
122	Medium Green	120
123	Dark Green	120
130	Blue	100
131	Light Blue	131
132	Medium Blue	132
133	Dark Blue	133

Figure 4.10 Color Ontology Example

All the items listed are colors, 3 families of color: Red, Green, and Blue. If one of these 3 words appear, the system knows it is dealing with a color. If the system sees Dark Red, the system knows the basic color is Red and so on. If the object has code 123, we infer the object is Dark Green in color.

Hence, Ontologies can imply characteristics based on the Ontology.

To summarize, consider this quote from DAMA's DMBOK:

> '... Master Data Management entails control over Master Data values and identifiers that enable consistent use, across systems, of the most accurate and timely data about essential business entities. The goals include ensuring availability of accurate, current values while reducing the risk of ambiguous identifiers.'
> – DAMA-DMBOK: DATA MANAGEMENT BODY OF KNOWLEDGE, 2nd Edition, p. 359.

When I think of organization schemes, the Dewey Decimal System pops to mind. Libraries adopted the Dewey Decimal Classification system in the late 1800s to organize their books topically. Today thanks to computers, we enter a word, a phrase, or a group of words, and the system searches semantically for books with the associated keywords and tells us which and where the books are in the library. This shift moves finding books from topical classification to keyword searches, which is a significant improvement. A book can only sit one place in the library, but that book can include many topics and hence be the result of many different searches.

Ultimately, **Master Data Management** is about consistency and managing differences.

4.5 Metadata and Metadata Management

Section Outline:

- Metadata Defined
- Metadata Management
- Metadata, Structured and Unstructured Data, and Big Data

Metadata

Metadata is literally 'data about data'. On the surface, this phrase is catchy and may seem adequate, but it is overly simplistic. The International Standards Organization (ISO) provides two similar but different definitions of **Metadata**, a simple definition and a more extensive definition:

'data … that defines and describes other data' [– ISO/IEC 11179–1:2015 (EN) 3.2.16 metadata. https://www.iso.org/obp/ui/#iso:std:iso-iec:11179:-1:ed-3:v1:en, June 5, 2022.]

'data about data or data elements, possibly including their data descriptions, and data about data ownership, access paths, access rights and data volatility' [– ISO/IEC 2382:2015, 2121505 metadata. https://www.iso.org/obp/ui/#iso:std:iso-iec:2382:ed-1:v1:en, June 5, 2022.]

The Data Management Association defines Metadata as follows:

'Metadata includes information about technical and business processes, data rules and constraints, and logical and physical data structures. It describes the data itself (e.g., databases, data elements, data models), the concepts the data represents (e.g., business processes, applications systems, software code, technology infrastructure), and the connections (relationships) between the data and concepts.'

– DAMA-DMBOK: DATA MANAGEMENT BODY OF
KNOWLEDGE, 2nd Edition, p.419.

At a minimum,

Metadata is the mechanism by which data elements are identified and the basis for establishing interrelationships among data elements and datasets.

Consider the number 100 and the word Jewel. What does the 100 represent? A quantity of 100? A price of $100? Is it 100.00 or just 100? Is it a location, such as 100 Main Street? Is it an item number, Item 100? In the case of Jewel, is Jewel a name? A first name? A last name? A middle name? A company name? Is it a street name? Or does Jewel refer to Jewelry? Without metadata these questions are impossible to answer although context is often helpful.

Consider a slightly different situation, a spreadsheet without column headings. The contents of some of the columns might be easily guessed while other columns, other sets of data elements, are left to our imagination. The values could mean many different things. If the value is an integer, we might assume a count. If the value is a decimal, we might assume currency. The decimal number could be related to price or cost … or some other value? The key to entangling the puzzle is the column headings, which are **Metadata**, the 'data about the data'.

Metadata answers these questions by identifying the Data Elements or the contents of columns on a spreadsheet or in a database. Hence, these values are data, or information, about data.

Metadata serves multiple functions, plays many roles, including at least the following:

- Metadata identifies.
- Metadata explains.

- Metadata establishes relationships.
- Metadata provides meaning to individual values.
- Metadata can 'tag' data elements.
- Metadata can identify source and lineage.
- Metadata can identify location.
- Metadata can track changes, including chain of custody.
- And more ...

When similar Data from different sources are combined, the Metadata identifies the common Data Elements across the Datasets without regard to their relative positions to each other. Remember the importance of position when working with flat files. If the data is scrambled, Metadata can unscramble the data.

The Data Management Association suggest two different sets of distinctions regarding **Metadata**:

- Business Metadata
- Technical Metadata
- Operational Metadata, and
- Descriptive Metadata
- Structural Metadata
- Administrative Metadata
            – DAMA-DMBOK: DATA MANAGEMENT BODY OF
                KNOWLEDGE, 2nd Edition, p. 422.

Wikipedia goes further identifying 6 distinct types of metadata as follows:

- Descriptive Metadata
- Structural Metadata
- Administrative Metadata
- Reference Metadata
- Statistical Metadata
- Legal Metadata
            – https://en.wikipedia.org/wiki/Metadata, 2022.

Where **Descriptive Metadata** names or describes data. For example, data element names.

Structural Metadata describes relationships such as customers and their orders and items and the customers who bought those items.

Administrative Metadata manages data over its lifecycle with controls such as version numbers and transaction dates.

Reference Metadata provides definitions or methodologies.

Statistical Metadata focuses on quantitative characteristics, statistical measures.

Legal Metadata defines legal concepts.

Doing a search on **Metadata**, one can come up with a myriad of different definitions and contexts as varied as images, text, document types, message types, posts, databases, a much longer list. The common elements are:

- Definition
- Classification
- Organization
- Description
- Spatial aspects
- Time sequence
- Relationships

Beyond these categories, **Metadata** can also relate to the following:

- **Business-related Metadata** identify the contents and conditions related to business data, such as entity names, attributes or characteristics of business data, and business rules.
- **Technical Metadata** focus on technical details such how and where data is processed and stored.
- **Operational Metadata** focus on details related to accessing and processing data.

Given this variety, the International Standards Organization (ISO) lays out a standard for Metadata Registries, i.e., a formal list and description of an organization's metadata, in ISO Standard ISO/IEC 11179.

Metadata Management

Where can **Metadata** be found?

Consider the most common methods for handling business data: Databases and Spreadsheets. In the case of spreadsheets, column headers typically contain nominative or descriptive information regarding the contents of the columns. This is Metadata, which names or describes the contents of the columns. This applies to databases as well where workbooks are replaced by databases, where spreadsheets are replaced by tables, and where the columns in the databases are equivalent to the columns in the spreadsheets. In databases, the full identification of data elements is expressed as the concatenation of the table name and the attribute name, i.e., tablename.columnname. Consider for example, customers.customname where customers is the table name and customername is the attribute or column name.

In environments utilizing 'tags' the tags typically identify the nature of the data element. Whichever the mechanism, there is a clear relationship between data elements and the tags or names that explicitly describe the data; hence, data about data. Consider the following JSON example:

```
{
    'customer': {
        'name':     'Fred James',
        'address1': '100 Pike Street',
        'city':     'Seattle',
        'state':    'WA',
        'zipcode':  '98101'
    }
}
```

In this example Fred James is a customer and his address is as shown.

A more expansive view of Business **Metadata** encompasses properties, origination, authorship, classification, storage, timing, keywords, access privileges, and lifecycle of the data. Discussing Metadata more expansively includes concepts such as 'electronic fingerprints' that provide information about data. The fingerprints can be descriptive and provide context.

Metadata not only identifies or describes data, but **Metadata** provides context and meaning enabling future uses of the data, such as evaluation and analysis.

To recap, Metadata provides 'Information about Data'.

Metadata and Structured versus Unstructured Data

Structured Data contains clear and easily accessible Metadata. Unstructured Data, in contrast, lacks an obvious structure. The structure may be minimal such as length, maybe 280 characters as in the case of Twitter. The structure may not be to our liking but there is still a structure.

Of all the places to find an insightful definition for Structured Data, consider below from the United States Securities and Exchange Commission (SEC):

> 'Structured data is data that is divided into standardized pieces that are identifiable and accessible by both humans and computers. The granularity of these pieces can range from an individual data point, such as a number (e.g., revenues), date (e.g., the date of a transaction), or text (e.g., a name), to data that includes multiple individual data points (e.g., an entire section of narrative disclosure).'
>
> – https://www.sec.gov/structureddata/what-is-structured-data,
> June 5, 2022.

Note especially the final element: '... data that includes multiple individual data points (e.g., an entire section of narrative disclosure).' While the SEC is talking about financial statement footnotes and narrative disclosures, the SEC is acknowledging there is a structure, i.e., the data is not structureless.

Data Dictionaries, like regular dictionaries, provide standard definitions for data and identify the business rules that apply to data. Business Glossaries, and Business Requirement Definitions (BRD) serve the same purpose, defining, explaining, and often providing examples. All three of these items document **Metadata**.

Metadata identification is a natural byproduct of the modeling process with the caveat that different analysts and designers may use different terms and may look at the same processes and elements differently.

Metadata Consistency exists at different levels.

- Within applications
- Among separate but related applications
- Among different applications within the same organization
- Among different applications outside of the organization
- And finally universal consistency

Universal consistency can be based on practice or fiat. If everyone refers to automobile vehicles as cars, to buyers as consumers, to items as products, consistency is based on practice. If, on the other hand, consistency can be dictated by fiat such as area codes, zip codes, country codes, airport codes and so on. Vehicle Identification Number (VIN) is an example of fiat-based consistency. Either way, increasing consistency makes the **Metadata** reusable beyond its original confines. Speculating at this point, the Internet, International Communications, and International Travel all conspire to promote consistency. Maybe the biggest international divergence is the metric system versus the English system of weights and measures.

Dictionaries and Glossaries enforce consistency within software development organizations. Data Stewards/Data Owners are responsible for developing and adopting standards for the data they oversee, especially in the case of Subject Matter Experts (SMEs) who are aware of the data's usage and ranges of variation. Technicians are often familiar with these terms and their variations by virtue of their technical work on the datasets.

Why is this important? Because consistency recognizes or imposes Structure on Data.

Over time a natural drift in terminology and usage occurs. Words, for example, pass in and out of vogue and their meanings can change over time. While **Metadata** are point-in-time expressions and notations, natural drift may result in cross-reference resources that link equal but different related **Metadata**.

DAMA illustrates the variety of **Metadata** in the following diagram:

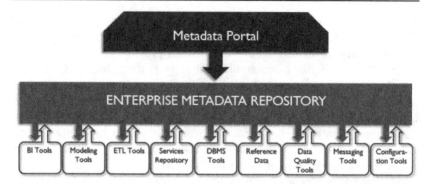

Figure 4.11 DAMA Centralized Metadata Repository
Reproduced with permission of DAMA International

Big Data, along with Unstructured Data, poses a particular challenge for **Metadata**.

We are familiar with the **Metadata** in our data. When we acquire '**Big Data**' from external sources, we may not be familiar with the **Metadata** in the 'Big Data' or worse, there may be little discernible or familiar **Metadata** in the 'Big Data'. This is a critical consideration for the import or ingestion of data. Data Wranglers constantly review and potentially revise ingestion processes in response to the **Metadata** they encounter. Even on routine imports, occasional changes to the data, its content, format and organization, can necessitate surprise revisions to the import protocols.

Obviously, the subject of **Metadata** is big enough for its own book. Suffice it is to say Metadata's big recurring themes are:

- Identification
- Description
- Explanation
- Classification and Organization
- Context, and
- Relationships ... at the least

Returning to the original definition of Metadata, yes **Metadata** is 'Data about Data' ... but much more.

4.6 Data Quality

Section Outline:

- Data Quality Defined
- High–Quality Data – Its Attributes or Characteristics

- Poor Data Quality – The Factors that Contribute to Poor Data Quality
- Data Quality Journey
- Data Quality and Business Rules

Data Quality

In the end, everything comes down to **Data Quality**. Data with poor quality is like a defective part. The defect in the part affects everything that depends on that part. Likewise, Poor Data Quality infects everything it touches.

An essential purpose of data is decision support. To be effective, executives and managers need access to accurate, reliable, valid data. How can executives ensure the data upon which they depend are accurate, reliable, and valid?

Posing this question several decades ago might elicit the following response: 'Garbage In, Garbage Out.' Today, that phrase ought to be something like: 'Bad Data In, Bad Decisions Out.'

The answer to the question of Data Quality is more nuanced today. For data to be Valuable, the data needs to be Accurate, Reliable and Trustworthy. The counter argument is that good Data Analytics can sort out bad data from good data and the good data can be used to make decisions. Regardless of which argument may be correct, the Higher the Quality of the Data, the greater likelihood for effective decision-making.

What constitutes 'Good Data'? The answer lies in the following contrasts:

- Accurate versus Inaccuracy
- Complete versus Incomplete
- Conforming versus Non-conforming
- Consistent versus Inconsistent
- Correct versus Incorrect
- Dependable versus Undependable
- Precise versus Imprecise
- Representative versus Misrepresentative, Misleading, Deceptive
- Reliable versus Unreliable
- Relevant versus Irrelevant
- Timely versus Not Timely
- Valid versus Invalid
- Standardized versus Not Standardized
- Lastly, 'Fit for Intended Uses'

T C Redman, Data Driven: The Field Guide, Boston: Digital Press, 2001, page 73., offered the phrase 'fit for intended uses.' This solidified the notion of 'fitness' as an appropriate measure of **Data Quality**.

The opposite of **Data Quality** is Erroneous, Misleading, Unreliable Data.

T. C. Redman's criteria sums up the practical side of data. Is the data fit or appropriate for what we are trying to do with it, for the decisions we are trying to make? The other criteria, i.e., accuracy and so on, help us determine the 'fitness' of the data for our purposes.

Poor Data Quality – What factors contribute to poor Data Quality?

- Silos of Data

  Data Silos are typically separate applications that are optimized for local efficiency instead of for overall effectiveness and efficiency. Data Silos are characterized by poor communications among the various parts of businesses such that differences and inconsistencies are inevitable.

- Standards – Lack thereof

  Lacking Standards, failing to enforce Standards, differences arise quickly.

- Inconsistent Development Processes

  This is especially true in businesses that develop their own applications. Different development teams may make their development decisions in a vacuum. The Lack of Development Standards promotes development 'on the fly' with little to no attention given to other applications and business processes re-enforcing 'siloed' systems, 'siloed' development, and inevitably 'siloed' data. Consider this simple example, FullName versus First Name, Middle Initial and Last Name. Both contain persons' names. In the first case, names appear as a single string. In the second case, the various parts of a person's name are explicitly identified.

- Poor Planning

  Which comes first, Poor Planning or Ad Hoc Behavior? If Ad Hoc behavior is the norm, don't expect much in the planning department. Conversely if planning is limited in scope and poor in quality, expect Ad Hoc behavior as the developers attempt to satisfy the requests made of them.

- Poor Governance

  Finally, and at the highest level of organization, what does IT Governance and Data Governance require? Weak Governance inevitably leads to less attention to standards, to less attention to established policies, procedures, practices, and processes, and to weak supervision. Governance is 'Tone at the Top' or 'Tone from the Top' regarding business process quality, application software quality, and Data Quality.

Trying to provide quality to an organization that doesn't care about quality is a losing proposition.

Finally, Data Quality, like so many other things, is not 'One-and-Done'. Data Quality is an ongoing attitude, direction, practice, commitment to maintain Quality Data.

Data Quality – What contributes to Data Quality?

- Data Quality begins with an overall commitment to Quality by business management and operations.

  This focus can be seen in a business' concern for its customers, its products, its services, its employees, its investments. Are effectiveness, responsiveness, and sensitivity in evidence relative to customers, products, services, employees, and investments?

  A singular focus on cost cutting has destroyed companies. Think of large enterprises that no longer exist or are a glimmer of their former glory. While cost cutting may not have been the only cause for their decline, it is often a primary factor. Consider IBM and General Electric. Arthur Anderson is another interesting case. In Arthur Anderson's case, a primary focus on revenue drove conditions that led to its downfall.

- Data Quality is the result of, is a byproduct of, an intentional commitment to Quality Data.

  Data Quality isn't automatic.

  Data Quality requires intentionality and commitment including adequate resources for systems, data and its processing and use.

  The most common problem I encounter is lack of adequate resources because of lack of adequate funding.

DAMA lists the following Data Quality principles:

- 'Criticality
- Lifecycle Management
- Prevention
- Root Cause Remediation
- Governance
- Standards-driven
- Objective Measurement and Transparency
- Embedded in Business Processes
- Systematically Enforced
- Connected to Service Levels'

  – DAMA-DMBOK: DATA MANAGEMENT BODY OF KNOWLEDGE, 2nd Edition, pp. 455, 456.

In my mind, everything begins, and ends, at the top with governance. From the Board of Directors and the C Suite down, an explicit commitment to Quality and Transparency is critical. Employees should be rewarded for mirroring this commitment. From this commitment flows Governance that supports Quality, establishes and enforces processes and standards that promote Quality. Ad Hoc behavior may have a place in R&D but not on the shop floor. Quality products and services should be mandatory. Quality should be inherent in the processes that make the products and services. Inspecting Quality in at the end of production doesn't work; Quality can't be tacked on at the end of the line.

The ultimate result of Data Governance should be High Quality Data that is dependable and reliable for valid decision-making. While Quality is an objective, it is also a natural consequence of a business' attitudes and behaviors.

So, our list looks something like this:

- Director and Executive Commitment to Quality.
- Established Business and IT Policies, Procedures, Practices, and Standards regarding Data Quality.
- Policies, Procedures, Practices and Standards that focus on Integrity and Quality.
- Adoption of Established Quality Frameworks and Standards to ensure Quality.

    We don't have to figure it out for ourselves; we can rely on the work of others.

- Measuring Process Quality and Data Quality.
- Adopting a Continuous Improvement attitude to ensure ongoing Quality.

Data Quality Journey

The Data Quality Journey begins with knowing what data you have and where it is. This is a two-part question for internally generated Data:

- What systems generate data?
- Where does that data reside?

In the case of internally generated data, if Quality is lacking, the organization is to blame.

In the case of external generated Data,

- From where does the data come?
- How was the data obtained?

- How good is the data? How consistent is the data?

Next, recognize that not all data is equally important. Structure data around importance, priorities and use cases.

- The most important data is data that will be used to make critical business decisions.
- Of equal importance, but in a separate category, is compliance requirements, i.e., data that needs to comply with business laws and regulations.
- Closely behind these is data needed for effective business operations.
- Closely related behind operations is financial reporting data.
- The remaining categories of data can be distinguished from each other based on operational and situational considerations.

'In 2013, DAMA UK produced a white paper describing six core dimensions of data quality:

- Completeness: The proportion of data stored against the potential for 100%.
- Uniqueness: No entity instance (thing) will be recorded more than once based upon how that thing is identified.
- Timeliness: The degree to which data represents reality from the required point in time.
- Validity: Data is valid if it conforms to the syntax (format, type, range) of its definition.
- Accuracy: The degree to which data correctly describes the 'real world' object or event being described.
- Consistency: The absence of difference, when comparing two or more representations of a thing against a definition.'

– DAMA-DMBOK: DATA MANAGEMENT BODY OF
KNOWLEDGE, 2nd Edition, p. 460.

These core characteristics with additions are illustrated in the following table:

Table 4.1 Data Quality Characteristics Defined

Data Quality Terms	Definition and/or Descriptions
Accuracy	Accuracy is a measure of correctness. The opposite is inaccurate, wrong, or erroneous data.
Completeness	Completeness means the data is whole at every step in its lifecycle. Yes, the data may be added to subsequently in its lifecycle but at each step in the lifecycle everything is there up to that point.

Data Quality Terms	Definition and/or Descriptions
Conformance	Conformance means the data conforms to standards, rules, regulations, mandates and so on. The opposite is data that does not conform to standards, rules, regulations, mandates and so on.
Consistency	Consistency means the data compares with, is like similar data, comparable data. The opposite is data that is not consistent with it 'peers.'
Correctness	Correctness means the data correctly represents reality. Correct data lacks errors and defects. The opposite of correct is inaccurate or misleading.
Dependable	Dependable means the data can be counted on, can be relied on, can be trusted. The opposite of Dependable is not being able to count on the data being correct.
Integrity	Integrity means the data is accurate, complete, and consistent. Integrity can include regulatory compliance. Lacking those qualities, the data is corrupted.
Precise/Precision	Precision is an extension of accuracy. How accurate does data have to be to be useful? Are integers fine or must the data be precise to 1 or 2 or 3 or 4 or more decimal points. The opposite of precise is inexact relative to the need. What is precision? Compare gold and dirt. With gold a high degree of precision is warranted. This is not the case with dirt.
Reasonable	Reasonableness asks if the data is consistent with expectation. Does the data satisfy the 'reasonable man' test? The opposite of reasonableness is unsubstantiated, unwarranted, flimsy, implausible, fallacious.
Reliable/Reliability	Reliability means the data is factual and can be reliable upon. The opposite is data that is dubious, uncertain, not dependable.
Relevance	Relevance deals with applicability. In other words, data that is applicable to, related to, pertinent to, connected with a particular situation, topic, domain or question.
Standardness	Standardness is like Conformance. Standardness means the data conforms to certain standards. The standards may be internal and/or external.
Timeliness	Timeliness has at least two elements. First, has to do with when events occur. Timestamps associate events with points in time. Second, has to do with up-to a time fence, for example these are the today's sales up to 12:00 noon. DAMA also recognizes volatility as an element in timeliness.

Data Quality Terms	Definition and/or Descriptions
Uniqueness	Uniqueness means each instance of data, be it an Entity or an Event is distinct from every other Entity or Event.
Validity	Validity means the data is consistent with domain standards. In other words, validity can be established based on domains requirements and standards.

Note that some of these terms are interrelated, like facets of a gemstone slightly different ways of expressing similar concepts, similar ideas.

DAMA drills into these dimensions and associated concepts in its 'Relationship between Data Quality Dimensions', Table 92. [– DMBOK, DAMA-DMBOK: DATA MANAGEMENT BODY OF KNOWLEDGE, 2nd Edition, 'Relationship between Data Quality Dimensions', Table 92, p. 463.] The diagram is quite busy, but it illustrates the interconnections among these various Data Quality characteristics.

For another resource, consider ISO8000, which is a global standard for Data Quality and Enterprise Master Data. The relationships among IS8000, Data Quality, Master Data, and Transaction Data, were discussed at the Electronic Commerce Code Management Association (ECCMA)'s WCF2017 conference. The workshop session summarized the relationships among IS8000, Data Quality, Master Data and Transaction Data in a diagram that can be found at: ECCMA, WCF2017-Workshop-A-ISO-8000-Data-Quality.pdf, slide 8. The workshop noted that **Metadata** plays an essential role in managing Data Quality by virtue of defining what the data represents.

Data Quality and Business Rules

Data Quality is an abstract concept, but achieving Data Quality is a practical, ongoing exercise.

The practical aspects of Data Quality are related to the applications that generate internal data, the Data Wrangling practices that touch the data outside of application control and the practices that control the ingestion and merger of externally generated data with internally generated data.

A variety of business rules apply to these circumstances.

For internally originated data,

- Rules that ensure that application data conforms to business objectives.

  In the same way that business demand drives purchasing, business objectives drive data generation, data use or consumption, data storage, data wrangling and data for decision-making.

For externally originated Data,

- Contractual agreements related to Data Quality of externally acquired data from Data Brokers or similar sources.
- Rules regarding schema changes that cause upload failure. (This is especially a problem when customers are left to discover schema changes on their own when uploads fail.)

General Data Quality Rules:

- Rules governing missing or blank values, especially no value and 'null' values.
- Data format standards, such as the formats for dates, telephone numbers, postal codes, and various entity and event types, and so on.
- Reference data that is consistent with the applicable domain and is used consistently, such as country and state codes and addresses that correctly identifying states and countries.
- Range limits are enforced, for example 60 minutes in an hour, 24 hours in a day, number of days in months, average number of sales order lines, maximum and minimum quantities on hand, and so on.
- Rules verifying uniqueness to prevent duplicate records and ensure transaction accuracy.
- Reasonableness tests that prevent or identify unusual values including blocking, flagging, quarantining, and alerting.
- Appropriate Timeliness requirements, for example when will yesterday's sales be available, when will today's sales be available, when will this week's sales be available, when will proforma numbers be available, when will the final numbers be available? When will results from the marketing campaign come in?

Types of Errors:

- Erroneous Data: Data entry errors where the wrong data is entered or selected from dropdowns such as selecting a wrong item or entering an incorrect quantity or overriding a correct price.
- Text Use Errors: Using or Overusing string fields beyond their intended purposes such as writing a treatise in a note field.
- Systemic Errors, such as faulty or incomplete validations.
- Errors caused by Business process changes.
- Drift over time in field usage where new fields should be added to ensure data consistency.

Preventive Practices:

- Validation rules that ensure accuracy and conformity to business standards.
- Data Sampling and Testing to confirm accuracy, consistency, and reliability.

Data Cleansing Practices:

- Standard procedures for parsing and reformatting data.
- Standard procedures for handling unknowns, blanks, and nulls.
- Standard procedures for handling errors including marking and quarantining.
- Profiling to detect blank fields, outliers, field length mismatch, reasonableness checks, format issues.
- Organizing and Re-organizing data to maximize its usefulness.
- Staging Data so that it does not become Production Data until it is completely vetted and processed.

Data Enrichment Practices:

- Accurately supplementing data to optimize and maximum its usefulness without denigrating the data.

Other Data Wrangling Practices:

- Managing Process and Data Drift, which is inevitable, so that data remains complete and has high quality.

Ultimately, business rules change and evolve over time. These changes may be easily accommodated by existing applications, or they may require changes to the applications that support the new business rules and processes. These changes, whether minor or major, can be evaluated in terms of:

- Business Process Integrity and
- Data Integrity

Furthermore, a variety of obstacles can interfere with Data Quality. DAMA's calls attention to the work of Danette McGilvray, James Price, Tom Redman, and Dr. Nina Evans and their barriers to managing data, which include:

- Lack of Executive and Practitioner Awareness of the subject.
- Lack of overall Business Governance, especially as it affects ownership and accountability.

- Difficulty justifying adequate Data Management based on cost, benefit, value, and demand.
- Ineffective Management and Leadership.
- Inappropriate or Ineffective Hardware, Software and Practices.
  – DAMA-DMBOK: DATA MANAGEMENT BODY OF KNOWLEDGE, 2nd Edition, p. 470.

In summary, nothing is more important to effective Operations and Decision-Making than **High Quality Data**, which does not come automatically. It is the result of a conscious, explicit commitment to Data Quality and the provision of adequate resources to achieve this objective.

4.7 Null Values

Null Values

Null Values are interesting topic by itself.

The big question: Do Null Values represent a value of 'nothing' or is the value merely missing?

A data element could be empty because its value is 'nothing' or because the value is unknown. These are two very different use cases. Consider this simple example, does a null mean an entity does not have a telephone number or the entity's telephone number is unknown? Was the telephone number not captured or not provided by the entity? Or does the entity not have a telephone number? This case raises several questions:

- Does the entity not have a telephone number?
- Did the entity intentionally not provide a telephone number?
- Was the telephone lost in a data pipeline?
- Was the telephone number intentionally deleted?
- Was there a storage failure?
- What effect, if any, does this absence have on subsequent data use?

If there was no value originally, how is this documented? One alternative is to insert a value that clearly communicates that the value was not originally present, such as #NULL. The problem with NULL is that it is routinely used by systems. So, an observer does not necessarily know if NULL was automatically inserted by the system based on system rules or if NULL was intentionally inserted to communicate that the field was blank. Hence, using NULL by itself does not fully convey a complete situation.

If the original value was 'nothing', do you leave the data element blank, i.e., a blank space with nothing in it, or do you insert a value such as #NULL to communicate to downstream users that there may be a value, but it wasn't present.

What about numeric data types? If non-numeric values are disallowed, the only choices are 0 or blank, depending upon whether or not a blank is allowed. Mandatory fill forces a 0. Either way, the question remains. Does the value exist and it is missing, or is the value really 0? This distinction can affect calculations. Consider calculating averages for example. If the value is 0 the numerator is unaffected but the count in the denominator is larger than it would be if 0's were ignored. This means including the 0's reduces the average, which may or may not be intended.

4.8 Data Modeling and Design

Section Outline:

- Data Modeling Introduction
- Data Modeling Defined
- Business Process Modeling
- Relational Data Modeling
- Object-Oriented Modeling
- NoSQL Data Modeling

Data Modeling Introduction

Data Modeling is Data Planning. As mentioned earlier, Data Modeling is essential for Data Management. As such, Data Modeling is worthy of an extended discussion regarding techniques and benefits for casual users and for professionals alike.

Data Modeling is, as its name states, constructing a model of the data.

Before beginning this discussion, consider Dr. George E. P. Box, a British statistician, and his aphorism:

'All models are wrong,
but some are useful.'

While arguments circulate regarding the accuracy of this statement, I interpret Box's words in two ways:

- First, models are Replicas.

  Models are simplifications, abstractions of complex situations. Consider photographs. Photographs are images of subjects. The photographs are real, but they aren't their subjects. They are representations of their subjects, be they people, buildings, landscapes, or other things. As abstractions, the photographs are inherently 'incomplete' copies of their subjects.

- Second, even though models are incomplete abstractions of reality, they can be helpful and beneficial, which is why I find them exciting.

Generally, models are helpful in at least three dimensions:

- They help us understand complex situations and display our understandings.
- They help us design solutions for complex situations, which can be tangible, such as buildings, and intangible, such as business processes and business software.
- Finally, models are a mechanism to document complex situations and processes, i.e., historical records.

So, if I was to restate Dr. Box's saying, it would be something along these lines:
'All models are inherently incomplete,
But if they help us understand and build useful solutions ... then hurray we win.'

Admittedly Dr. Box's expression is more compact than mine and delivers a 'punch' that mine lacks, but hopefully this 'tees' up the discussion about Data Modeling.

Data Modeling Defined

The Data Management Association's (DAMA) defines Data Modeling as follows:

> 'Data Modeling is the process of discovery, analyzing, and scope data requirements, and then representing and communicating these data requirements in a precise form called the data model. This process is iterative and may include a conceptual, logical, and physical model.'
> – DAMA-DMBOK: Data Management Body of Knowledge, 2nd Edition, p. 124.

In other words, Data Modeling is the process of discovering and evaluating the elements and interrelationships of data and building models of datasets based on this understanding. Subsequently these models can be used to design systems for handling the data, especially when business processes and decision-making are involved.

Consider business applications. They contain a Data Model. When the business application is installed, instantiated, the application automatically implements its Data Model. For smaller businesses, this is likely to become the business' default Data Model.

A side note: Interestingly the application data is stored in external databases in such a manner that the data is independent of the application that generated it. This independence allows businesses to access their data directly from these databases without having to go through the application. This capability may seem inappropriate but it has a host of benefits for businesses not the least of which is the ability to copy the data to another location where it can be easily analyzed without negatively impacting Business Production.

As DAMA's definition points out, Data Modeling is associated with two major topics:

1   Investigation, Discovery, and Analysis
2   Communicating or Using the results of the understanding derived from that discovery and analysis

Hence, Data Modeling can be used to:

1   To Understand Data,
2   To Design appropriate processing and storage mechanisms and
3   To communicate and document the resulting model.

Common Data Models include:

- The Relational Model, upon which Microsoft SQL, MySQL, Oracle, PostgreSQL, IBM Db2, SAP HANA, Amazon's Relational Database Service (RDS), and Azure's SQL Database depend.
- A Dimensional Model
- An Object-Oriented Model
- A Fact-Based Model
- A Time-Based Model
- A NoSQL Model

Usefulness of Data Models

How are Data Models useful? In several ways as enumerated below:

- To Understand Data – Constructing models enables the modeler to understand data.

    Hence, modeling provides a mechanism to explore data, to discover its attributes and the relationships among the various dimensions within the data.

- To Organize Data – Developing Data Models brings organization and structure to data.

Data's structure may be obvious or not. The structure may be unclear, confusing, obtuse, even hidden from view. Data Models give us tools to structure unstructured data, to organize unorganized data.

- To Document Datasets – Turning Data Models into diagrams provides a mechanism to document the analyst's understanding.
- To Support Stories and Narratives – Diagrams become visual elements that supplement narratives and lists regarding the data.
- To Manage Data – Models become the basis for managing data and for communicating among users, designers, and analysts about the data.
- To Store Data – Models organize and control the storing of data, the addition of new data and the removal of obsolete data.
- To Describe Data – Data Models provide coherent descriptions of the data that can be used in business operations to improve effectiveness and efficiency, and by Data Analysts and Scientists in their discovery and hunt for meaning.
- To Make Decisions – Ultimately, Data Models become the foundation for evidence-based decisions. The accuracy and relevance of the model are essential for valid decisions.

This list points to the importance and utility of Data Models to Understand Data, to Design Data Architectures, to Use Data in business operations and to seek Insight from Data through the analysis of that Data.

Data Models can be either Structure Oriented or Process Oriented.

- Structure-Oriented Models focus on Data Structures:
  - Data Structures are collections of related data elements. A quick way to understand these collections is to consider the Relational Data Model. The Relational Model includes databases containing tables which include columns and rows. All of the data in the database is related, for example the database for an ERP system.
  - Each Row is a Record, i.e., an instance of data, such as a customer or a customer order.
  - Each Column is an Attribute or Characteristic of the data in the table.
    - Among the Attributes is data that uniquely identifies each row in the table, be they Customers or Customer Sales Orders.
    - Attributes can indicate Relationships, such as Customers and their sales orders, sales orders and their line items.
    - Attributes show Commonality.

Commonality can be shared characteristics or shared categories, i.e., dimensions. How does this work?

Consider Product Types or Productlines that group related products together. Supermarkets and their departments are a great example. Supermarket departments include the vegetable department, the meat department, the dairy department and so on. Vegetables are in the vegetable department; meat is in the meat department; milk is in the dairy department.

These department can have subdepartments. Consider separate areas for beef, chicken, pork, seafood and so on. These becomes sub-departments of the meat department. This extends beyond Supermarkets to nearly every kind of retail store be they Supermarkets, Department stores, 'Big-Box' stores, Clothing stores, Hardware stores or DIY stores … the list goes on, i.e., this is a very common structure.

o Structure Models visualize data as sets of related Data Elements, whether the data is instantiated in databases, data tables or rows of data (tuples).

Consider business systems for example. They contain Customers, the Customers' Sales Orders, and the products in the Sales Orders, i.e., products within orders within customers.

- Process-Oriented Models focus on Business Process
In contrast to Structure Models, Process Models focus on work-flow, on business process, on sequential activities.
Sticking with Customers and their Sales Orders, below is a simpli-fied sales order process:
Customer → Sales Order → Credit Check → Pick → Pack → Ship → Invoice → Paid
This basic process happens millions of times a day around the world. This is the essence of the economic process, the selling and buying of products and services.
Process is the essence of business activity. Arguably much of the data that is created or captured daily is business-related data, whether it is sales or purchasing related data or sensor related data from a camera or a thermostat. The latter are examples of IoT, Internet of Things data.

Data Modeling – The Basics

The lowest common denominator in a Data Model is a **Data Element**, a factoid.

Consider again the components of a person's name: First Name, Middle Name or Initial, Last Name, and any prefixes or suffices, such as Mr., Miss or Mrs., and Junior, Senior, II or III. This combination of data elements may be handled individually or as a single item, i.e., full name.

When data is viewed structurally, a hierarchy is an apt construct. Consider several simple examples:

First Name/M.I./Last Name → Full Name → Customer Name
Nail → Box of Nails → Hardware
Beef → Meat → Groceries
Items → Sales Line Items → Sales Order

Each of these examples is slightly different but each have a simple hierarchy. These hierarchies can become very complicated in the case of a multi-level indented Bill of Materials (BOM) where the BOM has many levels.

Raw Material → SubSubSubComponent → SubSubComponent → SubComponent → Top Level Part

One can move up the hierarchy from the bottom item to the top-level classification or down the hierarchy from the top-level classification to the bottom micro detail. Whichever way, these hierarchies are examples of parent-child relationships, which are basic structure elements in a Data Model.

Uniqueness

Uniqueness is a critical data modeling factor.

Uniqueness differentiates similar items, such as customers and employees, and it is the factor that binds data together, for example, Customers and their Orders. Uniqueness binds sales orders to the customers to whom the sales orders belong. A collection of customers and a collection of sales without interconnection become a bunch of random events where nothing is related to anything else. Uniqueness plays a central role by establishing relationships among related items and is also the primary subject of Master Data Management.

In Relational Databases, every Entity has a Unique Identifier. The Unique Identifier is referred to as a Primary Key (PK). Excellent examples of Primary Keys are CustomerIDs, ProductIDs, VINs (Vehicle Identification Numbers). In the latter case, as mentioned earlier, every vehicle has its own unique number. Over the lifecycle of a vehicle, all its service and repair work can be compiled as well as its various owners and its accident history, if any, regardless of where the vehicle is in the world over its entire lifespan, from 'hunk to junk.'

Uniqueness is both a strength and a potential challenge. Consider a simple case where a person is an employee, a customer, and a supplier. This doesn't happen very often but occasionally I stumble across this situation. The person's EmployeeID, CustomerID and VendorID are all different. Now magnify this for an enterprise with many subsidiaries and the possibility of entities that interact with more than one or two parts of the enterprise. Herein lies the challenge, which is the focus of Master Data Management.

Relatedness

Relatedness and **Uniqueness** are not the same, but **Relatedness** depends on **Uniqueness** as described above. In relational systems, relationships are established by repeating the unique IDs, i.e., Primary Keys, in other tables. In graph systems, 'edges,' i.e., lines, are used to connect 'nodes' which are related entities.

In Data Analysis relationships are categorized as strong relationships and weak relationships. As a practice matter, strong relationships have an inherent characteristic while weak relationships are more coincidental. In the case of a business and its subsidiaries, there is an essential aspect of the relationship while in the case of a customer the customer is free to buy whatever it wants; hence, the relationship is more coincidental. However, if the items the customer buys are essential to the customer, the relationship is stronger than a coincidental relationship.

Attributes

Uniqueness and **Relatedness** are basic Data Modeling concepts, but they are only two or many **Attributes** Entities and Events can have. They are primary items that play a critical role in Data Modeling, and in the role data plays in business processes and in Data Analysis.

Attributes are characteristics. They express the complexity of Entities and their Events.

When thinking about **attribute** complexity, apparel is an excellent example of a somewhat more complex retail product. Clothing typically has many attributes, including at least GarmentID, Garment name or description, garment type, style, size, color, configuration, gender, age range, physical dimensions, season, collection, material, finishings, and so on. To appreciate the degree of complexity, consider the following from Amazon's Seller Central which identifies the following attributes related to apparel:

- Product Type, i.e., garment type
- Target Gender, such as Female, Male, Unisex
- Age Range, such as Adult, Kid, Toddler and so on
- Apparel Size Class, i.e., numeric, alphabetic, or age-based

- Apparel Size
- Apparel Size to Range appeals to show the maximum value
- Apparel Size Body Type
- Apparel Height Type
- And the customer-facing size description

For more details, see: https://sellercentral.amazon.com/gp/help/external/M6YJ5XPA58U99XM

A simple example of attributes is people and the attributes found on their drivers' licenses, passports, birth certificates and other identifying documents including ID, name, photograph, eye color, hair color, height and weight, address, even a footprint in the case of the birth certificate, expiration date, and so on depending upon the document.

A typical commercial product typically includes at least a name and/or description, size and color information and price and cost data. However, product data can get complicated quickly when replenishment rules are included, when the product is stocked in multiple locations, when manufacturing Bills of Material (BOMs) are included. In one small manufacturing ERP system, we counted the number of inventory item data entry screens, and found more than 30 separate data entry screens each containing multiple data elements relating to inventory items. If there were only five items on each data entry screen, the system would have over 150 attributes per item ... but all of the screens contained more than five data elements. Yikes.

Dimensions

Dimensions are **Attributes** that can be used to classify, to categorize, to cluster related items. These are the elements of multidimensional databases, which focus on dimensional attributes.

Let's begin with a simple case a ballpoint pen. The data elements for the pen include the following: SKU, name, description, product category, brand, color, point size, price, and quantity-on-hand. Brand, product category, color and point size are dimensional attributes so is the fact that the pen is a pen as opposed to another stationery category. The SKU is the Unique Identifier. Name and description are pen characteristics. Analysts could search by either of these characteristics to find all of the instances of this pen or similar pens. The price and quantity-on-hand are attributes of the pen. Again, analysts could search by price and quantity-on-hand to find similarly priced items and items with simple quantities-on-hand. So, there is some flexibility, i.e., determining dimensions can be fuzzy but clearly brand, product category, color and point size are dimensions.

Dimensions, Classification and **Categorization** play important roles in reporting, analysis, and decision-making. They provide the capability to group items based on common factors and are essential in determining group membership, such as wholesale or retail, public or private, profit or nonprofit, government or non-governmental, commercial, or military, professional or non-professional, bricks-and-mortar or online, and so on.

While business data can relate to item or static situations, business data is generally business process related, business workflow related. Entities are the subjects of the business process, but the 'action' is business process. In the case of business processes, data interacts with applications to stage and process transactions. For example, sales go through a standard process, and a sale doesn't get very far if it fails credit approval. The process depends on the data to determine which steps will occur and when they will occur. Process and workflow are inherent parts of business operations and Data Lifecycles.

An interesting side note, which I alluded to earlier in the book, Amazon has made or is making changes as this book was written. The change I mentioned earlier was abandoning packing lists and return authorization requests (RMAs). In 2021 both were typically in the box but sometime in 2022 these items disappeared from the box. If a customer wondered what is in the box or supposed to be in the box and/or wanted to return something, the customer now has to go to Amazon Orders to see this information. Two other changes this year stand out in the context of business process. First, encouraging customers to group their shipments to a certain day of the week, in my case Thursday. Second, encouraging customers to pick up their orders at local drop boxes. I suspect both are attempts to reduce shipping costs.

Data Lifecycle is the history of the data. In other words as processes occur, data is generated or collected. The data documents these processes from inception to completion. The data resides in the databases associated with the processes. The data may be copied to other repositories or series of repositories before it arrives at its destination.

Decomposition

As Data Modelers, we model data from its Inception to its final storage. Sub-models that focus on particular steps or aspects of the business process may be built. This is referred to as Decomposition or Granulation and may be expressed in levels of detail, where Level0 is the top of a pyramid that extends downward in sequence from Level0 to Level1, Level2, Level3, and so on down to the bottom level. Level0 is at the highest level of abstraction or summarization; Levelx, the bottom level, focuses on the details of a particular part of the process.

Data Models contain all of the information about the data, its components, its identifiers, its relationships, its attributes, its classifiers, its role in business process and ultimately its lifecycle. All these elements are candidates for a Data Model.

Metadata is an important aspect of Data Models. As the saying goes, 'metadata is data about data.' While this is simplistically true, metadata is much richer than this phrase implies. Metadata includes identifiers, descriptors, attributes, relationships, characteristics, categories all of which make data rich and provide context and content for Data Analysis and Decision-making. See the Metadata section for more information.

Presentation

How do Data Models Present this information? Typically, this is in a combination of diagrams and narrative. As previously mentioned, **Data Diagrams** show either static data structures, such as Entity Relationship Diagrams (ERDs) and Object-Oriented Diagrams (OOD), or data flows, such as Data Flow Diagrams (DFDs).

Over time, Data Structures have become more complex as data spreads across multiple tables to facilitate transaction processing and because of an increasingly complex business environment. Systems that embody this complexity include ERP systems such as those offered by SAP, Microsoft, Oracle, Infor, Sage, and others.

Structure focuses on data storage design.

- How data is stored in storage facilities. Is it stored in one or two tables or spread across multiple tables?
- How data is organized. Which data elements are in which tables?
- How data is identified in these data stores.
- How relationships are depicted.

If the data is transactional data, i.e., from business transaction processing systems such as ERP Systems, relational databases are the norm. The Data is shown visually as **Tables** with **Columns** and **Rows.** Each **Table** is a set dataset. The **Columns** identify the attributes, the **Rows** contain the specific instances, such as a particular Customer, Supplier, Product, Service, Purchase Orders or Sales Order.

A spreadsheet is a reasonable embodiment of this design. Spreadsheets involve Workbooks, Spreadsheets, Columns, Rows and Cells. Spreadsheets and relational databases have some structural similarities. Workbooks are like Databases; spreadsheets are like database tables, Columns and Rows are like columns and rows in a database table, and Cells are like the intersection of columns and rows in a database. However, spreadsheets are not databases; spreadsheets lack the structure, operations and controls which are inherent in, and essential to, relational databases.

Table Width is interesting in that it has shrunk as the Number of Tables has increased. These changes are directly related to the relational model and to differing needs between transaction processing and reporting, querying and analytics. Transaction systems use the relational model and therefore the number of tables has increased dramatically with fewer columns per table. These changes are partly in response to greater business complexity, for example businesses may now have many addresses not just a bill-to address and a ship-to address, which was the case for previous generations of business systems.

While more tables with fewer columns speed up transaction systems, it places more of a burden on reporting, querying and analytics tasks, which led to or at least capitalized on Data Warehouses and Data Marts. Data Warehouses and Data Marts have copies of the business' transaction data. As discussed earlier, transactional databases are normalized, more tables with fewer columns, while Data Warehouses and Data Marts are denormalized, fewer tables with more columns.

Normalization sped up transaction processing and adhered to the ACID principle. Denormalization reversed the processed and simplified reporting and querying with fewer reads and fewer JOINS that would otherwise be required to assemble the data for a report or a query.

Here is a simplified example:

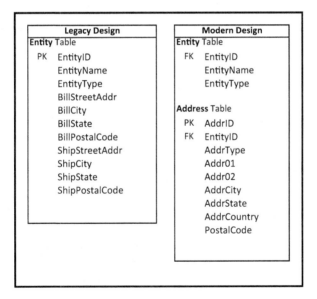

Figure 4.12 Comparison of Legacy Design versus Modern Design

This table shows the limitation of the Legacy Design that the Modern Design overcame. This change was as much a response to reality as an 'out of the blue' idea. In the modern design, there is no limitation. The database can encompass an unlimited number of addresses for every entity.

Transactional Database			Data Warehouse Database		
Customers			**SalesOrders**		
1	PK	CustomerID	1	PK	SONumber
2		CustomerName	2	PK	SOLineNumber
3		CustomerType	3		SODate
			4		CustomerID
SalesOrders			5		CustomerName
1	PK	SONumber	6		CustomerType
2	FK	CustomerID	7		ItemID
3		SODate	8		ItemQuantity
4		ShipMethod	9		ItemPrice
SalesOrderLines					
1	PK,FK	SONumber			
2	PK	SOLineNumber			
3	FK	ItemID			
4		ItemQuantity			
5		ItemPrice			

Figure 4.13 Comparison of Transactional Database and Data Warehouse Database

Figure 4.13 shows the difference between a Transactional Database designed for transaction processing and a Data Warehouse designed for querying and reporting.

While more details could be added to Table 4.13, this table was designed to illustrate the distinction between a Normalized Transactional Database and a Denormalized Data Warehouse Database.

Table Length, unlike **Data Width,** depends on the number of entries. Some Tables have a bounded number of entries, such as States, Countries, Currencies. Some Tables may be very limited, such as tables listing System States (not political jurisdictions), Statuses, Reason Codes, Approval Codes, Priorities, and so on. Transactions Tables, such as sales orders, purchase orders, employee time records, and so on occur grow in length over time. Consider an online retailer such as Amazon. How many entries does Amazon's retail operations generate daily? How many sales transactions does Starbucks generate daily? Their transactional tables are huge.

How big is big? Consider companies with hundreds of thousands of records in their databases. At this point we move beyond gigabytes (BG) of storage to terabytes (TB – 1,000,000,000,000 or 10^{12} bytes) to petabytes (PB – 1,000,000,000,000,000 or 10^{15} bytes) to exabytes (1,000,000,000,000,000,000 or 10^{18} bytes), and beyond. The website CalculateMe illustrates the difference between Terabytes (TB) and Petabytes (PB) with the following comparison: 1

TB could hold about 250 standard definition movies while 1 PB could hold about 250,000 standard definition movies and the website How-To-Geek illustrates Exabytes where 5 EX can hold all the words ever spoken by humankind. In a word, that's huge.

- https://www.calculateme.com/computer-storage/terabytes/to-petabytes/
- https://www.howtogeek.com/353116/how-big-are-gigabytes-terabytes-and-petabytes/

I do wonder how large future DVRs will have to be to contain the videos we love and the videos we think we might watch sometime in the future. This could be a sign to manufacturers to make really big DVRs to quench our thirst for entertainment … without or with pandemics that 'confine us to quarters'.

Table Size

Ultimately, the wideness or narrowness of database tables is an architectural issue balancing flexibility, scalability, future growth, business requirements, and performance challenges.

Figure 4.14 is a simple Entity Relationship Diagram (ERD) embracing the traditional relational format.

Flat Files are an older legacy approach. Today whenever we hear legacy, we presume we are talking about dinosaurs that are dead and gone. **But**, if something works and works reasonably well, why abandon it? Flat Files are significant because they continue to be used to move data. But Flat Files aren't the only 'game in town.' Alternatives include XML, JSON, BSON.

In Flat Files, the columnar aspect discussed above is implemented via delimiters to separate individual data elements. Delimiters separate individual data elements while Tags, the alternative, go a step further by identifying the individual data elements. Flat files using delimiters are the older traditional approach, i.e., legacy, while Tagged files using JSON or XML are the modern approach.

A significant difference between the two approaches is how blanks are handled. In delimited Flat Files, there is a fixed number of columns. If a column is blank, this is indicated by maintaining the delimiters; hence, two consecutive delimiters with no space between them indicates a blank. In Tagged files, such as JSON and XML, the Data Elements present are identified. Data Elements that are absent are just absent, no problem. The parser processes the data based on its tags without respect to their sequence, a marked difference from delimited files which are position sensitive.

Traditional Flat files depend on column integrity, including a pre-determined sequence, equivalent data in the same column and a method to indicate missing

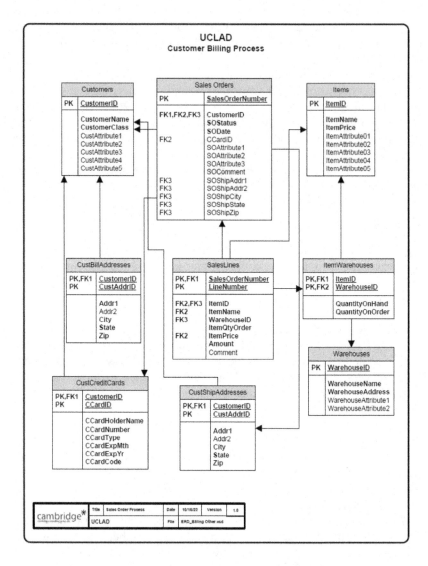

Figure 4.14 Sample Entity Relationship Diagram (ERD)

data elements. In contrast, Tagging does not require a pre-determined sequence and missing Data is simply absent from the record.

Below is a simple example of a Comma Separated Value flat file (CSV):

SOID,SOLine,SODate,CustID,CustName,ItemID,ItemName,Qty,Price
1001,1,16-Apr-16,C573,General Aerospace,C012,#12 Wire,10000,0.08
1002,1,21-Apr-16,C202,Gulfstream,S301,LowPressSwitch,1000,77
1002,2,21-Apr-16,C202,Gulfstream,S1000,Simple Sensor,25,155
1002,3,21-Apr-16,C202,Gulfstream,S1100,LowPressSensor,15,175
1002,4,21-Apr-16,C202,Gulfstream,SER100,Installation Services,8,150
1003,1,28-Apr-16,C253,Triumph,S1000,Simple Sensor,12,155
1003,2,28-Apr-16,C253,Triumph,S1100,LowPressSensor,24,175
1003,3,28-Apr-16,C253,Triumph,S1200,HighPressSensor,12,225
1004,1,5-May-16,C912,Rollys Royce,S1300,CorrosiveResistantSensor,24,380
1004,2,5-May-16,C912,Rollys Royce,SER200,Repair Services,12,150
1005,1,18-May-16,C742,Honeywell,RH711,Housing-Switch,50,35
1005,2,18-May-16,C742,Honeywell,RH811,Housing-Sensor,50,78
1006,1,1-Jun-16,C071,Boeing,S1200,HighPressSensor,100,150
1007,1,4-Jun-16,C436,MOOG,H301,HighToleranceSingleSwitch,50,110
1007,2,4-Jun-16,C436,MOOG,H302,HighToleranceDualSwitch,50,145
1008,1,13-Jun-16,C592,Rockwell Collins,H301,HighToleranceSingleSwitch,50,110
1008,2,13-Jun-16,C592,Rockwell Collins,H302,HighToleranceDualSwitch,50,145
1008,3,13-Jun-16,C592,Rockwell Collins,SER300,Design Services,12,250
1009,1,17-Jul-16,C071,Boeing,S1300,CorrosiveResistantSensor,75,300
1009,2,24-Jul-16,C071,Boeing,S1300,CorrosiveResistantSensor,35,300
1010,1,4-Aug-16,C912,Rollys Royce,S1300,CorrosiveResistantSensor,100,380

Figure 4.15 Sample CSV File

Below are three different examples covering JSON, XML and CSV for comparative purposes.

First, in JSON format:

{'name': 'Robert Smith'}

Second, in XML format:

<object>
<name>Robert Smith</name>

Third, in Comma Separate Value format where the delimiter is a comma as illustrated above:

…,Robert Smith,…

All three approaches accomplish the same objective. The question of which is better depends on the situation and what is available. Today there is a bias toward tagged Data Elements because tagging gets around the limitations of Flat Files, but Flat Files are still in use. The intention here is merely to show that there are alternatives.

Keys

As mentioned above, **Keys** play a critical role in the relational model. They uniquely identify Entities and Events and when repeated in other tables indicate relationships between tables. In relational databases, these are referred to as **Primary Keys (PK)** and **Foreign Keys (FK)** where the

Primary Key is the unique identifier, and the **Foreign Keys** establish relationships among related tables by repeating the **Primary Key** in other tables where it is referred to as a **Foreign Key**. Examples include Customers and their Orders, Suppliers and their associated Purchase Orders, Products and their Purchase Orders and their Sales Orders, Employees and their Time Records, and so on.

Customer Names could be suggested as Foreign Keys. As a practical matter, Customer Names may be unique, but they lack the inherent uniqueness characteristic of a **Primary Key;** hence, they are not good candidates for **Foreign Keys**.

The use of **Primary Keys** and **Foreign Keys** can be seen in Figures 4.13 and 4.14 above.

Relationships

Relationships can be:

- 1-to-1 relationships
- 1-to-Many relationships or
- Many-to-Many relationships

A simple way to illustrate the different is an example. Consider a person and a cellphone. In a 1-to-1 relationship a person has one cellphone. In a 1-to-Many relationship, the person has access to multiple cellphones. In the third use case, a Many-to-Many relationship means people share access to many cellphones. This may sound crazy making but hopefully the concept is clear. There are two additional cases, the 1-and-only-1 case and the zero case. In the one-and-only-one case, the person must have 1 cellphone. In the zero case, the person may have no cellphones. These two cases expand the options listed above.

As a point of reference, **Cardinality** is the technical term that applies to the various types of Relationships, 1-to-1, 1-to-Many and Many-to-Many.

The **Entity Relationship Diagram** (**ERD**), shown below in Figure 4.16 uses 'Crow's Foot' notation to show the various types of relationships: 1-to-1, 1-to-Many and Many-to-Many. In Crow's Foot Notation, a single vertical line, |, represents 1, the crow's foot, ◀, represents Many, and ⦿ represents the null case. Figure 4.16 is a revised version of the previous ERD diagram, Figure 4.13.

The two parallel vertical lines || represents the 'One-and-only-One' case. The symbols +O- and >O- represent the 'Zero-or-One' case and the 'Zero-or-Many' case respectively.

If the relationship is a 1-to-1 relationship, then the second table is effectively an extension of the first table and may be referred to as an Extension Table, i. e., an extension of the first Table.

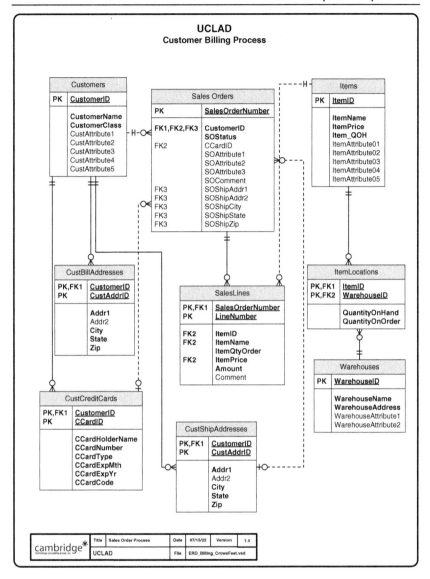

Figure 4.16 Sample Crow's Feet ERD

1-to-Many relationships are common and usually of business interest. Examples of One-to-Many relationships include a Customer and its Orders, a Product and its Suppliers, a Supplier and the items bought from it, and an Employee and their time entries.

Many-to-Many relationships are also common. Examples include Customers and their Orders, Suppliers and the Items they supply, Employees and their Time entries.

The curious thing about Many-to-Many relationships is that often the relevant question is a singular question. For example, which items did this Customer buy? When the sales system is deciding from which warehouse to pick an order, only one thing matters, which warehouse has sufficient quantity of that item to fulfill the order. This brings the discussion to associative or junction tables which link, in this case, many items and many warehouses. The typical operational question is which warehouse has this item. This is illustrated in Figure 4.17 below:

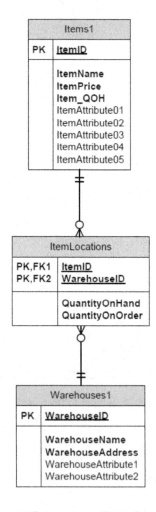

Figure 4.17 Associative Table Example

For the sake of completeness, there is another relationship, a recursive dependence. For example, consider a list of people including parents and children as members. The children are related to the parents. This is a recursive or 'unary' relationship because the parents and their children are listed in the same table, for example a people table. In Data Modeling, the relationship points back to another element in the same table.

Data Flow Diagrams show the workflow or process of which the Data is a part. Flow Diagrams have the potential to show how data triggers successive steps in the workflow. The process diagrams can be:

- **Conceptual,**
- **Logical – Digital**
- **Physical**

Conceptual flowcharts consider the process from a conceptual or theoretical perspective, the ideal without consideration of practical constraints. **Logical** or **Digital** diagrams consider the process in terms of data and how that data is handled at each step in the process. **Physical** diagrams show the actual physical process itself and the data stores that are involved in the process. The Physical and Logical diagrams typically mirror each other showing what is happening simultaneously in the Physical and Logical realms.

Object Modeling Alternatives

An alternative approach to modeling is Object-Oriented modeling, O-O. Object-Oriented Modeling begins with Objects, such as customers, suppliers, products, and so on. O-O defines the world in terms of:

- Objects – Objects are things or entities, such as people, places, products, events, even transactions.
- Attributes – Attributes are object characteristics. Objects can be thought of as nouns and Attributes as adjectives that modify nouns.
- Methods – Methods are tasks or functions related to an object. For example, customers buy items, customers pay for their items, customers return items and get money back.
- Messages – Messages initiate Methods. For example, BUY ITEMS, PAY FOR ITEMS, RETURN ITEMS.
- Classes – Classes are groups or categories of items.
  Recall the previous Data Modeling discussion regarding Supermarkets and their Meat Departments. Expanding on that reference, consider a Meat Department, which includes the Beef SubDepartment, The Poultry SubDepartment, the Pork SubDepartment, the Seafood Sub-Department, which could include the Fish SubSubDepartment and the ShellFishSubSubDepartment, and so on. In essence a Superclass, a Class

and a SubClass where the degree of granulation depends on the circumstances. Think of this in terms of a nested outline where the highest order is the leftmost item and as the outline progresses from left to right with each successive level of classification being further indented.

In addition, there are special attributes such as

- State – State is an Object condition, such as past, present (or current), future, or open and closed, each a separate distinct state.

Relationships allow Objects to communicate or interact with each other. Consider Customers, their Orders and the Orders' Line-items. Both are strong relationships, which can be described as Parent Child relationships in which the Child 'inherits' attributes from its Parent. In this example, the Order inherits Customer attributes, such as CustomerID, CustomerName, CustomerAddress, while Order Line-items inherit attributes from the Order, such as OrderID, Order Date, Order Payment, and so on.

Part of Object-Oriented Modeling are Use Case Modeling and Class Diagrams. Use Case Modeling shows process steps while Class Diagrams show object classes and their relationships. For example, Customers Put Items in their Shopping Carts, Select Shipping and Payment methods and Authorize the Order, four steps typical of the online shopping process. In addition, Class Diagrams can model Customers, their Orders, and their Order Line-items from different perspectives such as Purchasing, Suppliers, Selling and the Products involved in the orders.

State Transition Modeling shows how objects change from one state to another. Consider the following states through which Orders go, beginning with a Submitted or Pending state followed by the 'Pick-an-Pack' state, followed by the Shipping state, followed by the Shipped state, followed by the Paid state followed by an Archived state, for example.

Activity Diagrams and Business Process Diagrams show the progression of the events or actions from inception to completion as they occur in business processes.

Modeling NoSQL

The primary difference between SQL and NoSQL Modeling is that NoSQL Modeling does not use the relational data model. NoSQL emphasizes a more flexible design, a design that accommodates the different types of NoSQL data stores. SQL uses a 'schema' as discussed above, a more rigid approach. In contrast, NoSQL databases can be 'schema-less' providing flexibility without a precise database structure.

Consider the four basic types of NoSQL databases:

- Key-Value pairs model the 'Key' and the 'Value' associated with that key. Key-Value pairs are effectively a 2-column table that lists the Key and its corresponding Value, which could be in any form as diverse as text, or a blog post, or a video file, or an audio file, you name it. Depending on the situation, the 'Value' could be the actual value or a link to an actual value in the case of audio, image, or video files. Below are several examples of Key-Value Pairs:

Passwords: Key = 'smith', Value = 'dlC@89jz30nWep'
Telephone Numbers: Key = 'smith', Value = '+1–210–346–1394'
Account Number: Key = 'smith', Value = '750831'
Dictionary: Key = 'word', Value = 'definition'

- In the first case, Smith's password is dlc@89jz30nwep, Smith's Telephone number is '+1-210-346-1394 and Smith's account number is 750831. In the last case, the word's definition is stored in the Value.
- Key-Value pairs are normally shown in a 2-column array, such as the following list of fictitious telephone numbers:

Key	Value
Anderson	+1-404-350-8743
Jones	+1-312-456-7689
Smith	+1-210-346-1394
Vader	+1-212-500-7500
Zoro	+1-213-454-1000

Figure 4.18 Key-Value Pair Example

- A Document-based data store generally involves encoding, not to be confused with encryption, which it is not, such as JSON (Java-Script Object Notation), BSON (Binary JSON) or XML (eXtensible Markup Language). The data is stored in documents, which may be grouped in collections. For example:

Key: 1001
Document: {OrderID: '13583', CustomerID: 'C7458', OrderDate: 'July 15, 2023', ItemID: 'S1278', Qty: '5', Price: '59.75', ItemID: 'Z937', Qty: '12', Price: '975.00' ...} where the ellipse represents the other items in the order.
The Collection could include a single order, or multiple orders or a day's orders, or a week's orders or a month's orders or your choice.

- A Columnar data database stores data into columns, which are grouped into families which can be nested.
- A Graph-based data store uses a graphic model based on graph theory. Graph databases focus on relationships, which are called 'edges,' and objects also called 'nodes.'
  Neo4j has a variety of examples on their website and in their blogs. Take note of their Top 10 Graph Database Use Cases: Fraud Detection. Money Laundering and Fraud Detection are two great use cases for graph applications.

  > – https://neo4j.com/blog/enterprise-fraud-detection/?ref=web-solutions-fraud-detection

The bottom line, while SQL dominates the traditional ERP marketplace, other database technologies and other modeling approaches are available. SQL is not the only 'game in town,' however, as was noted in the Database discussion SQL has been incorporated into some of the NoSQL products and SQL has been extended to NewSQL and Distributed SQL. So, SQL isn't standing still either.

Reference Data Objects

Business systems have many Reference Data. They typically appear in dropdowns, where data entry is constrained to the choices provided, i.e., a predetermined list of alternatives. These lists or enumerations are used to ensure consistency and restrict choices to a pre-determined set of choices. Examples include the following:

- Priority: High, Medium, and Low
- Reason Codes: Better Price, Damaged Product, Bought by Mistake, Wrong Size, Did not fulfill Customer Expectations
- Item Status: InStock, Out-of-Stock, Restock, Repair, Dispose.

The Data Model should provide for these types of data elements. They are particularly important for operations, analytics, and future decision-making.

The Making of a Data Model

How are Data Models made?

1   The first step is Understanding the Process(es) involved.
    This information can be assembled by observation, process diagrams, documentation, and interviews. To the extent that the Business Processes are documented, this documentation is likely a reasonable starting point preceded by or immediately followed by observation.

As the saying goes, 'observation is worth more than a thousand words.' Well, at least it is a good adaption of a common saying.

2 The second step is gathering the data that will be modeled.

This is done through exploration and investigation.

It can include some combination of observations, interviews, document review, and identifying process inputs and outputs. IPO is used to describe the latter situation where I stand for Input, P stands for Process, and O stands for Output.

Reviewing forms, both blank and completed, is a rich resource ... to the extent forms still exist.

If there is existing automation, their database schema may be accessible and helpful.

3 The third step is identifying the Entities that are involved in the situation.

As you identify the Entities, consider Unique Identifiers, i.e., **Primary Keys**, associated with the various Entities.

4 The fourth step is identifying the relationships among the Entities. Simply put, how are the Entities interconnected in normal business operations.

5 The fifth step is beginning to build the Data Model. This involves a series of choices as described below.

Data models come in varying degrees of detail, which are technically referred to as Level0, Level1, Level2 and do on. (Note this concept was introduced a few paragraphs back.) The degrees of detail depend on the situation and the complexity of the Data involved. Level0 is the highest order of summarization or abstraction, the most summarized, the most generic version of the Model generally including the major items in the business processes.

While experts may disagree about the level of detail for Level0, at least the following elements are suggested here: Table Names, Primary Keys and Foreign Keys. If there are other data elements that are critical to the architecture, include them as well. Level1 includes everything that is in Level0 plus the additional data that needs to be maintained in the database. Level3 contains items lacking values and/or legacy items that will not be included in the future architecture or if included will be put in other tables.

At this step we are focused on making a Level0 diagram that includes the Entities, their Primary Keys and the Foreign Keys that establish the relationships.

6 The sixth step is to prepare a Flow diagram to accompany the structure diagram.

The diagram could be Conceptual, Logical or Physical, it could be Process Flow or Data Flow, or some combination of these perspectives.

Preparing the Flow diagram often reminds designers of elements what were overlooked in the initial diagrams.

7 The seventh step is to review the work with stakeholders. Get their input and feedback.

At this point, the architect is asking the stakeholders to verify what is in the diagrams, to identify missing elements and to clarify any ambiguities, not that the stakeholders weren't consulted during the design process.

(Hint, be sure they are included at every step in the process. Issues are easier to resolve the earlier they are identified.)

At this point, unusual or infrequently occurring situations may be considered. They may require additional data elements and greater levels of detail. They may be the subject of subsequent diagrams.

Knowing about these elements sooner rather than later is usually helpful.

8 The eighth and subsequent steps involve revising, reviewing, re-revising and re-reviewing until all parties agree that the data requirements are clear and complete.

9 The ninth step is the maintenance of this documentation over time as needs drift occurs and requirements change.

This should be a living document that both documents understandings and provides the basis for future development. It should be maintained under version control, which is to say, the various versions of the documents are clearly identified and maintained separately.

As designers step through this process, the perennial question is scope or boundaries. In other words, what should be included and what can be excluded from the model. In some cases, this is easy especially if the situation is established and stable. If, however, the situation is unstable and subject to changes, establishing boundaries may be difficult.

As I write this book, we are waiting for another wave of the COVID-19 pandemic. The Omicron variant has become the predominant variant in the United States with a large segment of the population unvaccinated or under-vaccinated. At this writing, most restrictions have been lifted but they could easily be re-imposed to control the spread of the disease. One disconcerting aspect of the situation is 'breakthrough' infections, i.e., vaccinated people who get COVID-19 and are contagious as well.

Why discuss the pandemic at this point in the book? Simply, it is an existential example of data in action. It is impacting our daily lives and despite everything there is still the gnawing question: What should we do to avoid or minimize the illness?

In terms of data, the newest wrinkle is home tests. The problem with home tests is under-reporting. People test positive, recover at home. The infection is never recorded; hence, the infection rate is understated.

These types of question are not limited to epidemiologic problems they extend to business as well. Collecting all the Data. Assembling the Data. Matching identical Entities identified differently in different systems. And ultimately making business decisions. They may not make newspaper headlines or the evening news, but they are as important to the life of the business as the pandemic is to the life of the population.

Data Modeling is an essential aspect of a System Development Lifecycle (SDLC), but Data Modeling can stand alone as an initiative to understand data and particular datasets. They might even initiate a new data project.

> 'Business and Data Architecture, Master Data Management, and Data Governance ... where the immediate end result is not a database but an understanding of organizations data.'
> – DAMA-DMBOK: DATA MANAGEMENT BODY OF
> KNOWLEDGE, 2nd Edition, p. 126

The importance of Data Modeling is well captured in the following words adapted from DAMA: If data is accurate, complete, and explicit, the chances of misinterpretation are reduced. To the extent, these items are not clear, misinterpretation is more likely to occur. [– DAMA-DMBOK: DATA MANAGEMENT BODY OF KNOWLEDGE, 2nd Edition, p. 135.]

4.9 Data Integration and Interoperability

Under the Hood

Section Outline:

- Introduction to Data Interoperability
- ETL – Extract Transform and Load
- Batch versus Online Processing
- Cloud Resources

A fascinating aspect of and opportunity for data is its ability to move among applications and databases. A big change for business software, which occurred back in the 1970s and 1980s, was the introduction of integration. Instead of a group of individual unintegrated applications, the new business software introduced integrated business suites, a major step forward at that time. Business has never looked back. Integration became the hallmark of business software. Consider a CRM system. The Suspect/Prospect data may originate in a CRM system and subsequently seamlessly move from the CRM system into an ERP System as Prospects are converted into Customers, and/or into a Marketing System for additional marketing campaigns, and/or on to other systems for a variety of reasons. Today we take this Integration, this Interoperability, for granted.

To be able to do this, the data needs to be suitably formatted, and the interconnections need to be available. This doesn't happen automatically; it needs to be planned and intentionally implemented.

For data to flow among applications, channels must exist to export data out of one application and import it into another application. These channels are called APIs, Application Programming Interfaces. One can think of these as the connectors at either end of a firehose. APIs are front and center for Data Integration. They are expediting Data Integration.

The simplest way to move data between applications is to export the data out of one application and then import it into the other application. There is even a name for this process, **ETL**, which stands for **Extract, Transform, and Load**. In this context, the Extract is the export procedure, and the Load is the import procedure.

The data that is exported may require some changes before it can be uploaded into the second system. This is the **Transform** function. The exported data needs to be fixed before it can be imported into the new system. This can be a manual process or automated via APIs and **Robotic Process Automation** (**RPA**), the newest option. The objective of **RPA** is to reduce if not eliminate manual procedures.

Business Purposes for Data Integration and Interoperability include:

- Making data available to users in formats and timeframes needed or expected.
- Moving data from one location to another location, which can be multiple applications and multiple databases.
- Merging/Consolidating data from various locations into a single dataset.
- Sharing data, making data available across multiple platforms.
- Connecting applications with each other allowing them to share their data with each other.
- Creating Data Warehouses or Data Marts for Querying, Reporting and Analysis.
- Obtaining data from Outside Sources and merging it into internal databases.
- And finally Archiving Data setting aside permanent copies of business data.

Extract, Transform, Load (ETL)

Extract, Transform, and Load (**ETL**) is a principal mechanism for moving and governing the movement of data between locations. The term implies that the Data Transformation happens after the data has been Extracted from a Source before it is Loaded into a Target. However, this isn't necessarily the case. In many cases, ETL may be the way to go, but TEL and ELT are both potential use cases depending upon the environments and objectives.

In the case of TEL, the Transformation occurs before the Extraction. This is often the case if the Source needs to include the transformed data. One could Export the Data, Transform the Data and then Import the transformed data into the Target and back into the Source as well but maybe it is easier to clean up the data before it is exported so the data in the Source is identical to the data in the Target.

In the third case, ELT, the Transformation happens after the data has been loaded into its Target environment. This approach may be better if the Target is a better platform in which to do the Transformation.

The bottom line, there is no one-size-fits-all. **ETL** or **TEL** or **ELT** depend on circumstances.

What are some examples of Transformations?

- Reformatting the data
- Reorganizing the data
- Making structural changes to the data
- Eliminating duplicates
- Adding additional data Values to the data, enriching the data
- Translating codes such converting CA to California or California to CA, or converting 75 to 75 degrees, or converting Customer-Type codes to new values based on the Target system
- And so on.

The three Use Cases, i.e., **TEL, ETL**, and **ELT,** are illustrated below. Keep in mind there are specific reasons why one of the three approaches may be superior to the other two in certain situations.

TEL

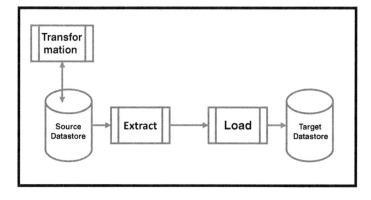

Figure 4.19 Transform, Extract and Load Diagram

ETL

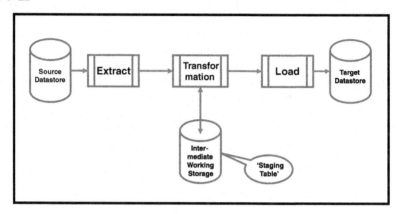

Figure 4.20 Extract, Transform and Load Diagram

ELT

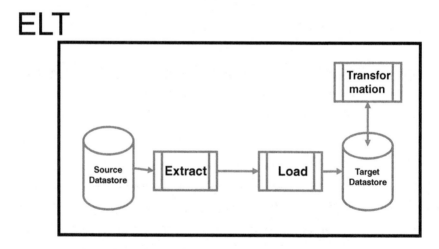

Figure 4.21 Extract, Load and Transform Diagram

Personally, I am a strong believer in 'Staging Tables' as places to do the Transformations and as places to maintain raw copies of data that is being moved from one place to another. These tables may be independent of both the Source and the Target; hence, that tends to put me in the ETL crowd, but I am always open to more efficient, more accurate methods.

Batch versus Online

Depending upon business needs, business processes can be either batch or online. As reporting strives to be more contemporaneous, business processes are being pushed to be more contemporaneous ultimately opening the door to online analytics where data is analyzed as it occurs. If up-to-the-moment is important, then the connection is live, online, and synchronous, which means changes in the Source system are immediately written to Target systems. This process is often referred to as Replication where the data is being Replicated to multiple places simultaneously and operational consumption can happen in the main system and analysis, querying and reporting can happen in up-to-the-moment ancillary data stores.

Consider financial systems that cannot afford downtime or breaks in service. They usually involve Replication such that if one system goes down the institution can continue to operate with little impact on the institution's employees and customers; however, if multiple systems fail simultaneously that is usually a real mess for employees and customers alike. Either way, IT will have its hands full restoring the failed system(s).

Data can be shared either directly between applications on a point-to-point basis or maintained centrally in a central shared facility. The point-to-point approach works well until the number of points become many; then a hub-and-spoke approach may be the better choice.

Cloud Services

Data Sharing cannot be discussed without talking about the Cloud. For a variety of reasons, data may reside 'in the cloud' either because the application is a SaaS (Software as a Service) Service, or the Repository is in the Cloud. Another use case is Data-as-a-Service (DaaS). Snowflake is making a big splash in this market. Microsoft Azure SQL and Amazon RDS are highly regarded offerings. Expect to see more vendors focusing on this marketspace.

In this case, internal and external data is federated in the Cloud as data in Database-as-a-Service (DBaaS) or Data-as-a-Service (DaaS). Given data volumes, it remains to be seen how workloads shake out between cloud and on-premises resources. I see articles that identify companies, generally large companies, that are repatriating some data back to on-premises resources typically because of cost.

An essential aspect of data in the cloud is third-party management and control. The customer is ultimately using someone else's compute capability. Cost, operational stability and reliability are major considerations in choosing cloud service providers and continuing with them.

Data Mapping, which is separately discussed, is an essential aspect of Integration and Interoperability.

Master Data Management, which is also discussed in detail in its own section, is a factor to consider in Data Integration and Interoperability.

The bottom line for Data Integration and Interoperability is that data is generated and consumed across a diverse group of business applications including Data Analytics. Inversely, data locked in applications is much less valuable to the business than data, which is shared across, is accessible to, the entire business.

4.10 Data Security

Section Outline:

- Introduction
- Three Protective Mechanisms:
  - Access Control
  - Intrusion Detection
  - Encryption
- Cybersecurity Frameworks

Introduction

A book about Data would be incomplete without a chapter on Data Security, especially today; however, the topic of Cybersecurity easily encompasses an entire book much more than would be appropriate for this publication. Nevertheless, knowing the cybersecurity landscape seems like a reasonable starting point.

The world has shrunk. Airplanes make it possible to be nearly anywhere in the world in 24 hours or less. Likewise, the Internet has shrunk the world. You can now be anywhere in the world and access your data, which means anyone with skill and motivation anywhere in the world can also access your data and in the process ruin your life. Wow, what an asset.

Potential adversaries are no longer limited to unhappy ex-employees and others with grudges to settle, the two traditional sources of cyber mischievous. They are focused on settling old scores. Another traditional adversary is those intent on satisfying their curiosity, i.e., can I break unto a well-known entity such as a government or a popular business and in the process get the recognition of their peers. These are the traditional Internet miscreants.

Two newer categories that sit at the center of the cyber landscape are Cybercriminals and Nation States. They differ from the traditional adversaries in that they have nearly unlimited resources, and they sit outside the United States Judicial System. Their motivations are different, and their knowledge, skills and tools are very sophisticated. They operate with little risk, with very little downside. Examples include North Korea's successful attack on Sony Pictures because Sony released a movie critical of the North Korean regime. Another example is Russia's attempts to influence US elections through misinformation and the Russian war on Ukraine which includes cyber conflict as well as traditional bullets, bombs and (ballistic) missiles. Just trying to keep the alliteration going. In between the North Koreans and Russia, the Iranians have been busy as well.

The point is that we live in an interconnected world with both positives and negatives. The Internet is now an essential foundation for communications and economics. Unfortunately, this capability has created opportunities for nefarious activity as well, and, more troubling, cyberadversaries that are well funded are in it for the money, and it has become an avenue for statecraft.

The implication for businesses: Businesses are up against considerable adversaries.

For cybercriminals or nation states, data is certainly a suitable target either to make money or to influence international behavior. But Data Security is not limited to cyberadversaries; data often has certain limitations or restrictions attached to it. The data may be Personally Identifiable Information (PII), or involve financial transactions, or be limited by contractual terms, or be intellectual property.

Hence, data can be the target of hostile parties because of its intrinsic value and because an adversarial relationship exists between the parties. Either way, businesses could find themselves in the crosshairs of formidable opponents with much to gain and little to lose.

The Data Management Association sums up the cyber landscape as shown below in its Figure 62:

Figure 4.22 DAMA Cyber Landscape Diagram

What is a business to do against such formidable opponents?

- First is awareness. Be aware of the adversarial landscape especially changes.
- Second, know the data the business has, its potential value to third parties, and restrictions and limitations associated with the data.
- Third, know where data is stored which is often in multiple locations.
- Fourth, know who has what kinds of access to that data.
- Fifth, as an article of Data Governance, develop and implement a Data Security program in the same way a business has a physical security program.
- Sixth, implement the Data Security.
- Seventh, maintain the Data Security program.
  The threat landscape is continually evolving; hence, the plan needs to be continuously reviewed and updated. This isn't a situation that stands still; it is constantly changing. This isn't something that is one-and-done, done and forgotten. It is an ongoing process.

Having surveyed the Cyber Criminal Landscape, let's move to the Second item. What data do businesses have? Obviously, businesses have data related to their business activities, such as data related to purchasing, selling, manufacturing, research and development, finance, and more. The less obvious may be data the business acquires from outside providers. Often this data is combined with in-house data.

A useful tool for memorializing a business' data is a Data Catalog. The actual format of the catalog can be adapted as needed. In any case, it could include at least the following elements:

- List of datasets and their principal contents

  o including sample Data to illustrate the complexity and variation of the Data

- Identify the restrictions and limitations imposed by external parties,

  o such as industry or governmental mandates and regulations

- Highlight data that might be of particular interest to an adversary

  o because there is a ready marketplace for it,
  o such as Personal Identifying Information (PII), and intellectual property.
  o Trade secrets also have a high value to competitors and would-be competitors.

Next identify the various locations where the data is stored including operational databases, data warehouses, data marts, backup storage, and archive storage and the interconnections among the various data stores. Determine how stable these repositories are. If the data is actively used outside of its original source, be sure the Data Catalog contains the additional locations.

The Data Catalog can include both Structured and Unstructured Data realizing that Unstructured Data has a level of complexity that the Structured Data doesn't have, or in reverse the Structured Data is organized for use while Unstructured Data isn't necessarily organized in a manner that makes it readily useable.

The Data Catalog should identify all forms and formats in which the data is used including queries, reports, analyses, dashboards, and visualizations.

Next identify the various users and user profiles that have access to the data, especially administrative access. Be sure to include user credentials embedded in application software. These are often forgotten after the initial connection is established or said differently forgotten once established.

In parallel with the above, develop or finalize a Data Governance plan that takes the Data Catalog into account and establishes the security mechanisms that will be implemented and maintained to control the Data. They could include

- Access controls with multi-factor authentication
  As a practical matter many segments of society have now implemented multi-factor authentication where a second factor such as a text or an email or a telephone call occur to confirm identity.
- Micro segmentation with additional access permissions
- DMZs
- Encryption
- Intrusion Detection and Prevention, including Firewalls
- Patch Management
- Virtual Private Networks (VPN) for remote connectivity
- Penetration testing
- Offline backup storage, 'air gap' the backups
- Incident Response and Contingency Planning
- Cybersecurity Training

Protective Mechanisms

This is not a complete list, but three obvious protective mechanisms that should be enforce:

- Access Control
- Intrusion Protection
- Encryption

Access Control

The purpose of Access Control is to control who has access to resources and services and what kind of access that is. This is a two-part question:

- **Who** are You? **What** access privileges do you have?
  - ○ **Who** determines Authentication
  - ○ **What** determines Authorization

- Authentication is simply confirmation that the user is who the user purports to be.
  Traditionally UserID and Password were sufficient; however, Multi-Factor Authentication, which has been around for years, is being increasingly adopted and is now a standard practice.
  By way of background. Multi-factor authentication is usually described as follows:

  - ○ Single Factor Authentication is typically UserID and Password, something the user knows.
  - ○ Two-Factor Authentication goes a step further and asks for something the User has, such as email or a cellphone by sending a message via email or text.
  - ○ Three-Factor Authentication is Two-Factor Authentication plus something the user is, typically a biometric measure, such as a fingerprint or other scan to confirm identity.

  Banks and other organizations now routinely text control numbers to users, which in turn allow users to enter the banking system. Duo.com, a subsidiary of Cisco, provides another mechanism for organizations to send authentication requests to users' phones, something they have.
  The use of mobile phones for access and for confirmations has made SIM Swapping a significant exploit. In SIM Swaps, the adversary poses as the owner of the phone, asks the phone provider to re-program a new phone for the lost phone. As a result, the adversary receives the second-factor confirmation instead of the real owner of the telephone number. How do you know that has happened to you? Your phone is bricked, i.e., shut down. Immediately contact your cellphone provider.

- Access Authorization is the set of permissions given to users.
  The access could be given on an individual basis or on a group basis, i.e., by being a member of a group, or on a combination of group and individual permissions.
  'Least privileges' is a best practice in this area. Users should have only the access privileges they need to perform their activities in the organization and nothing more. This means revising access permissions as users' responsibilities change and terminating access when users leave the company.

- The corollaries to this principle are regular, routine review of user privileges including confirmation and adjustments to user privileges when users change roles or responsibilities.

The bottom line is limiting the number of people that have access to your data and limiting their authorizations to the minimum required to perform their work activities so that if the credentials become compromised the potential damage is contained.

Intrusion Protection

Intrusion Protection are the locks, keys, and other methods to control access, the most common of which are firewalls, but they are by no means all the Intrusion Protection mechanisms.

These also include configuring all devices and software to reduce opportunities for intrusion, infiltration, and exfiltration. While typical firewall traffic, at least traditionally, is evaluated based on IP addressing, Intrusion Detection and Prevention software goes a step further and examines the contents of the traffic and based on this inspection decides whether to pass the traffic, whether to quarantine the traffic or whether to stop the traffic. Increasingly this additional layer of security is being built into firewalls.

Intrusion Detection and Prevention are primary Data Security practices.

Encryption

Encryption converts 'plain text' data into a complex code making the data useless without the ability to decrypt the data. Newer computer technologies, such as quantum computing, may make this option less effective as the quantum computers may be able to break the encryption by 'brute force,' i.e., trying every combination until the system discovers how to encrypt the Data, in a matter of minutes. As noted, adversaries with 'deep pockets' are now the rule, not the exception, and we should assume they have access to these computing resources, especially if they operate in the political sphere.

Data can be 'Encrypted at Rest' in Databases and in Applications. Data can be 'Encrypted in Motion', i.e., while the data is moving among databases and applications both locally and remotely. Parenthetically, HIPAA identifies encryption as a key protection for personal health information at Rest and in Motion.

The big question is: Can your business application software work with Encrypted Data. If the applications were custom developed, the ability to utilize encryption may be easier. If the application is commercial-off-the-shelf software, the software maker needs to be consulted.

Two wrinkles: If application users can see the actual text in the application, they are seeing the decrypted data and they could be in the position to copy the data. Second, as mentioned above, looking into the future and the advent of quantum computing, quantum computers will be able to decrypt today's encryption schemes. This reminds me of the client that went to his/her attorney and said make me an unbreakable contract. As soon as the attorney delivered the unbreakable contract, the client asks the attorney to break the unbreakable contract. So, with quantum computing, if they can break today's encryption schemes, then ask for encryption schemes that can't be broken. In turn parties will work to decrypt the unbreakable encryption scheme. How this plays out in the future remains to be seen but the scenario is much like the arcade game Whack-a-Mole.

Cybersecurity Frameworks

We don't have to figure this out for ourselves. There are numerous Cybersecurity frameworks the better-known ones include:

- ISO/IEC 27000 – The International Standards Organization – https://www.iso.org/standard/73906.html
- NIST Cybersecurity Framework – The National Institute of Standards and Technology – https://www.nist.gov/cyberframework
- CIS – The Center for Internet Security – https://www.cisecurity.org/

We don't have to re-invent the wheel. There are multiple superb resources to assist us.

In general, cybersecurity falls into three broad categories:

- Unauthorized use of computer resources without the owner's knowledge.
- Unauthorized actions that deprive access to computer resources. The obvious example is encrypting resources and demanding a ransom, i.e., ransomware.
- Unauthorized data access for malicious purposes, including viewing it, making copies of it, changing it and/or deleting it. All of which pose significant business problems.

Hence, the reasons for a chapter on Data Security.

Cybersecurity can also be boiled down into 5 issues:

- Unauthorized Unavailability of Data for authorized purposes – **Availability**
- Unauthorized Viewing, Browsing, Observing – **Confidentiality**
- Unauthorized Changes – **Manipulation**
- Unauthorized Deletions – **Manipulation**

- Unauthorized Use, which usually means making copies of the Data and subsequently using it inappropriately – **Confidentiality, Compliance**

With these issues in mind, consider the following user privilege distinctions:

- The ability to Read, Browse or See Data
- The ability to Enter or Insert Data
- The ability to Change existing Data and
- The ability to Delete Data from a system

Full control gives users the ability to do all four actions plus the ability to change directory structure.

In the end, **Data Security** comes down to three factors:

1   What data do you have?
2   What Protections does that data require?
3   What are the Protective mechanisms in place to Protect that data?

While much more can be said about Cybersecurity, while Cybersecurity is a current hot topic for discussion, alas, that discussion needs to continue elsewhere.

4.11 Data at Rest and Data in Motion

Section Outline:

- Data in Motion – A Copy
- Data at Rest in Source and Target
- Data in Motion

The phrases 'Data at Rest' and 'Data in Motion' may be familiar expressions. HIPAA's HITECH, for example, talks about Data at Rest and Data in Motion and the need for security protection for personal healthcare information both at Rest and in Motion.

Data is constantly in motion; Data doesn't stand still, especially when answers are sought.

Starting with the basics, **Data in Motion** doesn't 'move' in the conventional sense of the word. moving something from one place to another place. Data in Motion usually refers to copying data from one place to another. The original data remains in intact in its original location with some exceptions, such as 'tagging' or 'marking' the data to indicate it has been copied. This identification can be both a signal the data was copied and an indication of its destination.

Below are important terms to keep in mind for a discussion of Data at Rest and in Motion.

Table 4.2 – Important Terms Defined

Term/Terms	Definition/Description
Archive ≈	Is permanent, long-term data storage.
Concatenated Key ≈	Is a multi-part identifier. Both Primary and Foreign Keys can be concatenated.
Primary Key (PK) ≈	Is a unique identifier. Primary Keys refer to one and only one entity or event.
Foreign Key (FK) ≈	Is the repetition of a Primary Key (PK) in a subsidiary table. Foreign Keys establish relationships.
Data Broker ≈	Is a business that acquires data from other organizations and resells that data.
Import, Upload, Ingest ≈	Is the process of incorporating Source data into a Target. These terms are interchangeable.
Export, Download ≈	Is the process of coping Data from one location to another location. These terms are interchangeable.
Inbound ≈	Refers to Data that will be loaded into a Target repository. Imported and Ingested are interchangeable with Inbound.
Outbound ≈	Refers to Data that is being Exported, Downloaded or Exfiltrated.
Exfiltration ≈	Is the process of coping from a source. Exfiltration is a technical term. It appears frequently in Cybersecurity literature and typically refers to a negative, malicious export.
Pristine ≈	Refers to original data in its original form and format before any changes are made.
Source ≈	Source is origin of a dataset, i.e., from where the Data came.
Target ≈	Target is the location into which the Source Data will be loaded.
Staging Tables ≈	Are temporary, transitory workspaces.

Most of these terms were discussed in previous sections so they are not completely new at this point.

This section focuses on the 'ingestion' of data and its subsequent movement from one place to another.

Data in Motion – The Copy

In terms of data, our process begins with our receipt of the data. For us, this is the point of origination. The data may have history before we receive it, but everything begins when we receive the data, whether the data is internally generated data or obtained from external sources.

First, when data is received, making copies of that data makes sense and is an excellent practice. It has saved my life more than once or twice. If questions subsequently arise, having quick access to the original data in its original format can be a real time saver. Nothing is quite as frustrating as trying to find the original dataset regardless of the reason whether it is merely confirming the data or dealing with data corruption questions. Regardless of the reason, having a copy of the data in its original form close at hand avoids having to go back to the original source, which may be impractical.

This practice is frequently implemented using 'Staging Tables' or archive files. Staging Tables are workspaces, usually temporary, but their contents may be permanently saved depending on the circumstances. The typical difference between Staging Tables and Archive Files is permanence. The Staging Tables tend to be transitional workspaces, which may include 'pristine' copies of the inbound data. After the data is processed and copied to its next destination, the original copies of data may be archived permanently or for shorter periods of time.

Staging Tables are generally under the direct control of data technicians. They are typically quicker to access than archive files. The idea is to minimize delays and disruptions.

At times, things can be perverse. Keep a copy and it isn't needed; don't keep a copy and it is needed. So, adopting this practice as a standard operating procedure is generally a good idea, not something to gloss over. Failing to have a copy can come back to bite big time. This may be reality telling us our practices are sloppy at the best, negligent at the worst. I have the scars to support this practice.

An important distinction to keep in mind, unlike the physical world, data can readily move from place to place but that move is typically a copy not the relocation of the data from one place to another place although that can happen as well.

Data the Source and Target

The first consideration is typically where did this data come from. Is this data internal data or external data? In this context, internal refers to data generated or collected within the enterprise while external refers to data that comes from outside the enterprise. This can be an important distinction because we tend to know more about internal data and less about external data, especially with respect to its quality, its consistency, and its organization.

If the data came from internal business systems, we probably know a lot about the data including its characteristics, quality, and organization. If for some reason little is known about the internal data, obtaining additional information ought to be relatively easy (theoretically). However, if the data came from sources outside of the enterprise, less may be known about the data's characteristics, quality, and organization and additional information about these considerations may be difficult to come by. If our immediate source of the data is a Data Broker, the Data Broker may have the data but little information about how it was captured, generated, processed, maintained before it was received by the Data Broker.

In terms of outside data sources, contractual requirements regarding Data Quality are nice, but they are not operational guarantees. As with everything else, goofy things can happen to data from its inception to the file we receive, and changes may or may not be communicated to us or be obvious until something 'blows up' and we are left scrambling.

If the data is internal Data, we may be able to jump to the next step; if not, data assessment is the next step. This is often done by sampling the data using either a random or a stratified approach to confirm its contents, characteristics, and organization. If the data is as expected, we can move to the next step. If, on the other hand, the data is not as expected, we may have to go back to the source or do something else. The answer here, like in so many situations, is summed up by the word **depends**. There is no formulaic answer for this situation. One approach is to ingest the data into a separate workspace on a test basis allowing ingestion validation routines to identify issues in the new data. If issues are discovered:

- The data can be rolled back out of the workspace and/or
- The data elements with the issues can be quarantined and/or
- The ingestion validation rules can be revised.

The next step addresses the question of where we will put the data.

- In its own repository
- In a repository containing similar or identical data
- In a repository alongside other comparable data with tags, such as processing dates, to identify the new data quickly and easily for additional processing or removal. Timestamping is one tagging approach.

At this point there are a variety of options, but they really boil down to two choices:

- Keep the new data separate from the existing data, or
- Merge the new data with the existing data.

In the case of a separate repository or at least a separate area in an existing repository, the task is to understand the various data elements in the data, whether a primary key is present or not, and how the data is organized. A simple table such as Figure 4.23 illustrates what can be done.

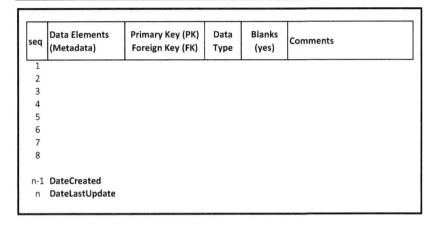

seq	Data Elements (Metadata)	Primary Key (PK) Foreign Key (FK)	Data Type	Blanks (yes)	Comments
1					
2					
3					
4					
5					
6					
7					
8					
n-1	DateCreated				
n	DateLastUpdate				

Figure 4.23 Basic Mapping Format Example

The idea is to identify elements in the data.

- Identify the data elements present in the dataset (the Metadata).
- Identify Primary Keys, or potential Primary Keys and Foreign Keys.
- Identify timestamps, which are particularly important for time-series Data.

These are arguably essential aspects of data. Typically, important questions at this stage are

- Is a Primary Key present?
- Is the data consistent?
- Are values missing or null?

Since Primary Keys, i.e., unique identifiers, are mandatory in relational databases, their absence would mean the records are indistinguishable for each other. Yes, the records are different but there isn't an inherent unique identifier that distinguishes one record from another. In these situations, proxy identifiers are adopted so that the records become unique even though they may contain duplicate or overlapping data.

When the answers to these questions are known, the repository, likely a database, can be appropriately structured. In a relational database, for example, the columnar organization of the data is known, and the data can be stored in one or more tables, as appropriate. If the database tables and columns do not already exist, they need to be created before the data is uploaded. If the database tables already exist, similar data may, or may not, be present. In No-SQL databases, Key-Value pairs or Document databases can be used where the tags identify and explain the data.

The next level of complexity is matching the data with the structure of the database and identifying issues. To explain this process, let's assume we are loading the data into an existing structure called a 'Target' and expand the previous diagram.

Figure 4.24, which is based on Figure 4.23, is simplified to focus on some of the problems that may be encountered. Rather than talk about these problems abstractly look at Figure 4.25.

Figure 4.25 presents a straightforward Name and Address situation.

Starting at the top, notice 'Source' and 'Target.' The 'Source' is the data that will be uploaded; the 'Target' is the repository into which the data will be loaded. As mentioned above, the number of columns was reduced to focus on common challenges. The actual number of columns is completely

	Source						Target				
seq	Data Elements (Metadata)	Keys (PK - FK)	Required	Data Type	Comments	seq	Data Elements (Metadata)	Keys (PK - FK)	Required	Data Type	Comments
1						1					
2						2					
3						3					
4						4					
5						5					
6						6					
7						7					
etc						etc					

Figure 4.24 Blank Source and Target Example

	Source						Target				
seq	Data Elements (Metadata)	Keys (PK - FK)	Required	Data Type	Comments	seq	Data Elements (Metadata)	Keys (PK - FK)	Required	Data Type	Comments
Name Address Table						**Name Table**					
1	ID	Yes	Yes	A(12)		1	NameID	PK	Yes	Integer	
2	Name		Yes	A(24)		2	Fname		Yes	A(48)	
3	Address		Opt	A(24)		3	Mname			A(48)	
4	City		Opt	A(24)		4	Lname		Yes	A(48)	
5	State		Opt	A(24)		5	Prefix			A(24)	
6	Zip		Opt	Numeric		6	Suffice			A(10)	
7	TelNo		Opt	A(18)							
						Address Table					
						1	AddressID	PK	Yes	Integer	
						2	NameID	FK	Yes	Integer	
						3	Address1		Yes	A(48)	
						4	Address2		Opt	A(48)	
						5	Address3		Opt	A(48)	
						6	City		Yes	A(48)	
						7	State		Yes	A(48)	
						8	Postal Code		Yes	A(12)	
						9	Country		Yes	A(48)	

Figure 4.25 Sample Source and Target Mapping

dependent on the situation, but these are a reasonable sample of columns. Specific requirements may necessitate additional columns, which is fine.

In this example, notice that the Source data is in a single table while the Target spreads the same data across two separate tables, a frequently encountered situation.

The first question: Are there places for the Source Data in the Target Dataset? The answer, in this case, is Yes. But, for the sake of discussion assume a seventh data element in the Source, Telephone Number. There is no place for a telephone number in the Target scheme. We are faced with changing the Target scheme or ignoring the data element because the Target dataset does not provide a field for this data element. If a copy of the Source Data is saved, we can always go back to the original copy should we subsequently need the telephone number.

Next question is a two-part question: Are there places for these data elements in the Target and the associated question: Is the Target organized the same way the Source is organized? Based on the data in Figure 4.29, there appears to be a place for everything, but the Target is organized differently than the Source, i.e., two tables instead of one table. That being the case, what problems do the differences introduce? We will come back to this question.

Next question: Will the source data fit neatly in the Target data scheme? Humm, there appear to be some issues, which are listed below:

- The ID in the Source is alphanumeric while the Target ID is numeric. If the ID in the Source is numeric no problem, but if the Source ID contains alphanumeric characters, i.e., non-numeric characters, there is a problem.
- The Source name field is a single field, the Target name field breaks the name into three pieces plus a prefix and a suffix, such as Mr. and Miss and Senior and Junior. If these values are present in Source Name, they will need to be separated out, i.e., parsed, and put in their respective places in the Target files.
  In the language of ETL, the name needs to be transformed. The values don't change but the organization of the data does change.
- While Name and Address data are in the same record in the Source, there are two different tables in the Target. So, we will need to split the inbound data to populate the two tables. No problem per se, except how Names and their Addresses connect?

So, what might be the intention of the Target that is different than the intention of the Source? The obvious difference, but by no means the only difference, is the Target can easily accommodate multiple addresses for a given name while the Source provides for only one address per name. One might wonder about this limitation in the Source. This raises the question of how multiple addresses were accommodated in the Source.

Coincidentally, there are several ways to accommodate multiple addresses for a given Entity. The simplest approach, but by no means the only approach, is to assign every address a unique AddressID and use a Foreign Key (FK) to associate the addresses to their appropriate Entities. An alternative approach is a 'concatenated' key whereby the NameID and the AddressID are combined, concatenated, to form a complex unique identifier. In this case, the AddressID might be a serial number, i.e., 1 for the first associated address, 2 for the second associated address, and so on.

Next question: Are there any data elements in the Target that aren't in the Source? And, if so, are any of these data elements required (mandatory)? In this case, Target requires Country; Source does not contain Country. Because Country is a required data element, it needs to be added to the Source data before the Source data can be copied into the Target. This means the Source data needs to be Enriched or Enhanced. Given City, State and Zip, this ought to be straightforward, but the upload procedure needs to have access to a Country list from which to populate the Country field and there needs to be a mechanism to ensure that countries are assigned correctly. This action could occur in the Source before the load, or it could occur during the upload process. Either way, programming and effort are required.

Other potential problems:

- Is the Target, the receiving, data element long enough to accommodate the Source data element? Or does the length of the Source data element exceed the length of the Target data field?
- Is the format of the Target data element compatible with the format of Source data element?
- Does the Source dataset include all mandatory data elements in the Target dataset?

Every No answer raises an issue or challenge that must be addressed.

ETL was covered earlier but here is a reminder:

- **Extract** the data (from the Source file)
- **Transform** the data (making whatever corrections and additions are required)
- **Load** the data (into the Target file)

The interesting aspect of this discussion is the Transformation. Where will it occur? ETL presumes the Transformation happens in an intermediate place between the Source and the Target after the data is copied out of the Source before it is uploaded into the Target. However, in special situations, the Transformation could happen before extraction or after the upload. Why these possibilities? Because by some measure, the Transformation may be easier to do in either the Source or the Target environments. ETL is the typical case, but TEL and ELT are potential use cases.

Consider the case of the missing Country data element. A strict reading to ETL is that the Source data would be extracted, copied out of its repository; then Transformed into the form and format required by the Target, and then Loaded into the Target. As was suggested, the Country could be added to the Source before the data is extracted or added to the Source data in between the Source and Target, in temporary storage and then Loaded into the Target. If Country was not a required field, then the data could be Extracted and Loaded without regard to the absence of the Country data element and then cleaned up later in the Target repository. So ETL can be TEL or ELT.

As always, there are other choices. In a NoSQL environment, the data could be loaded into the Target database without regard to form and format as just more unstructured data. This is one of the great benefits of NoSQL platforms, but if the data will be fed into an application, the question of structured Data and remediation arises.

Data in Motion

In terms of **Data in Motion**, the person handling the Data needs to be aware of all the issues that can arise and have the skill and experience to resolve them such that the data maintains its integrity. If you are a business executive responsible for Data Integrity, directly or indirectly, as a principal user, you need to satisfy yourself that the person or persons working with the data aren't unintentionally corrupting the data. If the corruption is intentional, you have an entirely different matter with which to deal. Either way, as a person in the process, there is responsibility for Data Integrity, either directly or indirectly.

The Terms **Data at Rest** and **Data in Motion** are often used in connection with threats to Data Integrity. In other words, Data at Rest or in Motion needs to be protected from unauthorized actions such as browsing, changing, and exfiltrating. This may be handled through access controls and encryption. Access Controls limit the ability to access, see, change, and exfiltrate the data while Encryption hides, obscures the actual data. Hence, the terms Data at Rest and Data in Motion are frequently mentioned in the context of protecting the data from unintentional and intentional unauthorized observation, changing, or copying. HITECH, for example, requires the following:

'(iv) Encryption and decryption (Addressable). Implement a mechanism to encrypt and decrypt electronic protected health information.' [– HIPAA

Administrative Simplification: Regulation Text, U.S. Department of Health and Human Services Office for Civil Rights, page 67.]

'(ii) Encryption (Addressable). Implement a mechanism to encrypt electronic protected health information whenever deemed appropriate.' [– Ibid, page 67.]

'Technical safeguards mean the technology and the policy and procedures for its use that protect electronic protected health information and control access to it.' [– Ibid., page 62.]

For additional information, see NIST, An Introductory Resource Guide for Implementing the Health Insurance Portability and Accountability Act (HIPAA) Security Rule, NIST, October 2008.

This section on **Data at Rest** and **Data in Motion** covers routine data migrations between repositories and special use cases, such as HIPAA's encryption requirement to limit access to Electronic Personal Health Information (EPHI) both at Rest in databases and in Motion especially over public communication lines. While the section identifies HITECH, this is by no means the only use case. Consider PCI-DSS (Payment Card Industry Data Security Standard), for example, which covers payment card transaction security.

4.12 Data Wrangling and Data Storage

Section Outline:

- Data Wrangling Defined with examples
- Data Storage Options
- Multidimensional Databases

Data Wrangling

In one sense, this book is really a summary of **Data Wrangling** and the terminology and techniques employed by those in the practice of **Data Wrangling** or **Data Munging**.

Data Wrangling, or **Data Munging**, is working with data. It encompasses at least the following:

- Data Aggregation
- Data Cleansing
- Data Collection
- Data Enrichment
- Data Exploration
- Data Mapping
- Data Migration
- Data Organization and Reorganization

- Data Structure
- Data Transformation
- Data Preparation
- Data Storage

Data Aggregation involves assembling data from different sources and combining them into a coherent assemblage that can be examined.

Data Cleansing, as noted in the definitions section, identifies and resolves potential errors in the data. Errors are not limited to incorrect or misleading values; they also include inaccuracies, inconsistencies, incompleteness, duplicates, formatting issues, and relevance, literally any condition or circumstance that compromises Data Quality.

Data Collection begins with determining what data is needed, where it resides and then how to collect it or scrape it in the case of websites.

Data Enrichment, as noted in the definitions section, involves adding data to a dataset to improve the quality and the usefulness of the data.

Data Exploration is the examination of the Data. It may occur before or after aggregation depending on the situation and needs. Data exploration may be used to determine the condition of the data including its structure and whether the condition and structure of the data will be useful or challenging. Data Exploration typically identifies data's characteristics and features, including data elements. Other considerations may include an assessment of missing, inconsistent, or incorrect data elements, identifying variables, especially independent and dependent variables, identifying appropriate data models, developing assumptions and hypotheses related to the data and estimating error margins.

The exploration might include a box or whisker plot analysis to identify the minimum and maximum values in the dataset, the median value, and the medians for the 2nd and 3rd Quartiles. Note that the 2nd and 3rd quartiles contain the middle 50% of the data. This range is referred to as the Inter-Quartile Range (IQR). IQR provides a formal mechanism to identify outliers, abnormally low or abnormally high values relative to the population as a whole, where an outlier is 1.5 times the IQR above 3rd Quartile and below the 2nd Quartile. This is a handy and quick analysis of the data to determine its central tendency and spread, i.e., whether it is a normal distribution or not.

An abundance of techniques is available to assess the data, such as scatter plots that allow the data to be visualized and identify challenges and issues early in the process.

Data Mapping is a method to understand data, especially combining data from different datasets and sources. It addresses questions regarding similarities and differences between datasets with the objective of combining the datasets.

Data Migration is the movement, generally the copying, of data among various databases and repositories.

Data Organization and Reorganization is one of the most common activities where Data may be re-organized multiple times for a variety of different purposes and analyses over its lifecycle.

Data Structure focuses on the structure of data and its impact on merging datasets and subsequent uses of the data.

Data Transformation is the generic term for activities that change the data. See the section on ETL for more discussion about Transformation and Mapping.

Data Preparation is a generic term for the activities identified above.

While Data Storage is the last item in the list, it is among the first and last issues with which the Data Wranglers must deal, i.e., where to put the Data when it is received and where will the Data reside after it has been Wrangled.

As described, Data Wrangling is a comprehensive term that encompasses a wide variety of activities performed by data technicians on and with Data. Some authors include Data Visualization too. Personally, I would regard Data Visualization as more reporting than wrangling, not that Data Wranglers don't generate Data Visualizations for a variety of purposes. I do suggest Box/Whisker plots and Scatter plots as potentially helpful wrangling techniques. I see Data Wrangling as preparing data for other uses be they operational or analytical or management related. The Data Wranglers are the Data Engineers and the Data Technicians that actively work with and on data.

A note in passing: These issues and challenges apply whether the Data is Structured or Not Structured; however, the techniques and the tools are different for Unstructured Data and tools and techniques tend to change over time.

Data Storage Options: Data Warehouses, Data Marts and Data Lakes

Data Warehouses (DW) are data repositories that generally contain copies of operational data. Interestingly, the operational data may be that of the host, i.e., inside data, or it can be data from external parties usually to provide a broader context. Operational data may be enhanced with relevant external data; hence, the Data Warehouse ends up with a combination of internal and external data.

Generally, the purpose of Data Warehouses is to consolidate data in a central place outside of the applications often for the purposes of Data Analysis, Data Queries, Data Reporting, Data Visualization and Dashboards. The idea is to support these functions outside of Production Systems to avoid adversely affecting them, especially their performance. The last thing anyone in IT wants to hear is that the system is running slowly because someone is generating a query or a report that sucks up system resources, not a pleasant situation for those responsible for high-performance operation.

Data Mart (DM) is like a Data Warehouse, but its contents are focused.

For example, Data Warehouse typically includes all business operational data including purchases, sales, manufacturing, and so on. Data Marts in contrast provide subsets of the total data, such a Purchasing Data Mart for Purchasing-related data and a separate Sales Data Mart for Sales-related data and so on.

Data Lakes

Data Lakes are large unstructured repositories for data, typically data that originated outside a business' systems. As external data is acquired, it is dumped into a Data Lake for holding purposes. Newer technologies offer the possibility of analyzing data 'as is' in a Data Lake without the traditional Data Wrangling to prepare the data for subsequent analysis. Select data from within the Data Lake may be incorporated into a Data Warehouse or a Data Mart in an additive and/or enriching process. Data in Data Lakes is typically in its raw forms while Data in Data Warehouses and Data Marts have been cleaned up, organized, and potentially enhanced.

The primary purpose of Data Warehouses and Data Marts is Business Intelligence activity while Data Lakes are typically storage facilities for large amounts of inbound external data often unstructured.

The design of Data Warehouses and Data Marts reflect an organization's business goals and objectives and the inherent structure of the business' data.

Data Warehouses and Data Marts are designed for querying, reporting and analysis unlike the operational databases from which they get their data. Data originating in an operational system is probably in Third Normal Form (3NF). In Data Warehouses and Data Marts that data may be 'de-normalized,' flattened, to reduce the number of reads and JOINs and therefore speed up query and report generation. For more information about Normalization consult the terms above and the Data Modeling domain discussion.

In Data Warehouses and Data Marts, **Metadata** are important. They become classifiers and dimensions that can be used for analytical purposes. For example, Products can be analyzed by Productlines or by Customer Types. Questions such as Who buys these products? Which Productlines are more profitable? Which Types of Customers are more profitable? These questions and their answers can lead to the fundamental question: How can we find more good Customers with similar extravagant purchasing habits? (Obviously a little tongue in cheek.)

Bill Inmon defined Data Warehouses as 'a subject oriented, integrated, time variant, and nonvolatile collection of summary and detailed historical data.' [– W. H. Inmon, Claudia Imhoff and Ryan Sousa, The Corporate Information Factory, 2nd ed. John Wiley and Sons, 2000.]

Note Inmon's list of characteristics:

- Subject Oriented – is organized by major business entities and/or transaction types.
- Integrated – is unified and cohesive.
- Time Variant – is time-stamped data, which means the same query will obtain the same results regardless of when the queries are run and regardless of specific time intervals.
- Non-volatile – unlike operational systems, data is not being continuous updated but rather amended; the data has a 'stateless' quality.
- Summary/Detail – Data Warehouses may include both granular detail and summarized Data.
- Historical – Data Warehouses are designed to store historical Data, often vast amounts, in contrast to Operational Systems that are focused on doing business now, in the present.

Another view of Metadata is shown below:

Figure 4.26 shows multiple potential types or dimensions of Metadata and the intertwining of Metadata depending upon its origin and purpose.

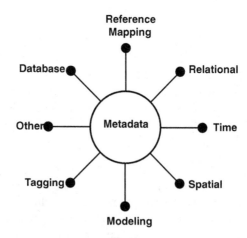

Figure 4.26 Metadata Dimensions

As noted elsewhere, **Staging Tables** play an essential role. As a best practice, when ingesting data, I always put data in Staging Tables before doing anything else for several reasons:

- First, as a matter of personal dignity, it is quite embarrassing if you can't easily retrieve the original data if you need to.
- Second, if I need to revisit the original data, I personally don't have the patience to hunt through multiple data stores to find data, I expect it to be readily available, i.e., impatience.
- Third, if I need to refresh the data, I prefer to go back to the original copy rather than an intermediate copy unless I specifically want to go back to a previous intermediate copy.
- Fourth, I typically use Staging Tables for intermediate working storage during Data Transformations, including cleansing, enhancing, organizing, and re-organizing the data, in part to make it easy to unravel changes if needed.

Note Staging Tables can be used to maintain original copies of data and copies of Transformed Data. The objectives are easily accessible copies of the original data and wrangling data outside of the data's ultimate destination. So, in a word, I use Staging Tables liberally.

As mentioned here and elsewhere, Staging Tables or Staging Areas play a central and essential role in ingesting data from operational or external sources into data repositories. The essential character of Staging Tables or Staging Areas is twofold:

- First, Staging Tables include intact copies of original data as they were originally received. These original copies are often characterized as 'Raw Data'.
- Second, Staging Tables are areas where Data Cleansing, Data Enrichment and Data Re-organization can occur.

Below is graphic representation of Stages Tables and where they sit in a ETL process.

Have a separate area for cleansing, organizing, re-organizing, and enriching Data. This means making copies of the data at each step in the process so that if the final outcome contains errors, the processing can be quickly unwound and quickly rewound as needed. Data storage today is cheap compared to the effort and cost that are invested in the data to get it to a place where it is reliable and useable.

Cautionary Advice: 'Don't blow your opportunity to be a Hero.' Be able to quickly, easily retrace your steps to adjust data and/or explain the why and how the data is dependable, reliable, and accurate. If you can explain these elements, you are in charge; otherwise, you are on the defensive.

Staging Tables

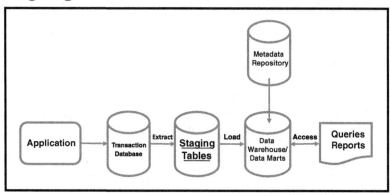

Figure 4.27 Staging Tables Example

Another piece of Advice: Write up what you did and the challenges you encountered, maybe not in excruciating detail but sufficient detail, and distribute that with the data. If nothing else that conveys, thoughtful, professional work and workproduct.

With respect to Data Warehouse and Data Mart Architecture, several choices are available:

- Mirror Operational Systems. As changes occur in the Operational Systems, immediately copy them into the Data Warehouses and Data Marts updating the existing data so that the data stores contain complete up-to-date copies of the Operational Data.
- Copy Operational Data into the Data Warehouses/Data Marts on an append basis rather than on an update or write-over basis so the changes in the data are evident.

Consider the following situation, a customer changes it's address. This means older orders have the old address and newer orders have the new address. Depending upon how the system is designed, the Data Wrangler may run the risk of overwriting the old address with the new address. This problem can be addressed by effective dates, start and stop dates. While this example deals with addresses, it applies to all master data that might change. Not to get tangled up in gender discussion but even that isn't as simple as male and female. Twenty years ago, who would have thought that there were more than two choices for gender.

Remember Murphy's Law, 'If anything can go wrong, it will,' … and its corollary, 'Murphy was an optimist.' In terms of these discussions, 'an ounce of prevention is worth a pound of cure.' Setting up start/stop dates makes systems more flexible and avoids downstream problems. Effective dates allow things to be reconstructed based on dates; however, applications do what they do. So, either the application must be revised if it overwrites the data or the Data Warehouse must maintain effectiveness date, such as start and stop dates, i.e., 'time fences', to preserve data integrity.

Specific advice for DW/DM architects, parameterize as many variables as possible so new data can merge with old data without having to change the underlying architecture and go through unload and re-load processes. Over time, data and datasets tend to drift with new circumstances, new products, new services, new categories of customers, and so on. This drift is completely normal. Design Data Warehouses and Data Marts with this in mind.

Self-service, an ancillary aspect of Business Intelligence, also impacts Data Wranglers. When data takes days or weeks to be ready for analytics, there is an inevitable push for self-service. This involves streaming data to analytic platforms quicker and pushing queries and reports to portals through which users can do their own analysis. An in-between alternative is allowing users to generate their own queries and reports as soon as the data is available without waiting for others to generate their reports.

The issue that stands between data and self-service is the extent to which the data needs to be reviewed and revised prior to becoming the subject of analysis. With new tools this time delay can be shortened, and AI can potentially shorten the time interval even more by automating much of the wrangling that is done manually.

As with everything, importance, quality, and timeliness play major roles in self-service decision-making.

Multi-Dimensional Data (MDD)

One last topic for Data Wrangling is **Multi-Dimensional Data** (**MDD**).

A basic characteristic of transactional data is multiple dimensions, where a dimension is a shared attribute that can be used to sub-set a sample population from a Universe. For example, out of all your sales you want to select sales of women's wear. Not only women's wear but blouses. Not only blouses but blue blouses in particular. This simple example relies on 3 dimensions: Wearer Type, Garment Type, and Garment Color. The same example could be applied to vehicles: Vehicle Type, Manufacturer, Model Type, Year, and any other shared vehicle characteristics. Another Sales example is: Sales can be analyzed by Customer, by Products Purchased, by Quantity Purchased, by Purchase Date, or by any Customer characteristic, such as State or City, and by any Product characteristics, such as price, cost, product types, product category and any other product factors.

In Multi-Dimensional Databases (MDD), Data is contained in two types of database tables:

- Fact Tables
- Dimension Tables

Facts are the Entities and Events; Dimensions are the attributes associated with the Facts, as noted in the examples above. These elements are contained in 'Fact Tables' and 'Dim Tables' or Dimension Tables where Fact Tables contain the 'factual' data, and the Dim Tables contain common characteristics or attributes related to the data. The Fact Tables contains the Entities and Events while the Dim Tables contain the values of the Dimensions used to evaluate Entities and Events.

Operational data inherently contains many dimensions as illustrated in the above examples.

Chapter 5

Data
Past, Present and Future

5.1 Data – The Past

History is Data, Data is History.

If an event occurred and it is not captured ... no Data, does that mean the event didn't happen? No, just that there is no record of the event. Do things exist in the world that we don't know about? Yes, there are things for which there is no data but that doesn't mean they didn't exist, they didn't occur. When we talk about the past, things that existed, events that occurred, our conversation is based on the data available to us about them. Without data everything is conjecture, or little can be said.

Data has an essential historic characteristic. A thing exists and its description, its characteristics, or attributes, describe the object. In business, these objects include suppliers, customers, products, services, employees, organization features, such as inventory storage locations and office locations, even rooms, time records, and more.

Arguably the most important things are about Us. Who we are. Our loves, our losses, our actions our inactions, our values, our behaviors. Some of this data, for example, is stored on our driver's license. It lists our name, our address, our age, the license number assigned to us, distinguishing characteristics such as our image (photo), our height, our weight, our eye color. These types of data are stored in databases, but there are other storage facilities like our minds. Our values and beliefs are stored in our minds. Our values and beliefs exist but they don't become data until they are expressed

DOI: 10.4324/9781003295228-5

and somehow recorded. Our thoughts and feelings are expressed in our speech, in our writings and in our actions, and with them information about our values.

In addition to objects and characteristics, events occur and are captured in a myriad of ways. We are born, our birth certificates. We get married, our marriage certificates. We die, our death certificates. We graduate from various educational institutions getting diplomas, degrees, and certificates. We work; we get paid. We buy things. We sell things. In each case, these actions are recorded. We go on vacations. We have hobbies. We have interests and passions. As we act on these, our actions are recorded. These recordings are data. In the case of events, they are often time-stamped, i.e., the day and time and potentially placed where the events occurred. Our diaries and biographies provide more data about us.

Data as a Business

Today, there are industries based on these records. Some of these industries are present in plain sight, such as the credit reporting agencies and the genealogy industry. Other lurk in the shadows, such as Data Brokers that compile data about us from various sources, package that data and subsequently resell it. Somewhere in between these entities are other businesses with whom we do business. Our transactions are saved. They are used by these businesses, and they are sold to other parties, such as Data Brokers. Governments also amass information about their citizens, in conjunction with government services and potentially for other purposes. Some of this data is in the public domain, some is not. Various government agencies, as diverse as the Department of Commerce, the Bureau of Labor Statistics, and the Security and Exchange Commission (SEC), collect and publish data. Data.gov, a service of the U.S. General Services Administration, lists over 343,000 datasets [as of March 2022] available from Federal, State, County and City Governments and Universities.

This function is not limited to the United States. The European Union has Eurostat. Eurostat is the statistical office of the European Union. Its mission '… is to provide high quality statistics and data on Europe.' The European Commission (EU) through 'Regulation No 223/2009 on European statistics defines Eurostat to be the statistical authority of the Union.'

> At Union level, Eurostat ensures the production of European statistics according to established rules and statistical principles, notably those laid down in the European statistics Code of Practice. Eurostat coordinates the statistical activities of the institutions and bodies of the Union, in particular with a view to ensuring consistency and quality of the data and minimising reporting burden.
>
> – https://ec.europa.eu/eurostat/web/main/about/policies/co-ordination-role, March 8, 2022.

The United Kingdom, Germany and Japan, for example, have their own national statistics agencies. GOV.UK and its Office for National Statistics '… is responsible for collecting and publishing statistics related to the economy, population and society at national, regional and local levels.' [– https://www.gov.uk/government/organisations/office-for-national-statistics, March 8, 2022.]

The Federal Statistical Office of Germany is available through https://www.destatis.de/EN/Home/_node.html, March 8, 2022. The Statistics Bureau of Japan '… play[s] the central role in the official statistical system in producing and disseminating basic official statistics such as Population Census, and coordinating statistical work under the Statistics Act and other legislation.' [– https://www.stat.go.jp/english/info/about_us.html, March 8, 2022.]

There are also private organizations, such as Statista, which '… establish[ed] itself as a leading provider of market and consumer data. Over 1,100 visionaries, experts and doers continuously reinvent Statista, thereby constantly developing … new products and business models.' [– https://www.statista.com/aboutus/, March 8, 2022.]

Society does not lack for businesses and organizations that capture and maintain data regarding people within their activities and jurisdictions. The idea of anonymity may be a relic of the past, now dead, and permanently gone.

This is not to diminish in any way the work of organizations such as the Electronic Frontier Alliance (EFA).

> The Electronic Frontier Alliance is a grassroots network of community and campus organizations across the United States working to educate our neighbors about the importance of digital rights. Participation is open to any group that endorses our simple principles.
>
> … we believe that technology should support the intellectual freedom at the heart of a democratic society. In the digital age, that entails advancing:
>
> 1 Free Expression …
> 2 Security …
> 3 Privacy …
> 4 Creativity …
> 5 Access to Knowledge …
>
> – https://www.eff.org/tl/fight

Data – The Past

The keys to '**Data – The Past**' are the collection, storage, organization, and distribution of data about past events, past actions, past situations, past objects. A primary objective of '**Data – The Past**' is having a complete and accurate record that correctly portrays past situations. Even with a complete and accurate record, interpretation is still required.

Here is an example from Hollywood, a quick flash in a movie of someone standing over a body holding a 'smoking gun'. Was the person a participant in a crime or a hapless observer who stumbled along? The image is there for the audience to consider. Killer or By-stander? The remainder of the movie focuses on answering this question; the remainder of the movie provides the audience more data with which to answer the central question, Killer or By-stander. That's the movie's plot. While this is entertainment, it is an example of questions about sufficient accurate data to answer pressing questions. In this case, 'Who done it'? And please pass the popcorn.

Starting at the beginning of the data lifecycle with the **Collection** phase, pertinent questions that need to be answered are the following:

- Is all relevant data available?
- Is anything incomplete, missing, or misleading?
- Are the facts, i.e., the data elements, correct? Do they portray the situation fully and correctly?
- Is this data consistent with other similar data with which it might be merged, with which it will be evaluated, as in the example above?
- Is the data misleading?
- Does the Data accurately represent, reflect the situation?

In a business setting, is everything about a business activity or a business entity known and recorded? And is the record accurate and complete? These questions can be difficult to answer. For example, early in the COVID-19 pandemic, there was the question about 'patient zero', or more accurately of 'patients zero'. Where did the infection start? While January 19th, 2020, is pegged as the official beginning of the infection in the United States, the actual origin may have been earlier based on the re-evaluation of issue and blood samples elsewhere. Without getting tangled up in the exact facts of the situation, the January diagnosis in Snohomish County outside of Seattle Washington appeared to have been the first diagnosis, but the virus may have been in the United States earlier in other areas. The problem pinning down patients zero and the date the infection arrived in the United States is shrouded in incomplete data. While Snohomish County may have had the first diagnosed person, other people may have gone undiagnosed. The point – Data is not always complete. We are often working with partially complete data and trying to make sense of things based on what we know, which isn't always complete. Evidence that points to earlier infections was found in the autopsy records in San Jose, CA. These deaths weren't associated with COVID-19 because personnel were not looking for COVID-19 early in 2020 … yet.

While history 'belongs to the victor', i.e., may be biased, to be useful the data needs to be accurate, reasonably complete, representative, and reliable, i.e., needs to be a truthful model of past entities, actions, and events. As the philosopher George Santayana points out: 'Those who cannot remember the past are condemned to repeat it.' The problem is not only one of remembrance; it is also one of accurately remembering what happened, which leads into the topic of Data Quality.

Data Quality

Data Quality is the discipline that answers at least the following questions:

- Accuracy – Is the data accurate?

- Precision – Does the data have the required precision?

  Precision and accuracy are closely related. For financial transactions, Data is typically expressed in 'dollars and cents' in an applicable currency be it dollars or euros or yuan or some other currency.
  At the other end of the spectrum, consider annual reports that are often rounded to the nearest million dollars.

- Correct – Is the data correct?

  Does the data correctly reflect, fairly represent, its entities and events?

- Complete – Is the data complete? Are items, elements, attributes or characteristics missing?

  For example, sales data should have a customer, a buyer, and the products or services sold to the customer. A sale without these data elements is incomplete. If movie attendance is the topic, who saw which films on which dates in which theatres or on which streaming services? Another example, someone gives you a recipe leaving out their 'secret' ingredient. The recipe is incomplete. You won't get the taste you expect; it just doesn't taste like it tasted in the restaurant or in their house … something is missing, in this case intentionally but not maliciously.
  As these examples illustrate, the incompleteness can be unintentional or intentional. If the data is intentionally incomplete, what does that say about the data and the circumstances being described?

- Consistency – Is the data consistent with similar Data?

If the Data will be merged with other data, this is particularly important. Ideally the new data will have all the attributes of the data with which it will be combined. For example, if epidemiologists are collecting data regarding diseases or pathogens from different sources, can this data be combined into a single dataset and used for epidemiological purposes? Does all the data contain the same information?

Consistency can also apply to standards, i.e., does the data comply with the standards that have been set for these types of data?

- Appropriate – Is the data appropriate for a given use?

We will return to this concept at the end of this list of questions.

- Lineage – From where did the data come? What is the data's history or provenance?

Lineage is often used as a substitute measure, a proxy, for quality. In other words, if the data's source is known, its accuracy can be implied. On the other hand, if the data is acquired on the open market, its quality may be uncertain. This is not saying the data lacks quality just that the acquirer does not necessarily know the quality of the data.

- Dependability/Reliability – Can one depend on the data? Is the data reliable?

Here are two measures of Data Quality that may be a distinction without a difference, i.e., dependability versus reliability. How are these characteristics different from each other?

- Valid – Is the data valid?

This question is like correctness but stresses conformity to specific validation requirements.

Does the data confirm with applicable rules and conventions completely, partially, or not at all?

- Verifiable – Can the data be verified?

By what process, can the data be verified?

- Timely – Is the data timely? Is the data up to date?

Timeliness typically involves currency. Is the data current to a point in time? Is the data complete up to that point in time? A frequent question is whether the data is complete up to a particular point in time, often its time of use. For example, is it complete through yesterday? Is it complete through last week? Is it complete through last month? Is the data complete up to the current moment in time?

A second question related to time is appropriateness and applicability. In other words, is prior data relevant and appropriate now. Has relevance declined over time? Has the data lost its relevance either because of the passage of time or because of events that make it no longer relevant? In other words, is the data too old to be useful? This situation is referred to as 'data rot'. Note: Data Rot is also used to refer to the decay of storage media. Here data rot is like old food that has lost its taste.

Has the value of the data declined over time or has something dramatic, such as a pandemic or a war or a replacement, invalidated the data's usefulness? Has the data lost its predictive value? Supposing a product is at the end of its product lifecycle. To what extent does its previous sales predict the future, especially if the item or the demand for the item no longer exists, at least not to its former extent? Think of blacksmiths and society's movement from horses to cars for transportation, a dramatic decline in the need for horseshoes and for people to shoe horses. Does horseshoes and horseshoeing predict anything regarding cars? Take the discussion one step further, if electric motors replace internal combustion engines, will electricians replace automobile mechanics?

On the other end of the spectrum, is the data too new and potentially incomplete? For example, when a business is making a sale, the sale is not complete until the seller invoices the customer, and the customer pays the bill. Lacking invoices and payments, the sales are not complete. Will the sales be disputed? Will the merchandise be returned?

So, too old, or too new?

- In the end as T.C. Redman noted, Data must be 'Fit for its Intended Purpose.'

– T.C. Redman, 'Data Driven: Profiting From Our Most Important Business Asset', 2008.

In terms of a checklist, data has quality if these boxes can be checked. Individually and collectively these criteria determine Data Quality.

A final note: Quality can be a relative judgment. In the extremes, High-Quality Data may not address certain concerns and by the same token poor quality data may still have some residual value. So, to some degree, Data Quality lives on a spectrum between high and low quality, very applicable and not at all applicable or appropriate versus inappropriate.

Assuming the data is reasonably appropriate for our intended use, it may still need a little tweaking. This gets us into the discussion of Data Cleansing, Cleaning, Correcting and/or Completing.

Data Cleansing/Cleaning/Correction/Completing

Data Correction, or as discussed in IT circles, Data Cleansing, is the discipline of correcting data. Data Correction involves three dimensions:

- Correcting errors in the data.
- Completing and/or Enhancing the Data, i.e., filling in the blanks.
- Removing erroneous data that cannot be repaired.

  This may involve quarantining the erroneous data to preserve the integrity of the original dataset and it may involve a subsequent re-examination of the data.

In the first use case, Data Correction, elements in the data are incorrect and the existing values need to be replaced by the correct values. This assumes the correct values can be determined and/or obtained. If not, the existing values may be replaced with placeholders, such as null, #null, n/a, or something else, which tells downstream users that the actual values were unavailable.

In the second use case, Data Completion involves finding missing values and adding them to the data. This is often referred to as **Enhancing** the Data. For example, if the Data is movie box office ticket sales, one can easily obtain data regarding the studio, the production company, the producer, the director, the stars, and so on, and that data can easily be combined with the raw box office data to provide a fuller picture of the activity. Pardon the pun. This data enhances the Box-Office Data and provides more dimensions along which to evaluate movie theatre patrons and their movie viewing habits.

In the third use case, where the missing data is not available and records remain incorrect or incomplete, the affected records may be removed from the dataset or tagged or otherwise quarantined because the data contains deficiencies, which cannot be remediated, and as a result the data may be unusable.

Coincidentally, in the era of inexpensive storage, data that is removed is seldom put in the trash. Rather it is copied into staging tables or quarantine areas and left for future re-examination and/or use depending upon future criteria.

Also, maybe, just maybe, more data may become available in the future to complete or correct the inaccuracies or maybe the data can be used for more narrowly defined purposes and so isn't completely useless.

An essential aspect of history is keeping it; in this case, keeping the records, keeping the data.

Data Storage

Data Storage addresses the issues of **Data Retention**, which include at least the following questions:

- Where will the data be stored?
- How will the data be stored? In what form will the data be stored?
- How long will the data be stored?

This question generally resolves itself into multiple storage facilities, not a single facility, and the repositories reflect the condition of the data, and its potential future uses, if any. Below are some options and their purposes:

- Production Data Storage
  Production Data Storage is for data that is in current use or will potentially be used in the foreseeable future.
- Working Data Storage
  Working Storage is reserved for data currently in active use and is typically in temporary storage while the data is not in actual use.
- Archive Data Storage
  Archived Data is data that is being retained but is not in active use and often is never used. Archive Storage could be the proverbial 'dead letter box'.
- Data Warehouses and Data Marts
  Data Warehouses and Data Marts are storage facilities for data that is used for querying, reporting and analysis.
  Data stored in Production or Working Storage are stored to support operations, whereas Data stored in Data Warehouses and Data Marts are stored for reporting and analysis, potentially in different formats than Production Data.
- Data Lakes
  Data Lakes are for vast quantities of Data typically in their native format. In Data Lakes little may be done to organize or optimize the Data. With more sophisticated tools, however, the data may be actively used for analysis and reporting while it is in the Data Lake in contrast to data that is stored Data Warehouses and Data Marts and are organized for specific purposes.

Addressing these options in sequence, Production is the business' operating systems. If the business' primary operational system is an ERP system, or something functioning in this capacity, it is likely to be using a relational database based on SQL (Structured Query Language). SQL was initially developed at IBM based on the work of Edgar F. Codd, which was published in his seminal paper entitled 'A Relational Model of Data for Large Shared Data Banks,' Communications of the ACM, 13. It was officially adopted as a standard by ANSI (American National Standards Institute) and ISO (International Organization for Standardization) in 1986.

While the name SQL stresses the retrieval aspect of this language, i.e., query, the traditional use of SQL databases is supporting business applications, such as ERP systems. As the name implies, SQL databases work with structured data and are uniquely suited to processing business transactions in volume. This technology favors Online Transaction Processing (OLTP) and Querying and Reporting, i.e., retrieving data easily and quickly. Hence, these databases process businesses' transactions and the data they contain is readily available for reporting purposes. For example, these systems process sales transactions, which in turn allows the business to generate sales reports. These databases are connected with their applications. The applications are designed to process many transactions simultaneously and their databases are designed to store large volumes of data measured in terabytes and more. Think of the transaction systems that support online retailers like Amazon or Alibaba.

At the other end of the spectrum is Archive Data Storage. These repositories generally include data no longer in active use. These repositories can be online or offline. If they are online, they can be accessed relatively quickly. If they are offline, access may require the movement of the data to an intermediate repository that is more readily accessible. Archive Storage is business' history.

Working Data Storage is a broad term. It refers to any data storage whose contents are used actively. They may be the Production Data Storage repositories or separate specifically designed facilities used for staging data, i.e., getting data ready for subsequent use or storage.

As noted above, Data Lakes are central repositories that store business data, structured and unstructured, at any scale usually from external sources. Data in Data Lakes is typically stored in its raw or native format, i.e., 'as-is'. In contrast, Data Warehouses and Data Marts are repositories that are specifically designed for reporting and analytical purposes. They typically contain Production Data that was copied into the Data Warehouses and Data Marts for subsequent reporting and analysis without interfering with actual Production.

With the Storage of large volumes of Data, a host of issues arise including at least the following:

Metadata

Metadata are names and descriptions, i.e., 'data about data'. By this we mean, metadata identify datasets and the data elements within the datasets.

In a SQL database or an EXCEL spreadsheet, the column headings are **Metadata**. Examples include Customer Name, Product Name, City, State, Zip, Telephone Number, Email Address, etc. Each of these is a distinct attribute that is related to a customer or a product or a location or something else.

An interesting subclass of **Metadata** are **dates**. Dates are essential for time-series data. Dates come in different formats, such as short dates, long dates, and date and time.

Consider this Date: October 15, 2022. It includes three components: Month, Day, and Year. Month, Day, and Year are the Metadata associated with the components of the date. Often in automated systems, the date is date and time. In this case the hours, minutes and seconds are included; hence, 12:01:01 is 1 minute and 1 second after 12 midnight. A full date-time stamp might look something like '2022-10-15 12:01:01'.

Hence, **Metadata** defines, describes, gives meaning to data.

Master Data Management

Master Data Management, which is also described above, is critical to effective data use. Master Data Management is, as the title implies, focused on Master Data, or put differently on Data that is Master Data. Master Data typically includes items such as Customer Master Data, Supplier Master Data, Product or Part Master Data, and so on. This could be as simple as a Customer's CustomerID, as a Supplier's SupplierID, or as a Product and its ProductNumber. By themselves, these IDs are crucial but so are the names associated with these IDs. Essentially, the Master Data are the Primary Keys for entities and events in business system and the names, descriptions and activities associated with these entities and events.

Where **Master Data Management** becomes critical is when businesses combine business activity from various separate systems into a single dataset. Consider the situation of a customer that purchases goods and services from different parts of an enterprise and in each part of the enterprise the customer has a different unique identifier, i.e., Primary Key. How can the enterprise reliably combine the sales activity of the customer across the various parts of the enterprise? The answer: Not easily, especially if the names or addresses are slightly different from each other. Now magnify this problem across a large organization with many divisions and many customers. Then extend this problem beyond a single organization. What a mess! Think of Credit Reporting Agencies that get data for many sources and must combine it into a coherent whole to generate our credit profiles. No small trick.

To further understand Master Data Management, look at exactly the opposite situation. Every vehicle, car or truck, has a distinct Vehicle ID Number. VINs tracks vehicles from manufacturer to dealer to customer to repair facilities to new dealers and new owners. The entire history of a vehicle can be compiled based on its VIN. How reliable is this? Several years ago, a client mentioned his impeccable black Mercedes Benz coupe had been stolen in, of all places, Palm Springs, California. Weeks went by until he received a telephone call from a police department of a city midway between Palm Springs and Los Angeles. The police said they had found his car in a field outside of town and they could fax him a picture of the car. He gave the police his fax number. They faxed him a photograph of his car. What did he see in the fax? Only the car's frame. How did the police know it was his car? Because the vehicle's VIN was stamped across the front of the frame. This was a real shame. His car was in mint condition. No matter where in the world that frame was found, it could be tracked back to my client based on the VIN. The VIN is an example of a Globally Unique ID Number, a GUID, a globally unique Primary Key.

The VIN is an example of a central identity authority, an organization or process that ensures consistency. In financial circles, this used to be Social Security Numbers (SSN), but as data breaches exposed this data, businesses abandoned the SSN as their employee ID because of liability issues.

In business situations, wouldn't it be great to be able to aggregate all of a person's or a business' purchases, to have a complete picture of an entity's buying habits ... that would be marketing gold. To do this, there must be a mechanism to aggregate identical entities and their business activities within the enterprise and in other external organizations.

Back to **Master Data Management.** Think of how reliable it would be if all entities that interacted with a business across all forms and formats had the same ID. Master Data Management would disappear as an issue. But Master Data Management hasn't disappeared because the practical reality is mostly the opposite of VIN Numbers and SSN Numbers. Every business gives an entity its own unique identifier and the problem of combining these entity's activities and their information can be a real challenge.

Not to leave readers hanging, there are techniques to handle this. These range from cross-reference tables to standardization across multiple divisions, to Soundex systems that identify alternative pronunciations for the same name, to inference techniques. For example, a business might infer identicalness based on similar named individuals residing at the same addresses, working for the same employers, registered owners of the same vehicles, using the same credit cards. Yes, even this may not be perfect. Think of families that have the same names, addresses, vehicles, credit cards, etc. How can a business distinguish them from each other? The point is that inference is just that, inference. Inference is not as reliable as GUIDs.

This section focused on Data and History and the related topics of Data Quality, Data Cleansing, Data Storage, Metadata and Master Data Management. These topics pertain to the accuracy and Quality of History, the need to cleanup and reorganize the data to see History appropriately. History needs to be stored to make its insights subsequently available. Metadata deals with the type and classification data such that meaning can be assigned to data, and finally Master Data Management deals with the aggregation of data, especially across multiple platforms and sources, to be able to see the entire picture, i.e., to see the entire History.

Without these elements, History is reduced to a bunch of random happenings and situations.

5.2 Data – The Present

Section Outline:

- Data – The Present
- Data Generation or Capture
- Data Identification, Characteristics and Relationships
- Data Storage
- Actively Used Data

Data – The Past focused on data as a record, a digital history, which can provide insights into what happened, why it happened and its implications for the future.

To use an analogy, consider moving from Data – The Past to Data – The Present is like moving from books in the library to events that will give rise to new books as yet unpublished. In terms of the analogy, yes, we are looking for a finished product based on how it was developed; we are asking this question in the context of how books are made today, i.e., Data in the Present.

Data – The Present looks at data in the present moment, the moment for which the previous moment is past, and the next moment is the future. The Present is perched precariously between Past and Future. This may seem overly philosophic, but it gets to essential, intrinsic characteristics of data. Data is both a record of the Past and an opportunity for Future actions; Data empowers the Present to move forward and reflects the Present as the Present becomes the Past.

Consider business data in terms of three dimensions:

- First, data is a digital record of present entities, events, actions, and situations as they occur.
- Second, data, unlike reality, can be updated, revised, dare I say, improved.
- Third, data enables future business activity.

To make sense of these three dimensions, consider an online Purchase. We are looking at items on an online retail site. We put several items in our shopping cart and check out. All of this is done in the Present. Out of our sight, a series of processes occur in the online retailer's retail system, processes that were initiated by our order. Several days later the items appear, one might say magically, at our front door.

- First, Our Order is a record of Purchases, a digital record. We can go back through previous orders and see everything that we have bought from the retailer, i.e., our purchase history. Hopefully, it is complete and accurate, including any returns we may have made.
- Second, Our Order was processed, potentially split into multiple separate Orders from different destinations with different delivery dates, i.e., the Order changed during the fulfillment process. The Order could also be changed by delivery delays or accelerated deliveries. Throughout the Process, the Order is updated, revised, and at least in the case of sooner delivery, maybe improved ... that old devil, instant gratification.
- Third, Our Order may cause the retailer to order additional product to replace the items which were purchased; hence, triggering future purchases by the retailer.

So, in this simple use case, we have The Past, the record, The Present, the fulfillment process, and The Future, decisions and actions triggered by our present actions. Past − Present − Future.

The moment entities are created, the moment events occur, they become the Past. This means data is essentially always history. It is always a record of past events and situations. The saying 'You can't unring a bell' captures an essential truth about the Present. Something occurs and data is the record of that occurrence. We may be able to apologize for what happened, we may be able to unwind the transaction by returning items, but we can't 'undo' the previous event, it happened. The occurrence may be forgiven but it still stands. 'Do overs' are reserved for science fiction.

However, unlike the bell, data can be updated. Data can be changed. While we can't change what actually happened, we can change the data, not by 'unringing the bell' but by revising the data. In this case, data and reality diverge. An essential characteristic of data is its historic nature, but data, unlike reality, can be revised ... for better or worse. The latter is particularly relevant at the time of this writing where denialism and revisionism are rampant among segments of American society.

But this isn't the end of the matter. As important as the Past is, data can trigger, data can initiate, actions, events, decisions in the present that will affect the future. As an aside, Alfred North Whitehead thought about and wrote about the nature of time. Whitehead saw each successive moment as a new beginning with different possibilities than the moment that preceded the current moment. His thinking could be visualized as a cone laying on its side where the tip of the cone represents the present and the opening of the cone represents future possibilities. So as time passes from moment-to-moment, new sets of possibilities arise, i.e., the cone moves forward with a new set of possibilities. The old possibilities are gone; a new set of possibilities has arrived. To complete the analogy, the new cone contains possibilities that weren't in the previous cone and the previous cone contained possibilities that are no longer possible. While scientists talk about an expanding universe, if our options do not similarly expand, they at least change from moment to moment based on what preceded them.

I recall an automobile accident on Pacific Coast Highway several years ago where a car crossed in front of us and crash. No one was hurt ... only the car. Afterwards I wondered what if I got to this point a minute earlier, the other car won't have been at that place trying to cross over into a driveway. What I if got there a minute later, the car would have pulled into the driveway before I arrived. What if the other car was less concerned about crossing into the driveway and more concerned about oncoming traffic. If ... if ... if, we can drive ourselves nuts. The point, at every successive moment, we have a new reality.

Switching from Orders and accidents, consider a prominent business theme today, Digital Transformation. Digital Transformation emphasizes the automation, the computerization, of business activities, of tasks that were previously mainly manual. Early on the clarion call was the 'paperless office,' i.e., switching from physical documents to digital documents. The idea was to replace documents with data in databases which could be more readily accessible, which could be stored electronically, goodbye file cabinets, and which could be less likely to be lost or destroyed because the data could be stored in a variety of geographically separated places.

Digital Transformation takes this concept a giant leap forward suggesting that businesses automate their business processes to the maximum amount possible so that the data of the entire business is digital and the opportunities for human errors, unintentional and intentional, are reduced as much as possible. Digital Transformation argues for an automated Present and Future in contrast to a Past that was manual by becoming increasingly digital over time.

In the ancient past, the recordings were carvings on rock faces or stories handed down from generation to generation. More recently the printed word became the recording mechanism of choice followed by photographs and video. Fast forward to today. Events happen, entities present themselves, situations arise. All of which are recorded if not initially digitally, then subsequently digitized, for example, scanning a photograph or a document to digitize it. All of this is to say that recording mechanisms have changed over time and will continue to change in the future. Consider augmented and virtual reality. Today it is digital, which means recording events, entities, and situations digitally, preferably online, real time, as they occur. This brings us to the first aspect of **Data – The Present**.

Data Generation or Capture

The Present is the generation or capture of data. Since our focus is on business, this digitalization is of normal business operations, such as buying goods and services, selling goods and services, making goods, managing human resources, managing financial affairs, and so on.

Data tends to fit into two general categories:

- Entities and
- Events

Entities are as diverse as things, people, places, and objects. Events are normal business activities such as selling, buying, making, managing, investing, and so on

Data regarding Entities and Events include three dimensions:

- Identification
- Characteristics and Attributes
- Relationships

The simplest piece of data is probably the name of a thing or its description. The problem is that neither of these are necessarily unique. Names can be generic. Names can also be descriptions. Proper names can become generic names, for example Kleenex, Google, and Xerox. These products now define categories. They no longer necessarily refer to specific products, services, or companies.

Consider the garment example again: A garment could have a name, such as 'shirt' or 'blouse', and a description which lists the garment's style, size, color, sleeve length, and so on. The name or description by themselves feel incomplete. The big question becomes are these characteristics a description or a list of characteristics? If there is no variation, the name and the description may be synonymous, like a 'short-sleeve shirt' or a 'baseball cap' or a 'tennis shoe'.

Events, especially business events, usually extend over time. Events could be as short, or even shorter than a lightning strike, or events could be of a longer duration such as building something. If the duration is long, the event is probably made up of many smaller events. In this case, the event is a series of sub-events, or in data parlance, **Time-Series Data**. Events can be captured as transactions or in streams of successive transactions, such as the output of a sensor, such as a security camera or a thermostat.

Events are often recorded as they occur in real time. Consider three alternatives:

- An online order
- A telephone order
- A mail order

In the first case, the customer goes online, puts items in a shopping cart and subsequently 'Checks out'. In the second case, a customer calls a sales rep who enters the order directly into a sales order system or records the order on a piece of paper and subsequently enters the order in the company's sales order system. In the third case, the order is created, mailed, or emailed to the supplier who then enters the order in the supplier's order management system.

In the first two use cases, the orders are recorded in real time or near real time; however, in the third use case, there is a delay between the order being created and the supplier's receipt of the order and subsequent entry into the supplier's order management system.

In all three cases, the order is created in real time. However, the time between order creation and digitization lengthens from the first use case to the second use case to the third use case.

In all three cases, the order includes not only the customer and the items ordered, but dates and times, and other order specifics, such as payment type and terms, shipping method and so forth.

As noted above, at least three important aspects of Business Entities and Events are

- Identification,
- Characteristics and
- Relationships.

Identification, Characteristics and Relationship

The first major element of data is Identification. What Entities and Events occurred? How are they identified in an automated system? How are they distinguished from other Entities and Events? How are specific Entities and Events identified and accessed, including all pertinent related data?

Primary Keys and **Foreign Keys** were previously explained. As previously noted, **Primary Keys** uniquely identify entities and their repetition in associated tables creates **Foreign Keys**, which connect related data elements in multiple tables. If the Entities already exist in the application, then the system merely creates a new event. If an Entity such as a customer does not exist, the system goes through a process to create an Entity record in the database to which the order is connected.

Note that the Identifier is not the object but the key to the object. The identifier is the digital representation of the Entity or Event, but the identifier is neither the Entity nor the Event itself. In some use cases, this distinction can blur. Consider Cryptocurrencies and their cousin Non-Fungible Tokens (NFTs). Both are unique digital assets that reside on blockchains. Their value lies in their uniqueness.

In business, how is Uniqueness established and why is Uniqueness important? Consider a vacation. We have purchased airline tickets for a fabulous get-away vacation. We arrive at the airline check-in counter and are immediately asked for our tickets and our passports. The airline wants to be sure it isn't giving our seats to someone else. In the background, a bunch of security confirmations occur to confirm that we are who we claim to be and that we aren't up to anything devious. The Entities include us, the airline, the flights, the destinations, the various agencies ensuring security, and so on. The Events are the check-in, the flights, the vacation, etc. All of this comes down to a bunch of Identifiers, our airline customer numbers, our passport numbers, our images, special anti-duplication elements built into the passports, all for the purpose of identifying us beyond doubt. Similarly, the airline has a Unique call sign, the flight has a flight number, the airplane has a tail number, the departure and arrival airports have airport codes. All of these are Unique identifiers to be sure we get on the correct flight to the correct destinations.

The purpose of Unique Identifiers is to identify a specific Entity or Event, in computer jargon, the 'one-and-only-one' relationship.

In database parlance, these unique identifiers identify the individual Entities and Events. They may be called **Primary Keys**. Ideally Primary Keys would be Globally Unique, GUIDs or UUIDs, as in the case of Airport codes. These Identifiers may be auto generated by a system, or they may exist outside the system. Either way they are distinct, no duplicates allowed. A note: systems often generate GUIDs in the background, for exclusive use of those systems, and use those identifiers to control their actions.

Primary Keys, as noted elsewhere, can be made up of a single segment or multiple segments, i.e., be concatenated.

Primary Keys can also be *Intelligent Numbers*. In the case of **Intelligent Numbers**, descriptors are embedded in the ID. Consider a Heating and Ventilation company that used Intelligent Part Numbers. The Part Number, the IDs, were descriptive. If one knew the abbreviations, one could quickly easily identify a specific part based on the various segments of the part number that identified different part characteristics, such as flexible versus rigid ducting, fans, louvers, dampers, vents, left-hand versus right-hand joints, 110 versus 220 motors, and so on right down to screws and nails. Get the part number, know the codes, and a picker knew what part to pick from the inventory.

Besides unique identification, **Primary Keys** in other tables connect related data elements, such as customers and their orders. In the foreign table, these keys are referred to as **Foreign Keys**. They are as important as the unique identifier because they connect related Data to each other.

Data Storage

As soon as the Data is generated or captured, the issue of **Data Storage** arises. Accurate **Data Storage** is essential for historical accuracy and for current and future uses of the Data. Basic **Data Storage** considerations include the following:

- First and foremost, the data must be stored dependably, reliably with integrity and fidelity.
- Second, the data must be available to support current business processes.
  The recording of the data and its subsequent retrieval must be swift enough to support process performance.
- Third, the data must be available throughout its lifecycle, especially for subsequent analysis and decision-making.
- Fourth, the data must be in such form and format that it accurately and completely reflects the situations that gave rise to the data and is therefore appropriate and ready for subsequent use.

Data Storage is a 2-part problem.

- First is the choice of type of Data Repository, i.e., type of database
- Second is the choice of Infrastructure

Storage must reliably store data and make the data subsequently available when and as needed.

Major drivers of the Infrastructure choice are performance, fault tolerance and the nature of existing complementary Infrastructure. From the performance standpoint, the infrastructure should be capable of storing and retrieving data in such a manner that transaction processing is not adversely affected. Fault Tolerance ensures that data is not adversely affected by malfunctions. One Fault-Tolerance mechanism is storing data on multiple separate storage environments to reduce the chances of Data Corruption or Data Destruction. Finally, most businesses try to maintain consistency to minimize maintenance issues, the greater the variety of infrastructure, the greater strain on maintenance resources.

Below are several Data Storage alternatives:

- The databases can reside on the business' own infrastructure.
  This is the traditional approach whereby the business is completely responsible for its data and it resources, including the amount of storage, the quality of the storage and the personnel that manage that facility.
- The now old 'new kid on the block' is the cloud whereby the business hosts its Data Storage on virtualized cloud servers.
  This shifts the focus, but not necessarily the responsibility, from in-house resources to the cloud vendor's resources.
- A third choice is Database-as-a-Service (DaaS) whereby the business uses database services provided by a cloud vendor.
  In this choice, the business is acquiring database management services from the vendor instead of just a place to store Data.

- The fourth option is a combination of the previous choices.
  In this option, the business is using a combination of on-premises and cloud resources to manage and store its data. Redundancy is typically a hallmark of this approach which means the data is stored in multiple locations and on multiple services and/or infrastructure. A note in passing, cloud vendors offer redundancy as a normal part of their offerings so that copies of clients' data are spread across multiple servers and facilities.

Database alternatives are separately described. No need to repeat them here. To the extent that you have questions about databases, see that section.

Archiving

A discussion of **Data Storage** is not complete with at least a brief mention of **Archiving**. Data that is no longer needed or is not particularly relevant is Archived to reduce the size of production databases and to reduce cost. Traditionally, Archives were offline. Traditionally data was spun off the Production systems onto tapes or removable hard drives. Today cloud providers offer low-cost alternatives for storing infrequently used data or 'cold data'. These services advertise low-cost data archiving and backup options at low cost. Typically, cloud vendors offer a variety of Storage methods at different price points for different service levels.

In general Archive alternatives include at least the following:

- Online or offline on-premises storage
- Major cloud vendors, such as AWS, Microsoft, and Google, offer a host of cloud storage options

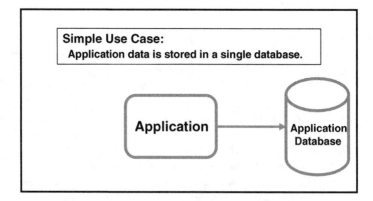

Figure 5.1 Simple Data Storage Example

- Non-major cloud vendor also offers their own specific cloud storage choices

The major driving force in this choice is cost, low cost.
Subtopics worth mentioning are:

- Replication
- Change Management
- Purging

Replication stores data on multiple storage devices. Replication spreads the workload among identical databases in support of a 'High-Availability' environment and as well as fault tolerance. 'High Availability' environment are structured to make data readily, quickly available. Fault Tolerance means the data is available and remains available if parts of the system fail.

Below are three examples moving from the simplest use case in which the data is written to a single database. Data in this approach could obviously be backed up later so this is not as onerous as it might appear to be. In the second use case the first database is automatically backed up to a second database to provide redundancy. In the third use case, data is automatically written to multiple databases simultaneously. In the example, three databases are shown but the number could be more.

Replication could be handled at the application level or at the operating system level. It can involve writing to an initial database that is mirrored; it can involve writing to multiple databases simultaneous; it can involve shipping log files to secondary databases.

The points are simply that there are multiple approaches and multiple technologies available to spread data around in such a manner that if any

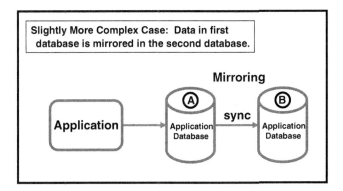

Figure 5.2 Data Storage Using Mirrored Databases

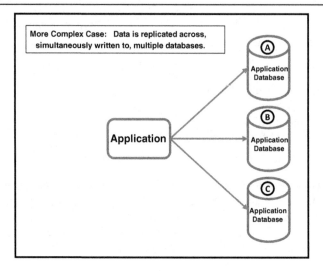

Figure 5.3 Data Storage Using Replication

database failed the data would remain available on different databases potentially at different locations.

Change Management, specifically **Change Data Capture (CDC)** addresses the question of what to do with minor changes in data. At the two extremes, an entire dataset can be refreshed, an inherently inefficient process, or the changes can be written to a subsidiary repository and tracked via version numbers or log files, a more efficient option.

When data approaches the end of its usefulness, it may be Purged, or it may be stepped down from an active repository to a repository specifically designed for inactive data from which it may eventually be purged when the data is determined to have reached 'end of life.' When storage is plentiful and inexpensive, decisions regarding purging can be postponed.

Moving from questions about Identification and Storage, consider data that is actively used in the Present.

Actively Used Data and Purging Inactive Data

An essential aspect of data is the role it plays in automation. Data is not only a record of entities and events, i.e., the Past, but data also triggers business processes. This is the foundation for business process automation, the ability of data to initiate and sustain business processes.

Consider online purchases. Customers go to online retailers, place orders, and subsequently receive their purchases. In the simplest use case, customers are registered with the websites including shipping address(s) and payment card(s) information. The purchase process is a series of sequential steps:

- Customers go to the online retailer's website and select items for purchase.
- The items are placed in the customers' shopping carts.
- Customers click a 'buy' or 'checkout' or 'place order' button to initiate the purchases.
- As customers begin the checkout process, the retailer automatically sends messages to the customer's credit card processors to reserve the cost of the purchases on the customer's credit cards.
- When charges are not approved, the retailer notifies the customers that the charges were declined and places their orders on hold pending a successful charge.
- When charges are approved, the retail process continues with the picking, packing, and shipping of the order.
- If the business process is entirely automated, the only person that physically touches the order may be the delivery person that puts the box or boxes at the customers' front doors.
  Even this touchpoint may be replaced in the future by delivery drones.

To process orders efficiently at scale, the process is performed by machines, not by people. If the reader is unfamiliar with Warehouse Automation, go to YouTube and search for Warehouse Automation. Numerous videos show warehouse automation in action, including how the picking, packing, and shipping is done without human assistance. A marvel unless your former job was that of a warehouse worker and machines now perform the work you previously did.

Consider this process from a Data perspective:

- When customers sign into a website, the customers may identify themselves or shop anonymously.
- If they shop anonymously, at some point, the website will ask the guests to 'create an account' or 'sign in,' hence, identify themselves to the business.
- As customers shop and place items in their shopping carts, various background tasks jump into action suggesting other items to consider based on past shopping data.
- When items are put in the shopping cart, the system records the items and their quantities and other characteristics such as color, size, configuration, etc.
- When the Buy or Checkout button is clicked, the system kicks into high gear.

- The system checks customer credit. If the charge is approved, the system records an authorization number.
- The system confirms the address to which the purchases will be shipped.
- The system confirms the delivery terms, such as overnight, 2-day, or longer.
- The system decides the locations from which the items will be shipped.
  - Orders may be split up into multiple sub-orders coming from different locations at different times.
  - The retailer may flip the order to a third party for fulfillment. In this case, the retailer is basically processing the order on behalf of the third-party.
- The system assigns the orders to various warehouse locations,
  - Sending picking instructions to the locations.
- As items are picked, the underlying database is updated to reflect the picks.
- The system determines how the shipment will be packaged, a box, an envelope, or something else.
  - This decision is based on the items being shipped, the amount of protection they require and potentially the shipping method.
- The items are placed in the appropriate packages.
- The system may confirm the contents of the packages before the packages are sealed noting the confirmation in the database.
- The system sends messages to the Carrier including class of service, weight, number of packages, and destination.
- The system receives messages back from the Carrier, including tracking number, delivery date, cost, and other related data.
- The system prints and attaches Shipping Labels to the packages and seals them.
  - In the old days, Packing Lists and Return Material Authorizations were part of the package but increasingly vendors are sending customers to their websites for order information and return authorizations.
- Finally, conveyor systems move the packages directly into semi-trailers waiting for the Carriers to pick up their trailers and take them to their distribution centers.
- When the custody of the packages passes to the Common Carrier, the retailer formally charges the customers' credit cards for the items shipped.

- In the background, the system crunches a lot of merchandising information to decide what to stock in the future in what quantities in what locations during specific time periods.

The key takeaway from this process is that each successive activity is handled and controlled by automation based on data. Data drives the automation, controls the process ensuring consistency and reliability, and records every step in the process.

The essential concept is that data drives the process and is updated as the process unfolds, including appropriate adjustments.

In the database behind the business process software, the Data Elements related to these actions both document the action and move the process forward to the next step.

From an Accounting perspective, the collection of this data as it happens is the sales order process documentation. In Accounting jargon, the data documents the Audit Trail complete with timestamps at each step in the process.

As can be seen in this example, a series of individual events occurred with each step in the process adding additional data to the order. This is **Time-Series Activity** with **Time-Series Data**.

The term **Time-Series Data** refers to a series of events that occur over time. These events are part of a single activity differentiated by time. **Time-Series Data,** as a practical matter, has at least two use cases:

- First, the technical definition: A series of observations that were obtained via repeated measurements over time. Think about thermostats, strip chart recorders, circular chart recorders, time lapse photography. They involve successive observations.
- Second, a broader use of the term: A series of events that can be aligned along a time axis, such as sales over time, yesterday, today, tomorrow. The time axis can be used to analyze the sales data as daily sales, monthly sales, annual sales, same day sales last year, etc. These analyses involve different time spans and different time horizons.

The point is that the term **Time-Series Data** has both a narrow definition and a broader application. Most business transactions, for example, generate **Time-Series Business Data**, which is the subject of many financial analyses. The underlying question could be: How are sales doing over time? Are they increasing, decreasing, or going sideways?

The simplest case is events that occur regularly in time, such as when stores open and close, when the sun rises and sets, daily high and low temperatures, and so on. Each of these events is associated with a specific time and these events recur either regularly at the same time or at on some other regular pattern. The simple case is a constant time interval such as hourly temperatures in contrast to the daily rising and setting of the sun, which is regular but the interval changes daily.

Some business examples include daily currency exchange rates, stock prices, commodity prices, consumer pricing and so on. Some of these items occur daily by definition, i.e., daily exchange rate, others constantly fluctuate giving rise to spot exchange rates.

Sensors and measuring devices, such as thermometers, barometers, microphones, and cameras record data, **Time–Series Data**. These devices can capture values or images over time on a continuous basis or at predetermined intervals such as minute by minute, hour by hour, day by day, or they may react to triggers like seeing a new image, detecting movement, feeling an earthquake.

Daily traffic flow is another example of **Time–Series Data**. Mechanisms associated with roadways record traffic flow to control traffic signals and provide a basis for subsequent analysis. In the food industry, freezer and cold storage temperatures are constantly monitored to ensure and document temperature over time. Should these temperatures vary beyond designated limits, alarms may sound, interventions may occur to ensure a constant temperature.

Hence, **Time–Series Data** is important to business for both operations and analysis. It is also important in our daily lives.

As mentioned, **Data in the Present** documents entities and events, such as acquiring new customers and selling products. Data accuracy is key for at least three reasons:

1   Data controls the business process.
2   Data is the evidence that substantiates situations and events.
3   Data is the basis for subsequent analysis and decision making.

If the data is inaccurate, process errors occur, such as picking wrong items or failing to pick items ordered. If the data isn't properly recorded, the record will be inaccurate and subsequent analysis and decision-making based on the resulting data will be inaccurate. The phrase used to be 'Garbage In, Garbage Out'. Today, that phrase ought to be 'Inaccurate Data, Terrible Decisions'.

5.3 Data – The Future

Section Outline:

- Predicting the Future
- Correlations, Patterns and Trends
- Exceptions

In other words, history, data, is a reminder of what happened in the past and might happen in the future as well, which could be good news or bad news depending upon what is sought. In business, what is sought is a better understanding of current situations and their implications for the future. Simply what are customers buying now and by extension what will they be buying tomorrow? Enter the realm of Analytics and Prediction.

Data Analytics offer a method for understanding past happenings and based on that understanding forecasting the future.

The previous chapter stepped through an automated sales order process where the data allowed the automation to proceed from purchase to receipt of goods. That process could span hours or days depending on circumstances.

As discussed already, Data serves multiple purposes:

- Data is created by entities and their business processes.
- Data documents these entities and their transactions.
- Data is 'process automation grease' allowing transactions to move through their workflow.
- Data has been and continues to be the content of numerous queries and reports upon which operations and management rely.
- Data is the raw material of Business Intelligence, Business Analytics and Business Data Science.

Data Analysis Data can serve several objectives:

- To describe previous situations and actions – Descriptive Analytics
- To understand current and previous situations and actions – Diagnostic Analytics
- To predict potential future situations and actions – Predictive Analytics
- To prescribe potential future actions – Prescriptive Analytics

To understand the differences among these objectives, take a simple example: Geolocation software, such as Google Maps, MapQuest, Apple Maps, etc.

The data used by these mapping and routing applications includes two major components:

- Digital Maps
- Traffic Data

The digital maps identify locations and potential routes. The traffic data provides both a historic picture and a current picture of traffic, which is constantly updated based on incoming traffic data from sensors, including cars themselves, and potentially observations by people, who are not necessarily thought of as sensors.

As users, we input our current location and the location to which we wish to go. In the background defaults were accepted, preferences were entered, such as shortest route versus quickest route, a preference for freeways over roads and streets or vice versa, the presence or absence of tolls.

Based on destinations, preferences, current traffic, past traffic patterns and current congestion, the map will calculate and display a route, often with choices. It may display several routes and alter the route in process based on current traffic data. With this data, these mapping applications show the route, give the distance, and forecast travel time and arrival time.

The digital map is the descriptive aspect. It knows the roadways, the destinations and historic traffic-flow. Combined, these elements describe past traffic patterns.

As we interact with these applications during our journey, the routing, mileage, and timing may quickly change as the traffic patterns change. The online changes are partly descriptive of current traffic, partly predictive relative to mileage and timing and prescriptive in suggesting a specific route or routes.

This example encapsulates four basic aspects of Data Analytics:

- Description – Understands routes and historic traffic patterns and flows.
- Diagnosis – Determines the current nature of traffic, including volume and incidents.
- Prediction – Estimates how long the drive will take and when you will arrive at your destination.
- Prescription – Suggests routes that reflect your preferences and current traffic density.

Descriptive and Diagnostic Analysis are a deep analysis of existing data, essentially historical data, looking for the following:

- Patterns
- Trends
- Correlations
- Exceptions – Outliers

The objective is to identify relationships among entities, events, and actions. Are these relationships coincidental or causal? This analysis could delve deeply into the relationships to determine whether they are merely accidental or whether there are inherent relationships among these items such that if one occurs the other always occurs.

Patterns are looser. Here we are dealing with tendencies. People tend to buy certain products at certain times. People tend to go to certain places at certain times. Items tend to be sold at certain times or in association with other items. Positioning items in a store may affect their sales. We are all familiar with the items placed next to checkout stands. This positioning is intentional. They are there for impulse buying. Sometimes the stuff at the checkout stand is as simple as candy while other items might be sophisticated, such as batteries, chargers, and cables.

Trends are long-term patterns, especially patterns that fluctuate up or down. For example, a trend may be increasing or decreasing sales over time. A trend may also be increasing sales at specific times of the year, often seasons, and a trend could be higher during the season and lower during the off-season.

Exceptions, which are referred to as 'Outliers,' are entities, situations, or events that are unusual. If orders typically range from $10 to $100, an order for $10,000 is way out of the normal range and probably an exception. If an event only happens once or twice in a thousand times, that would probably be considered an exception, out of the normal, a.k.a. an Outlier. How such situations or events are viewed depends upon whether the situation or event is positive or negative. If the situation/event is positive, how can we encourage this to happen more often. If the situation/event is negative, how can we prevent it from happening again? This gets into the realm of promoting or preventing certain situations/events. At this point, prediction tips over into prescription as supportive or preventive measures are instituted.

The '**Digital Gold**', so to speak, is an actionable prescription that achieves its intended results. What stands between us and our intended results? The future, which is in fact never certain. The future is inherently unknowable and uncertain … although some people offer certainty about the future, such as 'this is sure to make money'.

Discussions regarding future events become discussions of **likelihood/probability** and **impact**. How likely is an event to happen or not happen? How impactful will the event be, a ripple or a catastrophe? Data provides us with a foundation upon which to estimate the probability of certain situations or events occurring or not occurring. The simplest approach would be to plot sales up to the current moment on a graph and then draw a straight line such that the distance between the line and the existing points is the shortest amount possible. This is a 'Least Squares Regression'. In some situations, we can look at the points and accurately draw a line that approximates the Least Squares model. In other cases, the numbers are very different from period to period, so we need to use a computer program to calculate the intercept and slope of a line that has the Least Squares property, the least distance between the points and the line. Either way the line is made and then extended out into the future using the same slope, i.e., projecting the current trend will continue into the future.

However, suppose the sales trend has been a fairly constant 5% increase year on year and then takes a sharp drop. Is that a new trend or an anomaly that can be ignored? Suppose the sharp drop lasted two successive periods. Suppose the sharp drop lasted three successive periods. Under what circumstances would one decide the sales behavior was not adequately characterized by a straight line? If the sales were consistent over an extended period, what caused sales to make a 'sharp downturn'? Is a more sophisticated approach needed? Such approaches do exist. They are the province of Advanced Data Analysis and Data Science.

Underlying this discussion is the notion that the past is somehow indicative of the future. To the extent that this is an accurate analysis of the situation, the probabilities are higher; to the extent that this is not an accurate analysis of the situation, the probabilities are lower.

So, at the end of the day, we are left with predictions and prescriptions that may be likely but are never 100% sure, no guarantees.

To go back to the example of Digital Mapping, the arrival time becomes more accurate the closer we get to our destination. Supposing we have an appointment, and we arrive at the building in time for the meeting but can't find parking. The app was right, and we were late. Next time we add in the probability of finding parking and/or the average amount time required to find parking knowing that the average is merely the median, and others found parking upon their arrival while still others drove around, and around, and around to find parking. Is there one estimate, or are there really multiple estimates, i.e., average shortest times, average longest times, and overall average, i.e., best case, worst case and average case?

On top of this discussion sits disruptions, such as pandemics, earthquakes, military actions, and so on. In these cases, the question arises, how predictive are previous patterns? Will the disruptions be short-lived or long-term? Will long-term trends change in response to these disruptions? Did the probability of a situation or event decrease or increase, will life return to normal?

The questions for which we seek answers may to some degree be unanswerable unfortunately.

Chapter Endnote:

To appreciate the extent of warehouse automation, consider an empty box on a conveyor belt. When the box arrives at the point where an item is located, that item is retrieved using gravity feed racking or robotic arms or a person to pick the item and place it in the box. This activity is based entirely on data. The system has assigned an identifier to the box. The items are identified by labels, bar codes, RFID chips, maybe even location. When the box arrives at the designated location, the item is picked, and the system updates itself to reflect the picking. All of this happens automatically based on data and sensors that read the data.

Google provides a nearly limitless number of images showing warehouse automation and manufacturing automation.

Chapter 6

The New Reality

Section Outline:

- A New Reality
- An Abundance of Data
- An Abundance of Storage
- An Abundance of Tools and Techniques
- The New Landscape for Data
- The Situation Today

A New Reality

Over time, situations change. From a technology standpoint, where we sit today is much different than two decades ago and two decades from now it will be quite different as well. At the beginning of the 21st Century, businesses were relieved that Y2K wasn't a disaster. Businesses were able to continue without the potential disruption that pre-occupied much of the previous decade's thinking.

Among important events that happened during this time were the establishment of NetSuite and Intacct in 1998 and 1999, respectively, and shortly thereafter the creation of Tableau in 2003. These products ushered in two new choices made possible by new resources. NetSuite and Intacct ushered in Cloud-based Business Systems. Tableau offered a new Data Analytics platform that quickly became a favorite of many business analysts. Among its predecessors were SPSS Statistics, which was first released in 1968, and the programming platform R, which was created in 1995. Both products were designed by statisticians for statisticians. Tableau was different. It focused on Data Visualization, the ability to 'see' data, and understand and interrupt data based on charts and graphs ... not to oversell, or undersell, Tableau. In the first two decades of the 21st Century, data grew exponentially, and the list of available tools grew as well. For example, Microsoft's Power BI was released in 2015 based on Power Query, an EXCEL® add-on, and Alteryx, which was founded in 1997 as SRC LLC, released its first product in 2006. Talend traces

DOI: 10.4324/9781003295228-6

its roots back to 2005. These are examples of newer products introduced to address data wrangling and data analytics and make data more accessible beyond technical users.

As this book is being written, Russia's invasion of Ukraine is underway. We can see Russian columns on television. We can see drone combat footage. We can see drone coverage of utter destruction. We hear discussion of 'intelligent munitions.' Digital has become part of the battle for Ukraine. This battle is being played out for the entire world to see ... the bombs, the missiles, the artillery, the devastation. Realtime data is an important aspect of this war and data has become another dimension of the conflict. If you are reading this book a decade after the invasion, what new realities grew out of this invasion? While the conflict may be hard to understand, note that the boundaries of war have expanded to include cyber-attacks. The Internet that we depend upon and use daily has become another vehicle of war. Data, like dynamite, can be used for good and for bad.

I am reminded again of the expression 'If a tree falls in a forest and there's no one around to hear it, did it make a sound?' From the standpoint of data, if an event occurs and it leaves no digital breadcrumbs did it occur? The answer is obviously yes. Events routinely occur and are not necessarily captured digitally. However, if no digital evidence and no after-effects exist, we have no knowledge of the event. Our view of the world is shaped by our experiences and our digital history, which is constantly expanding and, even more importantly, instantly available at our fingertips. Books and libraries were great inventions. The new reality is that many questions can be quickly and easily answered via online search. No need to go to a library; no need to reach for a book, not that reaching for a good book isn't a pleasant experience to be savored. I love bookstores but things have changed.

Today we find ourselves in the worst inflation in four decades. Policy makers have a trove of data to analyze as they decide how to respond to the current situation. Different experts offer different advice. They say their advice is based on Data.

- Do different experts have different data?
- Do they focus on different aspects of the same data?
- Do they have different analytic tools and methods?
- Do they interpret the data differently?

The real answer is probably yes to all these questions. So how will well-intentioned policy makers decide what to do? And how quickly and precisely can they recalibrate their actions? For all the data, there are more questions. Today we hope the experts get it right.

Given these uncertainties, there are major trends that are shaping our lives in ways hard to image. We live in the middle of a New Reality that is changing. It includes:

- An Abundance of Data
- An Abundance of Storage to save the Abundance of Data
- New Tools and Techniques to mine this treasure trove of Data
- An Increasing supply of skilled data technicians, analysts, and scientists to evaluate the Data, explain our world to us, and recommend courses of Action.

An Abundance of Data

Between the proliferation of internal business data and the data available from third parties, any business can easily accumulate an enormous amount of data. Access to data is no longer reserved for big enterprises although they have the edge. The larger the business the more likely the business is to have access to ample data and ample technical resources to productively use the data to which they have access.

Businesses no longer determine what to stock, what to buy, what to sell based on observation by walking around a store or a warehouse and observing a physical inventory. This may still be a viable alternative for small businesses, but for large businesses with large product catalogs readily available data can extend their views well beyond what are on their shelves, in their inventories, and well beyond their immediate situations into the future.

As noted earlier, government and non-profit agencies collect and publish an enormous amount of data, a veritable treasure, as well. In some cases, the data must be subscribed to but in many cases the data is there for the public to consume for free. These data collections contain some of the same information for which larger businesses pay Data Brokers. This means even small businesses can access the data.

An Abundance of Storage

As data as grown so has affordable storage. In a relatively short span of time, conversations about storage shifted from kilobytes, when I first entered the IT profession, to megabytes to gigabytes to terabytes to petabytes to exabytes and larger. Looking at the larger arc of IT, this growth is to some extent astronomic. Even today we are buying larger and larger storage devices for our businesses and our personal use as well. The growth is astonishing.

The good news is the availability of an endless amount of affordable storage. This allows us to easily store our data that is accumulated from both inside and outside our business with little concern to how and where the data will be stored and the cost of storing that data.

In this environment, nothing need be deleted. So, what do businesses do with the inevitable errors and mistakes that occur naturally? They are a natural phenomenon. There is an urge to delete, remove, purge mistakes from our records. But, why? Even mistakes tell us something and they can be easily corrected without destroying the original entries. Leave the original entry intact, prepare offsetting entries and cross-reference the entries. Or, inactivate the original entry and add a new correct entry in its place cross-referencing the two old and new entries. The reality of the mistake is present together with the reality that should have been.

Why is this interesting? Because the human tendency is to remove mistakes to have a 'clean record' where mistakes are seen as indictments or distractions. In the case of intentional mistakes, there may be an explicit push to hide if not completely remove these mistakes. Accidental or intentional, the thrust is the same, remove the errors, but errors and mistakes are a reality, and it is possible to, as the saying goes 'have your cake and eat it to,' i.e., be able to see reality as it actually was and as it should have been. The difference is the correcting entries.

How a business deals with errors and mistakes, intentional and unintentional, is a topic for Data Governance. Data Governance should establish the policies and enforcement mechanisms for dealing with errors and mistakes and their correction. This includes whether to remove anomalies or not, includes having a complete history, and includes removing the opportunities for malicious entries, especially the ability to hide if not completely remove nefarious entries.

A potential trend to keep in mind. As one IT executive mentioned in the earlier days of the COVID-19 pandemic, 'the pandemic did more for sales [increased] than the regular sales force does in a year.' Rapid jumps like this could be referred to as the 'hockey stick affect', a sharp upward swing. As the costs of cloud services and storage increase, some businesses are reassessing their cloud utilization, which in some cases companies are bringing some workloads back on pre-premises. Accordingly, keeping executive eyes on IT workload and storage costs is prudent.

An Abundance of Tools and Techniques to Analyze Data

For a considerable time, statistics was arguably limited to scientists and scientific endeavors. In the absence of a commitment to statistical methods, most Data Analysis, especially in smaller businesses, was relatively simplistic. Businesses spoke of trends, up, down, and sideways, i.e., technically linear regression. This is easily accomplished with rudimentary products, such as spreadsheets.

Not that one can or should point to particular products, but Microsoft EXCEL®, Tableau, and Microsoft Power BI have garnered a lot of popular attention. Using these tools, non-technical personnel began to look beyond basic reports to more sophisticated data analyses and visualizations of business data.

Given an abundance of tools and environments and a demand for trained Data Analysts and Data Scientists, Data Analysis and Data Science have become darlings of College and University curricula creating a pool of trained graduates anxious to prove their worth in Data Science.

Hence, an abundance of data, an abundance of data analytic tools and techniques, and budding Data Scientists have increased interest in Data and Data Analysis. New computing platforms, such as Artificial Intelligence and Machine Learning will add more demand for data and resources to exploit the implications and ramifications of the data to make more informed, more educated business decisions.

A trend to watch is Data-as-a-Service (DaaS), Business Analytics-as-a-Service (BAaaS) and Data Science-as-a-Service (DSaaS). As these services become more readily available and more user accessible and friendly, the incentives for businesses to deploy more data in more sophisticated business decision-making increase. Aspects to keep in mind are the following:

- Business Analytics and Data Science will become a daily requirement for business.
- Sophisticated Analysis and Design will become readily available to decision-makers at all levels in business.
- These Tools or Services won't require a Ph.D. in statistics to operate.
- Hence, nearly anyone anywhere can point these tools and services at data and get an informed analysis with recommendations.
- Which also means having data will become even more important as businesses struggle to keep up with each other.

An interesting sidenote here. For a long time, PivotTables were considered a pinnacle for spreadsheets. In Microsoft EXCEL, the command to create a PivotTables is Insert > PivotTable. EXCEL 2013 Microsoft expanded the choices to include Recommended PivotTables, which meant the software would analyze the identified table and construct a group of PivotTables, from which a user could choose. At this point, users didn't necessarily need to know how to make PivotTables, it was now automatic, and all a user had to do was choose the PivotTable that most closely matched their need. The point – This is also happening with Data Analytics. New services allow users to associate the data analysis service with a dataset and get a set of analyses back. They don't have to build the analyses that activity is done automatically by the service. At least at this point, users must still interpret the results. The big question – What will the future bring in this department?

The New Landscape for Data

In traditional ERP and CRM systems, the center of the universe is entities, such as customers, suppliers, items, and employees, for example. These entities interacted with each other: The business bought items from suppliers; the business managed items in their custody; the business sold items to customers. Or put the other way around, customers bought items from businesses. These entities were at the core of traditional business applications. They reflected the purchasing and selling activities of businesses. All these pieces fit neatly together. From the perspective of data analysis, the analysis that was performed on this data was performed on clearly organized and easily understood data with little ambiguity; in other words, the data was highly structured Data.

Then the Internet emerged. Suddenly data in which we were interested, i.e., 'data of interest,' existed outside of our systems. An abundance of relevant data was rapidly accumulating outside of our systems and that data lacked the structure of our internal systems. Data Analysis became more challenging as questions, such as how do our sales compare with our competition? How do our customers assess our products and services relative to the competition? How are customer needs and wants changing? For these and similar questions, we now look outside of our traditional systems and the data they contain to data living in 'the wild,' so to speak. The big questions then became how can we manage large volumes of external data and how can that data be utilized in our business decision-making?

Questions of this sort and the abundance of Data that originates outside of traditional systems, such as ERP and CRM systems, turns the traditional model upside down. By this, I am referring to new methods and tools to capture and manage online data, such as Apache Kafka, for example. Kafka 'is an open-source distributed event streaming platform used by thousands of companies for high-performance data pipelines, streaming analytics, data integration, and mission-critical applications.' [– https://kafka.apache.org/] Kafka, which originated in LinkedIn, is now owned and managed by the Apache Software Foundation. Kafka and similar products turn the conventional model on its head.

The traditional model focuses on Entities and their Actions. It is, as mentioned above, very structured. Traditional business transaction systems usually maintain their data in SQL databases. These highly structured systems are the mainstay of many businesses; however, today we also have continuous streams of events, of actions, ranging from web blog posts and logging applications to messaging applications, location services, Internet of Things (IoT), and so on, each with their own streams of data. What these applications have in common is time-series data, i.e., events happening in sequence such as blog posts and threaded discussions or online traffic measurement or temperature readings, all of which occur over time. Returning to sales for a moment, a business' sales are sequenced by time of purchase; hence, the first sale, followed by the next sale followed by the third sale, and so on.

The emphasis is capturing sales events as they occur and, at the least, storing them in such a manner that they can be subsequently sequenced allowing the businesses to determine daily sales, weekly sales, monthly sales, and so on. These events could be rapid fire, consider applications that monitor traffic to recommend appropriate routes.

All of this leads to something like Kafka, which is built around five APIs (Application Programming Interfaces).

- Producer APIs capture events as they occur and publish them as streams of events.
- Consumer APIs allow applications to subscribe to these events streams.
- Streams API handles the actual streaming function.
- Connector API enables developers to build Producer APIs and Consumer APIs that can be reused as needed.
- Administrative API manages Kafka.

In other words, Kafka is built around events in contrast to tradition business systems that are built around entities. These new tools shift the focus from entities to events providing a fuller, larger tapestry of data.

A notion central to Kafka is Topics. Topics are the streams of data, where each instance or event is a separate item in the collection. Consider JSON and tagged Data, one tag includes a timestamp while the second tag includes the event, whatever it is. Remember NoSQL and Key-Value pairs. The timestamp could be the Key and the event however it is captured becomes the Value; hence these instances could be thought of as partitions within the topics, as shown in the diagram on the next page.

Central Themes in this new environment include:

- Online, Realtime Data Capture and Publishing
- Preserving events in their time sequence
- Decoupling Producing and Consuming processes so that they work independent of each other based on an underlying messaging protocol, which means analysis can occur without adversely impacting transaction processing.
- Clustered architectures for both speed and resilience, i.e., gaining 'two birds with one stone'

Hence, the New Landscape shifts the focus of attention from Objects and Entities to Events and Transactions. With this change came new technologies to manage this unstructured Data.

The Situation Today

Disruption has become today's big theme. For Silicon Valley, disruption began as a verb and became a technology. Initially disruption meant using technology to disrupt established processes. Then disruption became one

```
                    ( Producer Applications )
                              |
                              v

  Kafka Cluster
  ┌─Broker 1─┐   ┌─Broker 2─┐   ┌─Broker 3─┐
     Topic          Topic          Topic
  ┌─────────┐    ┌─────────┐    ┌─────────┐
  │Partition│    │Partition│    │Partition│
  │ ┌─────┐ │    │ ┌─────┐ │    │ ┌─────┐ │
  │ │Data │ │    │ │Data │ │    │ │Data │ │
  │ ├─────┤ │    │ ├─────┤ │    │ ├─────┤ │
  │ │Data │ │    │ │Data │ │    │ │Data │ │
  │ ├─────┤ │    │ ├─────┤ │    │ ├─────┤ │
  │ │Data │ │    │ │Data │ │    │ │Data │ │
  │ └─────┘ │    │ └─────┘ │    │ └─────┘ │
  └─────────┘    └─────────┘    └─────────┘

                              |
                              v
                  ( Consumer Applications )
```

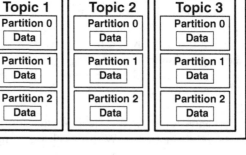

Figure 6.1   Apache Kafka Design

technology disrupting another technology, i.e., disrupting the disruptors. The big question: Given all this disruption, are we any better off than we were before the disruptions. I suspect the answer is both yes and no. Yes, in that some technologies have been very beneficial, and No because not all technologies were beneficial or they had major unintended negative consequences. Lithium batteries may be an interesting case in point. On one hand, Lithium batteries power cars, tools, cellphones, all sorts of portable devices, but Lithium is difficult to mine, harmful to the environment and toxic to animals. We may look back on all the Lithium that was mined for batteries and wonder how this very toxic element will be recycled and/or rendered harmless.

To evaluate Data and the Tools and Techniques to manage it, consider the following questions:

- Did Data help us understand and deal with the Pandemic? Did it help us prepare for the Pandemic? Did it allow us to deal more effectively with the Pandemic?
- Were our assumptions about Supply Chain accurate? Could Data help predict the Supply Chain disruptions with which we struggled and continue to struggle?
- Can Data help us deal effectively with the worst inflation in 40 years?
- Can Data resolve the conflict in Ukraine? (As of this writing, the outcome is far from certain.)
- Can Data help democratic societies thrive and grow and in so doing improve society?

Maybe the answer is in the wisdom of the movies. Yes, granted, a strange place to look, but what did Oliver Hardy say to Stan Laurel, 'Well, here's another nice mess you've gotten me into' or as I would paraphrase the quote 'Look at another fine mess we have gotten ourselves into.'

Every day there are new perspectives on these topics, but the big questions remain:

- How can Data help us better manage an open society?
- How can Data help us resolve conflicts?
- How can Data help us to deal with major health crises more effectively?
- How can Data help us deal with a constantly changing world?
- How can Data help businesses be more effective and profitable?
- How can Data help us live fulfilling lives?

Is it too much to hope that an Abundance of Data with Quick and Easy Access can help us more effectively deal with these problems and in the process improve society, improve the lot of all humanity? This must sound a little like 'Mary Poppins' but a dispassionate look at data may tip us off to impending crises earlier and give us more time to prepare for the next crises and/or deal more effectively with them ... like climate change.

The promise of Data Analytics and Data Science is that previous patterns and relationships, which are captured in the data, can hint at, if not tell us about, upcoming situations and how best to cope with them. The watch words appear to be those of Dr. Anthony Fauci, the former director of the NIH's National Institute of Allergy and Infectious Diseases, 'what does the data tell us,' 'what does the data say'?

Chapter 7

Data – Use Cases

Section Outline:

- Use Case in Healthcare
- Use Case in Healthcare and Business
- Use Case in Business

Throughout this book, numerous examples were provided. The most frequent example is based on customers and sales. In this chapter, five examples are presented.

- The COVID-19 Pandemic
- The Movies and the Pandemic
- Business Innovation
- An Outsource Marketing Company
- A Typical Business Dilemma

The COVID-19 Pandemic

The COVID-19 Pandemic is an excellent example of data playing out in plain sight. You didn't have to be a Data Scientist to find the data. All major news outlets were filled with data, statistics, graphs, and interpretations.

Remedial measures were based on the data, 'what the Data says'; including the various recommendations and mandates, such as getting vaccinated, wearing masks, social distancing to reduce transmission and hand washing to remove any virus from our hands. These remedial measures were based on data, although as more data was gathered, some of these recommendations changed.

So, what could possibly go wrong?

Early in the pandemic, I recall situations where data anomalies, variations, were attributed to failure to report timely. In some cases, problems were attributed to demand overwhelming resources with samples accidentally

DOI: 10.4324/9781003295228-7

being set aside. Various jurisdictions were accused of underreporting because the data was unfavorable.

These problems are not reserved for pandemics; they happen in business as well. If new data points in a different direction than previous data pointed, the new data may be ignored or pushed aside, the problem of an inconvenient truth.

Infection rates, hospital utilization, intensive care utilization, recovery rate and morbidity rate are examples of **Time-Series Data**. They reflect circumstances or actions at points in time.

Taken together, these situations call for agreement on data standards. The ultimate question: What constitutes complete, accurate, reliable data upon which to base policy?

Take a simple question: When and where did the pandemic first appear in the United States? While this example was previously mentioned in this book. Consider a deeper dive into the situation. Answering this question took some deliberate forensic work. The first case of COVID-19 in the United States was confirmed in Snohomish County, Washington on January 18, 2020 and the initial epicenter of the pandemic in the United States was at a nursing home in Kirkland, Washington. [–www.cdc.gov/museum/timeline/covid19.html]. However, data sleuths in Santa Clara County, California reviewed the county's death records early in 2020 and discovered the virus was present in Santa Clara County prior to the Snohomish County infections.

'The fact that there were deaths related to COVID back in early February is very significant, because it means the virus was around for a lot longer than was initially realized,' Jeff Smith, a physician and the county executive in Santa Clara, told The Washington Post.

> 'It's been around for a while, and it's probably been spreading in the community for quite some time. It is not yet known exactly how the two people became infected [in Santa Clara County], but Sara Cody, the county's public health officer, told The Post that the cases are thought to be community transmissions.' Cody … credits the discovery of the infections to the county's 'thoughtful, astute medical examiner,' who sent tissue samples from the two people to the CDC. The positive test results were confirmed Tuesday. These two fatalities, along with a third on March 6, also indicate the coronavirus was probably spreading earlier and farther in the San Francisco Bay area than local officials initially thought.
> –https://www.washingtonpost.com/nation/2020/04/22/death-coronavirus-first-california/.

How did this confusion arise? Simply, coroners lacked the necessary tests to confirm the presence of the virus at that point in time. Only after

COVID cases began climbing did Santa Clara County officials review previous autopsy specimens and discover the presence of the virus. Lacking tests, the deaths were not initially attributed to COVID. Remember the tree falling in the forest. That no one saw it fall doesn't mean it didn't fall. Silence is not absence.

This example highlights several classification problems.

- Did COVID-19 kill an individual?
- Was COVID-19 present but the death was attributed to something else like a pre-existing condition or something as mundane as a traffic accident?

Based solely on what was mentioned in the general non-medical press, we see several common Data Management themes, including

- Data Collection Issues
- Classification Issues
- Timeliness Issues
- Interpretation Issues

A contributing factor was the lack of COVID tests early in the pandemic and the accuracy of early tests illustrating issues related to both the collection of data and its interpretation.

The point is, without digging into specifics, several common Data Management issues occurred. These issues are not limited to epidemiology, they occur in business as well. How and when is data collected? How is it classified? How is it interpreted? These differences played out in public making the pandemic, despite its destruction, a readily accessible example for those who lived through it and remember it.

The Pandemic and the Movies

This example deals with the collision of Business and the Pandemic. 'Superlative Theatres' is a hypothetical composite of various cinemas and cinema chains. In this example, the Pandemic shut Superlative down for nearly two years. When it was time for Superlative Theatres to reopen, Superlative had to decide when and how to reopen and which films to show as people became comfortable with going into theatres. Parenthetically, customers were most comfortable going back into theatres when only a few other patrons were in the auditorium, i.e., social distancing on a grand scale. Great for patrons but wreaked havoc on the theatres' economics.

Back to Superlative and the business questions it had to consider:

- Which theatres to reopen?
- When to reopen them?
- What movies should be booked/scheduled?
- What renovations need to be made?
- Are there cinemas that should not be opened?
- Are there movies that should not be shown? And so on.

Can Data help answer these questions?

Superlative could examine its Box Office records. The Box Office Data includes which films were shown on which screens on which dates at which price points. This is a good beginning but what are the sales patterns? What were the characteristics of the most successful films; what were the characteristics of the least successful films? What were snack bar sales and how did they relate to the films being shown? All important business questions as Superlative decides when and how to reopen.

These questions, however, reach beyond the Box Office ticket sales Data. Film characteristics and seasonal trends also need to be considered. Film characteristics include type or genre of the movie, who starred in the movie, who released the movie, who directed the movie, MMPA rating, audience ratings, and so on. Seasonal factors might include holidays, school holidays, and vacations and of course weekend attendance versus weekday attendance.

Delving into profitability, Superlative also needed to consider snack bar sales as well as its portion of the ticket revenue. Snack sales information isn't part of Box Office Data.

If we really want to get in front of everything, we might also look for data to indicate how customers' tastes may have changed. What types of films did movie patrons want to see after being cooped up at home for months on end? What types of films and entertainment were they looking for to distract them from the social isolation the pandemic wrought on us … movies like comfort food?

Questions about refurbishing theatres and closing theatres could be economic decisions that include profitability and patronage, i.e., empty theatres don't make money neither do partially full theatres. Issues like leases could come into play, i.e., can the leases be renegotiated, can the theatre walk away from a lease?

For Superlative Theatres and its competitors, they were many facets to consider as the movie theatres decided when and how to move forward into the future. These decisions were based on the data in their systems supplemented as needed to provide a broader basis upon which to make their decisions. This is a practical example of data enrichment, i.e., adding external Data to internal data to get a fuller picture of reality.

Restaurants were another industry profoundly impacted by the pandemic. For them as well, the question of survival or failure was front and center.

An interesting study might include the data restaurants used to decide their future. For small restaurants, the primary issue was probably how to survive; however, for larger restaurants, restaurant groups and restaurant chains, data could determine which locations remained open, how they were staffed, and the items on the menu.

Empire Enterprises …

'Empire Enterprises' is a hypothetical conglomeration of previous clients. Empire makes special purpose sensors. Before the advent of the pandemic, their sensors were used in commercial applications. With the advent of the pandemic, Empire decided adapted its expertise to the COVID-19 pandemic and in the process expand from commercial and military aviation into the consumer products market.

Empire decided to adapt its R & D capabilities into developing a COVID-19 sensor. Yes, this is hypothetical. Why – because I really wanted something like this during the height of the pandemic, especially before vaccines became available.

Looking at the data aspect of this initiative, what data did Empire have in its systems that will help it make these kinds of decisions? What data did Empire need from outside sources that could affect its decisions? Obviously, data about consumer demand for this type of product would be relevant. Think of all the businesses that began making masks many with no previous experience making masks.

Combining Empire's expertise with a brand-new need born out of the Pandemic, what might consumer demand be for a COVID-19 tester, some sort of a test mechanism that could detect the presence of the COVID virus? Probably every household, maybe every person in a household would want their own personal tester that would tell them when the virus is present in the air or on surfaces. If Empire could develop such a sensor given its expertise, how would that affect its existing productlines? Could existing products be adapted to the new application? Would entirely new manufacturing processes be required to make the new sensors? Empire's existing business targeted commercial applications; how would Empire enter the consumer market? Would this involve an entirely new production facility, entirely new distribution channels, entirely new pricing models? Would this new product dwarf its existing products and sales?

All questions that could be addressed with the right data. But where would this data come from? What skills and resources would Empire need to develop or acquire to manage this data? While this is a fictitious business, imagine the businesses that sprang up to provide masks and COVID test kits. Some of these businesses were already in this realm, i.e., those that made surgical masks or medical test kits, while others were new ventures. Some adapted existing products, others started entirely new ventures.

Arguably the greatest innovation was the development of mRNA vaccines. Yes, this was the adaption of a preexisting technology, but the truly remarkable aspect was the speed with which the new mRNA vaccines were developed, tested, and released. All of this involved enormous amounts of data from research studies to develop the underlying technology to clinical studies to confirm the efficacy of the vaccine, i.e., its effectiveness in preventing illness without creating troublesome side effects.

Ace Marketing

Ace Marketing is also a conglomeration of previous clients. Ace provides Data Management, Marketing Campaign design and Marketing execution to its clients. Every campaign is tailored to a client's specific business requirements and data. The data generally came from some combination of the client's internal systems and outside Data Brokers that had client-relevant data.

To be profitable, Ace needs a Data Warehouse that can receive and ingest similar data for similar clients in similar markets. The similarities mean Ace needs a Data Architecture that allows it to ingest relevant data from its clients and Data Brokers regardless of its form, format, and content. Our job was to develop such an architecture for Ace. Previously Ace had different Data Warehouses for different clients. That worked but wasn't efficient. The design criteria we were given was to design a Data Warehouse that was robust enough to contain similar but different data for similar clients coming from different sources in different formats, with different contents, truly an exciting challenge.

The Data Architecture was designed with many parameters that could trigger different storage options and different processing options all within a single application and allow Ace to add new clients and options without creating additional architectures. The new architecture was more complex than the existing architectures, but a single process could now handle a variety of clients with slightly different data and slightly different needs in a single workflow. This was significantly more efficient, and it avoided having to process different clients with different applications.

A Typical Business Dilemma

There are times in many businesses where business is reasonable, but the trends are unsettling. Consider this Use Case:

A consumer products business has been operating smoothly for years. Sales have been steadily increasing between 8% and 12% year over year, except that during the first two years of the pandemic, sales were up 40%. The business' profit margin is in the low 20s seldom dropping below 20%. The company's combination of domestic and foreign suppliers allowed it to avoid some of the issues that impacted its competitors.

Everything is roses ... well not exactly. Competition is getting more intense. While sales are increasing, seven large customers are becoming dominant, accounting for 65% of sales. Sales derived from the remaining customer base are slowly decreasing, down only 2% and the decrease continues despite increasing marketing efforts.

The owners of the business feel good but unsettled, especially about the sales concentration. Are they becoming too comfortable in their success? What will sales look like in five years? In ten years? What happens if one of the big customers moves all or part of their business to a competitor? There are no indications that this is on the horizon but there are occasional product and service issues which may be increasing in frequency.

The business has four facilities spread across the United States, each with its own business systems. One of the facilities was an expansion; two were acquired, the last three years before the pandemic. There was a push before the pandemic to move all facilities onto the same system, but the pandemic put that plan on hold where it remains.

In summary, this is an established business with steadily increasing sales, which got a big boost from an extraordinary event, in this case the COVID-19 pandemic. While the customer base is reasonable broad, sales are increasingly concentrated in a small group of accounts and there are occasional product and service issues. As the pandemic recedes from the national psyche and a potential economic slowdown looms on the horizon, will sales return to pre-pandemic levels or go even lower as the economy adjusts to a new reality. How will this business fare? What does the data say?

Ignoring the specifics, I presume your business may have these or similar issues and these issues may be intensifying for a variety of reasons including but not limited to hyper-competition and situations outside of our direct control such as changing economic conditions, changing climate, and manmade disasters, such as war.

From the perspective of Data, what might be needed by your specific business situation:

- Comprehensive data that is appropriate to, that aligns with you business' Needs and Objectives.
- Sufficient Internal and External Data for Decisions to be Informed and well founded.
- Changes to the Data to improve the Data and make the Data easier to use, including but not limited to

   o Cleansing the Data
   o Enhancing the Data
   o Organizing and re-organizing the Data
   o Ensuring consistent, adequate Metadata and Dimensionality for Classification Analysis

- ○ Managing the Data across various platforms and storage modalities
- ○ Managing Master Data Equivalence

- • Data of Quality appropriate to the Decisions that need to be made.
- • Access to Appropriate Skills and Resources to Work with, to Wrangle, to Analyze the Data.

Summary

Each Use Case is different emphasizing different aspects of Data Management and Analysis and illustrating the need for intentional Data Governance and Data Management techniques and tools. The art of being able to make decisions by looking out the window is long gone. Decisions today and in the future are and will be based on data and its analysis using sophisticated tools and techniques.

Chapter 8

To Sum Up

To Sum Up,

- Data exists in a myriad of forms.
  Some forms of data are easier to use in decision-making while other forms of data are harder to use. Digital Data obviously is easier to use than data that is not digitalized.
  Text, or narrative, sound, and video present their own challenges and may require advanced tools as well as specialized skills and techniques to accurately interpret.
- Data describes both Entities (Objects) and Events (Transactions and Processes).
  Entities are the objects involved in events. Entities are related through events and shared characteristics.
  Shared characteristics may include common ownership, such as departments within organizations, or common membership by virtue of categories or grouping, or a commonality based on time or location. These are structural relationships.
  Events also relate entities by virtue of activities such as buying products and services, selling products or services, or making products. The nature of the relationship may be strong or weak, causal or coincidental.
  Events are objects themselves involving Entities in actions. The emphasis is on the actions rather than on the entities. Event-centric systems capture events as they occur and makes them available for subsequent analysis.
  Entity-centric systems are highly structured, Event-centric systems may be less structured and may have no obvious structure other than being an action that occurred, maybe even a random event.
- The key is recognizing these distinctions and how they affect decision-making. For example, are we looking for structural

DOI: 10.4324/9781003295228-8

relationships involving entities or transactional relationships, involving events? And how do these differences affect our decisions?

- Data my come from Internal or External sources.

Essentially, we know, or we can know, more about our own data and by extension have more control over it than we have over data received from third parties. In general, we tend to know more about internally generated data and less about externally generated data. This distinction can have a big impact on the effort needed to effectively use the external data; however, external data offers depth and richness to internal data.

In the case of internally generated data, there is fewer excuses for faulty data. The data is the organization's data from the organization's systems. To the extent the data is faulty, the deficiencies should be resolved in the systems that generate the data. Why make problems for ourselves? The data may be sufficient for the systems that generate and use it but without further effort that data is insufficient for other purposes including decision-making.

Early in the COVID-19 pandemic, for example, the question of 'patent zero' was a big question. How, where, and when did the virus enter the United States? Initially the answers were thought to be Washington State in February of 2020, but later investigation revealed COVID in Santa Clara County as early as December of 2019. The evidence, the data was present, but no one was looking for it. Only subsequently through post-mortems were the infections identified. The data seemed fine at the time and only subsequently did a more complete understanding of reality emerge.

In the case of externally generated data, we are dependent on the data's source and the degree to which the data was altered for better or for worse on its path from source to us. Data Lineage deals with this topic. Hence, in the case of externally generated data, buyer beware. The ultimate end user will have to contend with the data's quality and its usefulness. To the extent that the external data is inaccurate or not representative, end users must decide about its real usefulness and make their decisions accordingly.

There is an in-between use case where the data is sufficient for the systems that generate it but is insufficient for certain subsequent use cases. In this situation, the data may need to be organized, re-organized, refined and enriched to meet the 'fit-for-the-intended-purpose' criterion, articulated by T.C. Redman.

- Data may be Stable or Volatile over time.

Ideally, Data streams are stable over time. This reduces the amount of discovery required and increases the reusability of previously established data techniques and procedures.

If the data is volatile, extensive investigation and evaluation may be required to determine the degree of Data Quality and the amount of Correction and Enhancement that will be required to make the data useful increasing the need for Data Wrangling resources and expertise.

- Data Usefulness and Data Quality are arguably among the two most important characteristics of Data.

   Granted these concepts are interrelated; however, data can be viewed from the perspective of accuracy and completeness independent of the question of whether the data is useful or not and to what extent the data is useful. The later question deals with appropriateness and relevance.

- Data may be interrelated Causally or Coincidentally.

   From the predictive standpoint, causal relationships have a higher level of predictability than coincidental relationships. It is nice to know the degree of interconnection between entities, situations, and events before making business predictions.

- Finally, Data may have Predictive qualities.

   Arguably one of the biggest benefit of data is predictability, being able to reliably predict the future in the face of uncertainty. We routinely predict the future in business and in our personal lives. Prediction can involve complex decisions regarding how best to deploy scarce resources, such as money, or as mundane as laying out our clothes for tomorrow before going to bed.

   Today climate change is a major issue. As this book is being written, the northern hemisphere is experiencing unprecedented heat and drought, which interestingly were accompanied by torrential rains in some parts of the country and record snowfalls … not enough followed by too much. The ultimate result was large scale destruction. Questions such as the amount of water available now versus the future, and for farmers what crops to plant if at all, agonizing decisions.

Hence the purpose of this book – to provide Decision-makers with the terms and tools to understand, to effectively communicate with Data stewards and to make the best decisions possible.

Chapter 9

Data – Optimization
Subtitle: Finding Value Hidden in Data

Section Outline:

- The Process to Optimize Data
- The Challenges to Data Optimization

If we were starting a data project from scratch and we could organize our data anyway we wanted, where should we start? What should we do in what sequence? Consider the following as a general approach. Adapt it as needed for your particular circumstances.

First, Build a Data Catalog listing all the Datasets and certain basic elements, including:

a   Identification of the Data
b   Description of the Data
c   Ownership and Stewardship of the Data
d   Lineage of the Data
e   Storage Locations
f   Usage information
g   Anything else that is relevant to your project

A typical question at this point is: How much detail?

Let business needs drive the determination of the amount and level or detail. If business needs are not clear at this point, then begin at the dataset level and explore the detail as needed. As the saying goes, 'let's not try to boil the ocean' at least not at this point.

Detail can always be added later as needed when needed.

Second, Understand the applications that generate Data and Understand the applications that use the Data.

To understand the data, we need to understand the applications that generate the data, how they work, the data they generate, and how that

DOI: 10.4324/9781003295228-9

data is subsequently used in that application and in other applications, and how this data is subsequently analyzed and used for decision-making.

In essence, we need to understand how the data is generated and subsequently used by all applications, or in other words, we need understand the Data's Lifecycle.

Third, Identify the external Data that enters the enterprise, including

    a   Identification of the Data
    b   Description of the Data
    c   Ownership and Stewardship of the Data
    d   Sources of the Data
    e   Storage Locations
    f   Usage information
    g   Anything else that is relevant

This is the same list as before except that item d now relates to the external Data sources.

Additional questions include.

- Of what Quality is the Data?
- How stable or volatile is the Data?
- Is the Data consistent from batch to batch or does it change periodically? If so, how often? Occasionally or Routinely?
- How Reliable are the Data Sources? Some sources may be more reliable and some less so.

These questions are obviously important to the extent this Data is used for decision-making.

Fourth, Group, Prioritize and Assess the various Datasets in terms of:

    a   Importance
    b   Role in the Enterprise

        Is this Data used in decision-making?
        Are the decisions operational decisions or strategic decisions?

    c   Data Quality Issues
    d   Compliance Demands

Ultimately, if the data is used to make decisions, be sure the data is of appropriate quality for reliable decisions. If the data isn't used for decisions, then why collect the data? Why keep it? The answer could be operational as opposed to decision-making.

Fifth, Evaluate the datasets in terms of Quality, Integrity, Importance, and potential future Usefulness.
Prioritize the datasets based on importance.

Sixth, Cleanse the Data, Enhance the Data, Organize and Re-organized the Data, as needed.

Seventh, Once the Data is of appropriate Quality and Content, organize the Data for its subsequent uses, including Data Analysis.

Eighth, Resolve any limitations and shortcomings in the Data.

Ninth, Find out what the 'Data says'.

Tenth, In parallel with cataloging and gaining an understanding of the Data, understand the Business Processes which use or affect the Data.

- Understand how those processes work.
- Understand how those processes interact with the Data.
- Understand how the business processes depend on the Data.
- Understand how the business processes interconnect with each other. Ultimately, understand the integrity of the Business Processes and the Data.

Typically, the slate is not a clean slate; there are existing circumstances, existing use cases and existing sources and uses of the Data. So, you are some where between a clean slate and established policies, procedures, practices, and standards. Not a bad position, hopefully further along in the process.

The seeming simplicity of this process belies the many challenges that can be encountered in taking control of Data and using it productively for business.

The Challenges

Executing a program such as the one outlined above will inevitably involve challenges. Below are some common challenges that may be encountered.

Hidden Data

The first challenge likely to be faced is finding and aggregating all of the enterprise's data.

The obvious sources of data are the enterprise's prominent applications, such as its ERP, or equivalent, systems. Focusing only on the big systems can overlook smaller, often departmental specific applications. This can also ignore data hiding in spreadsheets and data hidden on paper.

The initial thrust of Digital Transformation was digitalizing data 'hidden in plain sight' on paper. The objective was to move this data from file cabinets to databases for a variety of reasons which extend beyond just making the data more accessible, i.e., don't have to find the right file in the right file cabinet. Digital Transformation projects depend on moving data out of functional silos, including divisions and departments, and file cabinets, spreadsheets, and smaller applications. The goal is to make the data accessible to the entire enterprise rather than limited to certain parts of the enterprise. In a Digitally Transformed business all, or nearly all, of the enterprise's data should be in data repositories that can be easily accessed by the organization for analysis and decision-making. Data locked away in departments is data for which the enterprise gets only a small part of its potential benefit and value.

Finding this hidden Data can require significant effort roughly the equivalent of an 'all hands' effort to find and catalog a business' hidden data. There may be an exception however. Data that is deemed to be sensitive or intellectual property of the business may continue to be managed on a restricted basis.

Data Quality

Data that lives outside of major business applications may be fine for its present purposes but when businesses attempt to use that data, let alone merge it into enterprise-wide data stores, significant challenges can arise.

In a simple case, entity identification may not be consistent across the enterprise. Supposing the data involves customers and is maintained on Sales or Marketing spreadsheets. The data could easily use different IDs and in some cases may be merely a list of names and addresses. Recall the Master Data Management discussion.

The enterprise may need to revisit its Master Data standards. The ideal choice is standardizing IDs across the organization such that all departments and functional areas refer to the same entities the same way. If that is not possible, develop and maintain cross-reference tables that establish equality. The big tasks here are establishing an accurate cross-reference scheme and maintaining the scheme for new entities and for entity changes. The last choice, dare I say the worst choice, is not to standardize the data, exactly the opposite of the first choice.

This is a case where Artificial Intelligence and Machine Learning can shoulder part, if not all of the burden by examining all of the entity characteristics and deciding which entities are likely the same, which entities are not likely the same, and a third group which requires the 'human touch' to run the differences to ground. The problem: Entities may be equivalent, but the equivalence cannot be confirmed based on the information in the organization; hence, additional research is required.

Accountability

Accountability is about subject matter knowledge and responsibility. Owners and Stewards of Data are responsible for their data. Do they also understand the data, its degree of Quality and Reliability and its importance to the enterprise?

Taking these questions in sequence, Data Owners and Stewards are probably the closest personnel in the enterprise to the data. If they aren't working with the data daily, they are at least overseeing the processes that routinely generate and use the data. Their familiarity with the data gives them 'expert' knowledge about the data, its characteristics, and its usability.

In addition to Owners and Stewards, other parts of the enterprise may have a stake in the data. Governance frameworks, such as COBIT®, teach stakeholder involvement. Stakeholders include anyone who has an interest in the data and as such may have unique concerns regarding the data, its use and reuse.

Accountability for the Data shifts or broadens depending how Data is stored. Data stores are typically under the responsibility of IT at least in terms of maintaining the integrity of the data store and any processes that are applied to the data in storage. For example, data can be copied from transactional systems into data warehouses for storage and subsequent analysis and reporting. At this point, the data moves outside of the original owner's sphere of influence but that doesn't necessarily relieve the original owners of their responsibilities relative to Data Quality and Data Reliability. These responsibilities are now shared with the engineers who are responsible for the storage facility.

I recall a conversation several years ago with a CIO who was asked about providing application support. His response was that IT was responsible for the integrity of the platform on which the application operated, but Data Quality and Process Integrity remained the responsibility of the personnel that used the application. This may be a good caution for overly zealous IT personnel. Process owners are responsible for their business processes. They are responsible for the data their processes spawn, and they are responsible for the uses of that data, especially operational uses. They may be less responsible for subsequent decision-making uses. Accordingly, they must have adequate resources to maintain and sustain Process Integrity and Data Integrity.

Another Data Cataloging challenge relates to use. Who will use the data? For what purposes? Obviously as the cataloging progresses, the users and uses may change. The challenge as the project unfolds is to determine who is accountable at the various stages of Data Generation, Data Wrangling and Data Use. These could be different departments, different personnel.

For more discussion in this regard, refer to the section on Data Governance.

Business Purpose

Central to any understanding of data is business purpose, which relates to the generation or acquisition of data and the purposes for which data is subsequently used.

When talking about business purpose, consider COBIT®, which mentions several concepts that are on point to business purpose. They include alignment of IT and IT resources with corporate goals and objectives, the inherent value of business processes and the data they generate to the organization, and the roles business goals and stakeholders play relative to the data. COBIT's point is that IT provides value to an organization to the extent that its products and services align with the organization's overall goals and stakeholder concerns and expectations. These elements reflect the business' culture and play a primary role in business activity. In this context, stakeholders are anyone inside or outside the business that has a stake in the business processes and by extension in the data generated by these business process and used by them.

Hence, stakeholders and enterprise governance artifacts are places to look to understand business processes from the top down. From the bottom up, those who are directly involved in the business processes have first-hand knowledge about the business processes and issues related to Process Integrity and Data Integrity.

To understand data uses, current and potential, the business' goals and objectives need to be understood as well as business process contexts. If the Business Processes and Data do not align with business strategy and objectives, the business is handcuffed from the outset.

Chapter 10

Epilog

Recalling my public speaking class, the teacher suggested the following approach to public speaking:

1 Tell 'em what you are going to tell 'em
2 Tell 'em
3 Tell 'em what you told 'em

Following this advice, our conversation about data is important on two levels:

- First, the importance of Data Integrity
- Second, the role of Data in Decision making.

When it comes to decision-making today either we are either making important decisions, or some combination of Artificial Intelligence or Machine Learning is making these decisions. Either way, we and they are reliant on the data available to them and its Integrity. There is an argument that sophisticated mathematical models can detect and work around data lacking integrity, but why go there? It is one thing if lack of integrity cannot be avoided; it is an entirely different matter if we enforce Data Integrity. As one might imagine lack of Data Integrity could be more detrimental if decisions are automated. Will automation be smart enough, sophisticated enough to question the quality of the data fed to it. Of course, one could ask, will people be smart enough, sophisticated enough to question the data fed to them. By some measure, society seems to struggle with reality and truth.

At least now a distinction exists between humans being able to adjust and adapt to new situations and machines being less capable of adjusting to new situations. However, there are tasks at which machines excel. Think of CNC machines and their ability to mass produce identical machine parts quickly, i.e., tighter tolerances and faster than skilled machinists.

Will this change in the future? It may very well change, but at least now there is a spectrum of human-machine interactions. At one end of the

DOI: 10.4324/9781003295228-10

spectrum, machines help people, at the other end of the spectrum, machines replace people. As one ponders his/her future career(s), the question in the back of many minds is: What is the future of this career? What impact will automation have on this career? Will it be safe from automation, or will automation prevail? We may only know looking back.

Data Analysis, Data Science, Artificial Intelligence and Machine Learning are in ascendance, no question about that. Consider the splash that ChatGPT made in November 2022. They are becoming increasingly important for businesses to compete effectively in our hyper-competitive marketplace. If I design something that is outstanding and it takes the market by storm, I can rest assured that someone somewhere will 'knock-off' my invention and sell their product for less. Arguably Roomba invented the floor clearing robot and Dyson reinvented the vacuum cleaner. Now there are a long list of competitors selling all sorts of imitations many less expensively. One place where businesses can get an edge is mining their data and obtaining complementary data from outside sources to fully understand their business, the marketplace, their place in that market and the avenues available to them for success in that market. Data Science and Artificial Intelligence will undoubtedly play important roles in the quest to understand markets and plan effective responses.

Throughout the book, multiple good practices are identified; some active, some proactive, some reactive. They are typical practices used by successful Data Wranglers. Feel free to adapt them to your situations. Feel free to adapt them as new technology emerges. This is an evolving field with lots of opportunity for the 'fleet footed.'

Be an effective advocate for good practices and wise decisions based on good data.

Ultimately, this discipline comes down to the following:

- Data is the doorway to understanding.

- Data is the foundation for informed, evidence-based decisions.

- Data has a lifecycle. This lifecycle involves at least the following: generating, collecting, formatting, cleaning, organizing, enhancing, storing, and distributing data.

  Data Wranglers are the engineers of this process.

- Data Quality is absolutely essential.

  Information Technology (IT) used to talk about 'Garbage In Garbage Out'. Today I suggest that the more appropriate phrase is: 'Bad Data Poor Decisions'.

High-Quality Data is essential for High-Quality Processes and High-Quality Decisions.

- Numerous resources are available to assist new Data Wranglers.

  Re-inventing 'the wheel' isn't necessary. We can learn from others. DAMA, and others, are wonderful resources. Avail yourself of their wisdom.

- The ultimate gauge of data success is effectiveness:
  - Getting the right Data
  - Of appropriate Quality
  - To the right Place
  - At the right Time
  - Accurately interpreting the Data
  - Making the Right Decisions based on the Data

Good Luck working with Data. Data contains all kinds of amazing insights and predictions.

Index

Note:- Page numbers in *italics* and **bold** refers to *figures* and **tables**respectively.

Printed in the United States
by Baker & Taylor Publisher Services